CATHOLIC &
CHRISTIAN

A BOOK OF ESSENTIAL
CATHOLIC CATECHESIS

PATRICK MIRON

Order this book online at www.trafford.com
or email orders@trafford.com

Most Trafford titles are also available at major online book retailers.

Print information available on the last page.

ISBN: 978-1-4907-7559-3 (sc)
ISBN: 978-1-4907-7561-6 (hc)
ISBN: 978-1-4907-7560-9 (e)

Library of Congress Control Number: 2016912358

Trafford rev.   09/08/2016

North America & international
toll-free: 1 888 232 4444 (USA & Canada)
fax: 812 355 4082

To Al and Maureen Glombowski,
who first suggested this book and then made it possible.
God bless you. Thanks seems insufficient.

CATECHESIS. That form of ecclesiastical action that leads both communities and individual members of the faithful to maturity of faith. Because of varied circumstances and multiple needs, catechetical activity takes on various forms.

In regions that have been Catholic from past ages, catechesis most often takes the form of religious instruction given to children and adolescents in schools or outside a school atmosphere. Also found in those regions are various catechetical programs for adults, whether in preparation for baptism or reception into the Church, or to deepen one's understanding of the faith. Sometimes the actual condition of the faithful demands that some form of evangelization of the baptized precede catechesis.

In churches that have been established recently, special importance is placed on evangelizing in the strict sense. This becomes the well-known catechumenate for those who are being introduced to the faith in preparation for baptism.

For individuals whose minds are open to the message of the Gospel, catechesis is an apt means to understand God's plan in their own lives and in the lives of others. Having come to know this divine plan, they can more effectively co-operate with God's grace and become better instruments for the extension of Christ's kingdom. (Etym. Greek *atechizo*, to teach by word of mouth.)

—Father Hardon's Catholic Dictionary

Contents

Foreword

I'm a now-retired midlevel retail executive and a lifelong Catholic, who was blessed with twelve years of *solid* Catholic school formation and education in grades 1–12, when Catholic education was still very well done, in the pre–Vatican II period. This faith formation would later be extended by several more years of intense study, which was associated with my becoming a trained and certified Catholic catechist.

Now retired after having been involved in several of the parish's religious education programs for twenty-plus years—which included grades 3–12, confirmation preparation, and RCIA (Rites of Christian Initiation for Adults), which is normally required faith formation for entry into our Catholic faith by those of differing faith backgrounds—the Holy Spirit led me to develop a *totally free-of-all-cost* home study, weekly e-mailed lesson course, to augment and supplement the gaps in formation wrought by time constraints often associated with RCIA programs. It's impossible to teach well and thoroughly our two thousand years of developed and Holy Spirit–guided traditions and teachings in the times allotted. Thus, there is a period of "mystagogy," advanced and prolonged study, required but sometimes overlooked.

My retirement ministry is now into its seventh year and has led to this book, which consists of some of the e-mailed, shared lessons from my "e-course," which Al has encouraged me to publish.

The course is entitled Building Blocks of Our Catholic Faith because that's the approach I try to take. That same mind-set is found in this book, which covers instruction in our Catholic faith *in an individual lesson format*. Many topics I address are seldom taught in parish catechesis programs because of time restraints or are simply being overlooked by them. A secondary goal of this book and my course is to provide the evidence of our beliefs and practices and thus enable others to also share our faith with facts and confidence.

Just a note about the format of this book: this is not a novel. The book's format introduces category chapters and lesson numbers and the titles of the individual lessons. Some chapters for this book will only have a single lesson, while others will have multiple lessons.

God bless you. Please pray much.

May Mary be ever on our lips and remembrance of her always in our hearts.

—*Fr. John A. Hardon's Catholic Prayer Book*

CHAPTER ONE

Discovering Our God

And God spoke all these words, saying, "I am the Lord your God, who brought you out of the land of Egypt, out of the house of bondage. You shall have no other gods before me."

—Exodus 20:1–3; emphasis added

I will take you for my people, **and I will be your God.**

—Exodus 6:7; emphasis added

What agreement has the temple of God with idols? For we are the temple of the living God; as God said, "I will live in them and move among them, and I will be their God, and they shall be my people."

—2 Corinthians 6:16; emphasis added

The Mystery of Who God Is

What's your image of God? When you think about God, is it only Jesus? Does it really matter?

Certainly, all thoughts of God are in and of themselves "good." But who is, what is, and where is God for you? And where are you for God? (I'll leave this part for you to answer for yourselves.)

Does it really matter? It does for a fuller understanding of the divine mystery of who God is and a better understanding of how God has chosen to interact with us. And it's important because we are able as humans to respond more readily with "persons" than with "spirits." God, of course, knows this, and it is complementary to God's desire for a highly personalized relationship with each of us. Our God therefore has chosen to reveal himself as the divine triune Godhead, the "blessed Trinity," to share a bit more about the mystery of who God is. Keep in mind this is for the benefit of our understanding and in no way benefits God, who, being perfect, cannot be added to or improved in any way or even changed.

234 The mystery of the Most Holy Trinity is the central mystery of Christian faith and life. It is the mystery of God in himself. It is therefore the source of all the other mysteries of faith, the light that enlightens them. It is the most fundamental and essential teaching in the "hierarchy of the truths of [our Catholic] faith." The whole history of salvation is identical with the history of the way and the means by which the one true God, Father, Son and Holy Spirit, reveals himself to men "and reconciles and unites with himself those who turn away from sin."

237 The Trinity is a mystery of faith in the strict sense, one of the "mysteries that are hidden in God, which can never be known unless they are revealed by God." To be sure, God has left traces of his Trinitarian being in his work of creation and in his Revelation throughout the Old Testament. But his inmost Being as Holy Trinity is a mystery that is inaccessible to reason alone or even to Israel's faith before the Incarnation of God's Son and the sending of the Holy Spirit . . . .

253 *The Trinity is One.* **We do not confess three Gods, but one God** [each sharing fully 1 perfect and divine nature] **in three persons,** the "consubstantial Trinity." The divine persons do not share [as in split up] the one divinity among themselves **but each of them is God whole and entire:** "The Father is that which the Son is, the Son that which the Father is, the Father and the Son that which the Holy Spirit is, i.e. by nature one God." In the words of the Fourth Lateran Council (1215), "Each of the persons is that supreme reality, viz., the divine substance, essence or nature."

261 The mystery of the Most Holy Trinity is the central mystery of the Christian faith and of Christian life. God alone can make it known to us by revealing himself as Father, Son and Holy Spirit. (Catechism of the Catholic Church; emphasis added)

This mystery of God—Father, Son, and Holy Spirit—has had numerous attempts at being explained by saints and teachers *far brighter* than I am. It is and shall remain a mystery, until God himself explains it to us in our promised life to come.

Still, there is a profound example used by Saint Patrick: the shamrock, with its three separate leaves still being *only* one shamrock. When I was teaching high school students, I came up with another visual example. It's not profound, but it does nevertheless give an illustration of the "three in one" possibility.

I had three identical clear glasses and a clear glass pitcher of water. I marked the glasses one inch from the top and filled them water from the glass pitcher carefully to the line. I then had the class look closely to see if there were any differences. None were found. I then took premade labels with "God the Father," "God the Son (Jesus)," and "God the Holy Spirit" written on them and stuck them to each of the three glasses. And I asked if everyone thought the contents were "equal." "Yes, they are!" So I went on to explain that each of the three divine persons are "coequal" and "coeternal," meaning that they are very much "the same." They share *fully*, not a section of only one divine and *perfect* nature. But each contains the entirety of that one divine and perfect nature. What one knows, *all* know; what one desires, *all* desire; what one commands, *all* command. They cannot disagree with one another because they share the same *one* divine nature fully and completely. I then fielded their questions.

I then poured the water from the three glasses back into the same pitcher while naming each of the divine persons and ended the demonstration with the words "three in one," only one nature, only one God but three separate persons.

We then shared some catechism teachings and this passage from the Bible: "Then Jesus came from Galilee to the Jordan to John [Saint John the Baptist], to be baptized by him. John would have prevented him, saying, 'I need to be baptized by you, and do you come to me?' But Jesus answered him, 'Let it be so now; for thus it is fitting for us to fulfil all righteousness.' Then he consented. And when *Jesus was baptized* [the Son of God], he went up immediately from the water, and behold, the heavens were opened and he saw *the Spirit of God descending like a dove* [God the Holy Spirit] and alighting on him; and lo, a *voice* from heaven [God the Father*], saying*, 'This is my beloved Son, with whom I am well pleased'" (Matthew 3:13–17; emphasis added). All three "persons" of the blessed Trinity are at one time and in one place for our benefit.

Three in one. Every thought, every teaching, every dogma, and every doctrine in the Bible is there because God wants it there. That's the primary reason the Bible ought not be altered, and as Peter himself points out in 2 Peter 1:20–21, "First of all you must understand this, that no prophecy of scripture is a matter of one's own interpretation, because no prophecy ever came by the impulse of man, but men moved by the Holy Spirit spoke from God." And Paul explains who God assigns to handle this task in Ephesians 3:9–12: "And to make all men see what is the plan of the mystery hidden for ages in God who created all things; that through the church [singular: the Catholic Church] the manifold wisdom of God might now be made known to the principalities and powers in the heavenly places. This was according to the eternal purpose which he has realized in Christ Jesus our Lord, in whom we have boldness and confidence of access through our faith in him."

254 *The divine persons are really distinct from one another.* "God is one but not solitary." "Father," "Son," "Holy Spirit" are not simply names designating modalities of the divine being, for they are really distinct from one another: "He is not the Father who is the Son, nor is the Son he who is the Father, nor is the Holy Spirit he who is the Father or the Son." **They are distinct from one another in their relations of origin: "It is the Father who generates, the Son who is begotten, and the Holy Spirit who proceeds." The divine Unity**

is Triune [which explains why this is a mystery, and by definition, "a mystery" is not comprehensible].

264 "The Holy Spirit proceeds from the Father as the first principle and, by the eternal gift of this to the Son, from the communion of both the Father and the Son" (St. Augustine, *De Trin.* 15, 26, 47: PL 42, 1095). (Catechism of the Catholic Church; emphasis added)

It might surprise you to discover that this mystery of the blessed Trinity was actually introduced in the Old Testament's first book, Genesis.

St. Paul used the concept of the "re'shiyt" or the "firstborn" when he wrote about Christ as the "firstborn," meaning the head or first in rank, "of all Creation" and the "the Beginning, the firstborn from the dead," meaning that as the heir of the Father Jesus was the first in rank and in order in leading his brothers and sisters in the resurrection from the dead: *He is the image of the unseen God, the* **first-born** *of all creation, for in him were created all things in heaven and on earth: everything visible and everything invisible, thrones, ruling forces, sovereignties, powers—all things were created* **through** *him and* **for** *him. He exists before all things and* **in** *him all things hold together, and he is the Head of the Body that is the Church. He is* **the Beginning**, *the* **first-born** *from the dead, so that he should be supreme in every way . . .* [emphasis in original].

St. John spoke of Jesus' pre-existence in John 1:1–2: *In the beginning was the Word: the Word was with God and the Word was God. He was with God in the beginning.* **St. John** also spoke of Jesus' pre-existence in verse 15: *John witnesses to him. He proclaims: "This is the one of whom I said: He who comes after me has passed ahead of me because he existed before me* (repeated in John 1:30). St. John identified Jesus as the force behind Creation in John 1:3–5 and verse 10: *Through him all things came into being, not one thing came into being except through him . . . .*

The Church teaches that the Creation event was the unified work of the Most Holy Trinity [emphasis mine]: *The Old Testament suggests and the New Covenant reveals the creative action of the Son and the Spirit, inseparably one with that of the Father. This creative cooperation is clearly affirmed in the Church's rule of faith: "There exists but one God . . . he is the Father, God, the Creator, the author, the giver*

> of order. He made all things by himself, this is, by his Word and by his Wisdom," "by the Son and the Spirit" who, so to speak, are "his hands." Creation is the common work of the Holy Trinity. (AGAPE Bible Study)

God chose to speak through ordinary men whom he made very special (an early indication of the future role of Peter and the new faith, church, and new covenant of the New Testament) and slowly began unfolding the mystery of who God is to humanity in a manner never before revealed, and such was beyond the comprehension of the early Jewish fathers; his name (Yahweh) which they would not even say out loud for both fear and awe of him.

It is highly significant that, in doing so, God chose to reveal himself directly to only one nation (the Hebrews' or Jews') but allowed other nations and other peoples to "look on" and gaze in wonder and awe upon him. Why God chose to do this is also a mystery without an immediate answer. "For my thoughts are not your thoughts, neither are your ways my ways, says the Lord. For as the heavens are higher than the earth, so are my ways higher than your ways and my thoughts than your thoughts" (Isaiah 55:8–9). This is a great example that "faith as a requirement" is conditionally imposed upon us; it's God's right to choose. And it's God's right to limit our understanding. "You turn things upside down! Shall the potter be regarded as the clay; that the thing made should say of its maker, 'He did not make me'; or the thing formed say of him who formed it, 'He has no understanding'?" (Isaiah 29:16).

Later on, God used the kings and the prophets; and through pain and patience, the understanding of one *true* God slowly became evident, which is also supported by Deuteronomy 10:17, Joshua 24:23, and Daniel 2:47.

God's self-introduction was somewhat of an on-again-off-again series of his reactions based on the degree of obedience shown by the Hebrew nation. While God never deserted the Hebrews, they often abandoned him. Similar to an onion being peeled layer by layer, God made himself more fully known with and through "just judgments," continual adjustments, and the "carrot and the stick" type of reward and punishment, dependent on the choices that they freely made relating to their level of understanding of Yahweh, who was demanding to be their "one God, their *only* God, and *the* one true God," amid the proliferation of pagan religions with their numerous man-invented gods, which was constantly an opposing influence and a conflicting stimulus on their acceptance of "the One"—one God, one faith, and one chosen people. That same struggle still exists today in the very many Protestant faiths and churches, who too struggle mightily to grasp the reality of "just one." At that point in time in history, Yahweh was focusing solely on the Hebrew nation, which he would use as a model for all to see and the choice that Jesus would later affirm in choosing to establish only one God with just one faith in and through just one true church, from the time of its formation until the End Times.

God guides, guards, and protects only his one Catholic Church with the fullness of his truths and sort of leaves the man-made, come-along, competing faiths to deal with the realities of trying to cope, live, teach, and believe with only partial and/or incomplete truths. Exodus 34:14 says, "For you shall worship no other god, for the Lord, whose name is Jealous, is a jealous God." Deuteronomy 4:35, 39 states, "To you it was shown, that you might know that the Lord is God; there is no other besides him. Know therefore this day, and lay it to your heart, that the Lord is God in heaven above and on the earth beneath; there is no other." Deuteronomy 5:7 says, "You shall have no other gods before me." From this foundation, it seems logically to express clearly and exactly what Jesus both desired and accomplished—one God, one faith, and only one church (Ephesians 4:1–7).

Here, to clarify for us, are some of the things that really seem to stand out in the Bible history of Christianity that can aid and should direct our understanding of God, not in any specific order, rather only as they occur to me.

The Bible always seems to be pointing forward, predicting what's to come, what needs to be done, what has to be obeyed and followed. There is an amazing continuity of prophesy and forewarning from the beginning to the end of the Bible. Clearly, this is, as it "must be," a guide of sorts inspired by God's accounting. There is an inherent optimism, at times partially hidden yet always present, that is astounding. The realization of God's love for us is clearly evident throughout the Bible. "Therefore, beloved, since you wait for these, be zealous to be found by him without spot or blemish, and at peace. And count the forbearance of our Lord as salvation. So also our beloved brother Paul wrote to you according to the wisdom given him, speaking of this as he does in all his letters. *There are some things in them hard to understand, which the ignorant and unstable twist to their own destruction, as they do the other scriptures. You therefore, beloved, knowing this beforehand, beware lest you be carried away with the error of lawless men and lose your own stability"* (2 Peter 3:14–17; italics added).

The most profound and thought to be correctly understood message by many, if not all, Christians in the entire Bible is the undeniable, persistent love of God for sinful humanity, which is articulated clearest in this statement from Saint Paul: "But God shows his love for us in that while we were yet sinners Christ died for us" (Romans 5:8). This we ought never to forget.

Also evident is God's incredible patience in dealing with the Hebrew nation of the past and equally sinful man in our time and displaying astounding tolerance for our many sins, which are ever increasing in number and severity and led on by secular humanism's ramped, unabated existence and warped morality, eagerly sought and embraced by so many; atheism's rapid growth; and the ever-present relativism, which teaches that "all religious or nonreligious opinions are of equal value and equal merit if I say so." These lies are believed by uncounted millions and are competing successfully with our Catholic faith as are Christianity's many varieties—Buddhism, Islam, Mormonism, and everything else so often seen as being "equal choices" to Catholicism, which are believed to be able to be freely chosen without consequences. Yet in the end, God reigns supreme (Matthew 16:19).

God's benevolent love for all of his created humanity, like a single candle in a darkened dungeon, makes evident the need "for his light of truth and love" and permits the virtue of hope to exist. This is yet another indication of God's unyielding, unquenchable love for us. Christ's preferential candle continues to be his Catholic Church.

To be clear here, I am not suggesting that salvation outside of the Catholic Church is impossible. It is less likely and certainly less than assured, but conditional salvation might be possible for those who through no fault of their own are unaware of the Catholic Church as God's chosen path to his salvation, which is why, mysteriously, all salvation must and does flow through her (the Catholic Church).

God is "just," according to Hebrews 6:10: "For God is not so unjust as to overlook your work and the love which you showed for his sake in serving the saints, as you still do." Revelation 2:23 says, "And I will strike her children dead. And all the churches shall know that I am he who searches mind and heart, and I will give to each of you as your works deserve."

What God permits is a great mystery—abortion, wars, natural disasters, the many competing "Christian faiths"—and can only be understood and judged by God, while we stand in the background in bewilderment of God's seemingly infinite, patient endurance. Trying to understand the "justice" of cancer, early death, lack of faith, secular humanism, divorce, and an explosion of government-imposed "forms of morality," from lawful abortions to same-sex "marriages," and who knows what is next on their agenda? Divine patience is further aggravated and tried by the exodus of millions of "once Catholics" to either complete agnostic unbelief or mortal man's invented beliefs of their own choosing.

Countless numbers have abandoned the bark of Peter by insisting on some nonexistent "right" to have "worship services" that "they like" as if these services are actually for them and trashing the reality that true worship is *for* God, not primarily for our pleasure or even necessarily to our personal liking. Our liking or disliking is irrelevant; all divine worship is to be God centered and God focused, and every other consideration is secondary to this truth. This is the first and third commandments, and abandonment of the Catholic faith is succinctly and precisely addressed in Hebrews 6:1–8. Both they and, at times, the ones given responsibility for their souls might well share the guilt and the blame.

One might think of divine justice as a huge axlike pendulum that is still moving to the high left, just waiting to fall forward and make evident God's *just* anger and displeasure with what we have done or perhaps what he has only tolerated, with no or very little effort on our part to influence corrections. Our own souls and our influence on others both by our actions and by our inactions will have a part in deciding where we choose for ourselves to spend eternity. We ought to take advantage of the time that God has granted us to make amends and take God at his word. Be assured that "the ax will fall." In Deuteronomy 32:35, "Vengeance is *mine* (emphasis added)," says the Lord. Yet God remains a god of mercy and love and fairness. Hope is still available to us.

It appears to me, no matter how bad things seem to get, there is still room for optimism—a sure sign of faith, a light at the end of the tunnel, a sign of hope. The book of Job recounts how God's patience, mercy, and love permit him to remain completely and totally in charge, even in the darkness of the nights, which we so often make for ourselves. At times, God permits us to experience suffering so that we can show evidence of our love for him. God asks of us—no, demands from us faith, hope,

30

x

and charity. And God himself models these very divine attributes for us. "Listen to my words, and follow the example I set for you."

Were it possible to ask anyone of the Old Testament era to describe God, I suspect we'd hear words like powerful, vengeful, swift to act, compelling, kind, merciful, and loving. Do these same terms apply today? What terms would you use?

Now returning to the present, how God does make himself known to us through his Son, Jesus? In trying to gain personal insights of God, can one actually know him on their own terms, in the time and manner they choose; or is there a more precise, expected, and required manner of attaining this knowledge? Is it based on opportunity, luck, predestination, or something else?

Assuming that everyone is familiar with the incarnation—the birth story of Christ—I'll proceed to what seems to be the obvious question: *why?* Why did God do this? Why did God himself not only permit but also actually command the incarnation, passion, death, and resurrection of Jesus?

God is the cause of *all good*, yet God can and does permit evil to befall us in order to accomplish his own purpose. Permitting evil is not the same as causing evil. God can and does at times transform an apparent evil to gain a "good" from the dung heap of evil in our lives. This is God doing things his way, which at times is not clearly evident to us (Isaiah 55:6–10). Such is the will of God. Full understanding and complete comprehension is not for this world; rather, it is reserved for the eternal destination we choose for ourselves.

Recognizing that God is "all-knowing" tells us that there are no surprises for God. However, don't confuse "preknowledge" as automatic approval by God. Even though God knew before creating Adam and Eve that they would "fail him" as did Satan, as did Judas, as did Peter, as do we, God permits our free will to act independently of his influence, without the stimulus of external pressures, enabling us to freely choose good or evil (Ecclesiastes 15:18). Take a moment to think about this in relation to God's mercy and love and its inevitable effect, divine justice.

This tidbit of information is very revealing about God's nature: when God commits to something, he does not change his mind. Job 23:13 says, "But he is unchangeable and who can turn him? What he desires, that he does." This is not to say that prayer does not work, only that God is ever aware of all contingencies and accounts for them; no surprises ever.

God knew that Adam and Eve would fail him. And God knew from all time what actions he would take because of this momentous failure. God could have said, "That's your mulligan. Don't mess up again." God knew the seriousness of the sin and factored in all that he had provided Adam and Eve (a literal perfect existence) to encourage them not to sin. Yet they freely chose to fail God. One of the highly significant effects of this "original sin" was God closing access to heaven before anyone even had an opportunity to use it. God knew from all time what this would later lead him to do and what he would and could only accept as appeasement or "full repayment" for man's original sin. Only an offsetting action by God himself could and would satisfy divine justice. Only the abused Godhead could make full and equal amends for the abusers. God ordained the incarnation from the beginning of time.

What does that tell *us* about God? If we go back and reread Genesis chapter three, God speaks of labor, work, pain, and suffering as penalties for original sin; and these are parts of the punishment that will not be removed until the "final judgment." But even more reflective of the enormity that God perceives original sin to be is heaven being put into "lockout status," which is not even mentioned in this particular text but nevertheless is a doctrine of the Catholic Church as evidenced by "Limbo of the Fathers" and affecting all the deceased souls that merited heaven prior to Christ's resurrection. While the effects on humanity are many, the overriding one—the "natural tendency to sin"—will be immediate and last through the ages, until our death and final judgment. This effect has the theological name of "concupiscence," defined by *Fr. John Hardon's Catholic Dictionary* as "insubordination of man's desires to the dictates of reason, and the propensity of human nature to sin as a result of original sin."

Through original sin, man's reason becomes subject to ignorance, his will becomes subject to malice, the influence of concupiscence's sense appetite loses its subjection to reason and so is wounded by failures, and his irritable sense appetite loses its strength in the face of difficulty and so is said to suffer the wound of weakness, what is commonly termed "a natural tendency to sin." While this is indeed true, I hasten to point out that the "supernatural" grace from God is intended and sufficient to overcome these sinful tendencies that each of us has. Revelation 22:14 says, "Blessed are those who wash their robes [in the blood of the Lamb], that they may have the right to the tree of life and that they may enter the city by the gates." John 10:3, 11, 14 states, "To him the gatekeeper [Jesus] opens; the sheep hear his voice, and he calls his own sheep by name and leads them out. I am the good shepherd. The good shepherd lays down his life for the sheep. I am the good shepherd; I know my own and my own know me."

Original sin was so grave, such an affront to God, in great part because of all that God had bestowed upon Adam and Eve. Short of actually "being God" was the sin of Satan and would also become their own freely chosen sin; they lived a life of truly perfect existence. Every conceivable need and want was met, except for actually "being God" themselves.

Genesis 3:1–5 says, "Now the serpent was more subtle than any other wild creature that the Lord God had made. He said to the woman, 'Did God say, "You shall not eat of any tree of the garden"?' And the woman said to the serpent, 'We may eat of the fruit of the trees of the garden; but God said, "You shall not eat of the fruit of the tree which is in the midst of the garden, neither shall you touch it, lest you die."' But the serpent said to the woman, 'You will not die. *For God knows that when you eat of it your eyes will be opened, and you will be like God, knowing good and evil* [emphasis added]."

The result of Adam's original sin (CCC 404) co-opted by Eve, in a sense, "caused" or led God himself to conclude that he alone could set things right again, that he alone could restore the original friendship between the creator and the created. This was sought by God even more fervently than by man. Only God alone could make amends equal and of sufficient value to offset the "lockout" of heaven. In a real sense, the birth, life, passion, and death of Jesus were "absolutely necessary" for God to do. *Why?*

It was because heaven and a greatly desired personal relationship with God's created humanity, made in his image (Genesis 1:26–27), would have gone to waste, thereby nullifying the very reason for our creation: to enable us to be in a very personal relationship with God, one focused on man freely choosing divine worship and displaying gratitude (Isaiah 43:7, 21), which otherwise could not and would not have taken place unless God himself made atonement.

All that took place was ordained by God from the very beginning of time. It was not simply known but planned and caused by God's need for divine justice and God's incomprehensible "need," not "absolute" but in the sense of a very powerful desire, to be in personal relationship with his created humanity, which then was the overriding factor. Isaiah 43:7, 21 says, "Every one who is called by my name, whom I created for my glory, whom I formed and made. The people whom I formed for myself that they might declare my praise."

The Old Testament has many prophecies about the coming Messiah (Savior). First Samuel 16:1 says, "The Lord said to Samuel, '. . . Fill your horn with oil, and be on go; I will send you to *Jesse the Bethlehemite*, for I have provided for myself a *king* among his sons'" (from David's line, and the birth of Jesus was in the "city of David," in Bethlehem, which by the way means "city of bread"; emphasis added). Isaiah 25:9 states, "It will be said on that day, 'Lo, this is our God; we have waited for him, that he might save us. This is the Lord; we have waited for him; let us be glad and rejoice in his salvation.'" Isaiah 56:1 says, "Thus says the Lord: 'Keep justice, and do righteousness, for soon my salvation will come, and my deliverance be revealed.'" Isaiah 7:14 declares, "Therefore the Lord himself will give you a sign. Behold, a young woman shall conceive and be a son, and shall call him Imman'u-el." Micah 5:2 states, "But you, O Bethlehem Eph'rathah, who are little among the clans of Judah, from you shall come forth for me one who is to be ruler in Israel, whose origin is from of old, from ancient days." According to Hosea 11:1, "When Israel was a child, I loved him, and out of Egypt I called my son." Isaiah 9:6–7 states, "For to us a child is born, to us a son is given, and the government will be upon his shoulder, and his name will be called 'Wonderful Counselor, Mighty God, Everlasting Father, Prince of Peace.' Of the increase of his government and of peace there will be no end upon the throne of David, and over his kingdom, to establish it, and to uphold it with justice and with righteousness from this time forth and for evermore. The zeal of the Lord of hosts will do this."

John 1:29, 36 says, "The next day he saw Jesus coming toward him, and said, 'Behold, the Lamb of God, who takes away the sin of the world!' And he looked at Jesus as he walked, and said, 'Behold, the Lamb of God!'" Saint John the Baptist speaks of Jesus, who is "the Lamb of God" and the Paschal Lamb of sacrifice, planned from all eternity. Jesus Christ is the Paschal Lamb on the feast of Passover in Jerusalem—from God, of God, and by God. That, dear friends, is how much we are loved by our creator.

Matthew 26:63 says, "But Jesus was silent. And the high priest said to him, 'I adjure you by the living God, tell us if you are the Christ, the Son of God.'" Matthew 16:16 states, "Simon Peter replied, 'You are the Christ, the Son of the living God.'" Matthew 14:33 declares, "And those in the boat [the apostles] worshiped him, saying, 'Truly you are the Son of God.'" Matthew 27:54 also says, "When the centurion [the captain of the Roman guards who supervised the crucifixion of Christ] and those who were with him, keeping watch over Jesus, saw the earthquake and what took place, they were filled with awe, and said, 'Truly this was the Son of God!'"

This, friends, is the key to understanding the mystery of who God is. "Seek, and you will find" (Matthew 7:7).

God came to redeem all and to save many—all those who would or could choose to hear him and, in humility, obey him, thereby forming a personal relationship with God and fulfilling God's own desire for humanity (John 3:17) and at the same time our own destiny, conditional on our avoiding, with God's help, mortal sin by applying correctly our minds, intellects, and free will in conjunction and in full conformity with God's divine will for us and making frequent use of the sacramental confession and God's offered grace (John 20:19–23).

Only humanity can literally love and thank God. That too is another key to understanding God and why God seeks a personal relationship with us.

Redemption is not the same as salvation. Even though Jesus has an active role in both, Christ's "redemption" refers especially to the reopening and unlocking of the gates of heaven, unused by humanity from the time of Adam's original sin, thus permitting those who had cooperated with God's plans for them but were still denied access despite having "merited" the "right" to be in heaven. For them, the fathers of Limbo, the time of their personal salvation had come, and it is tied directly with Christ's resurrection and ascension. They were at last able to be "face to face" (actually "intuitively") with the God they lived and died for. (We will actually know God intuitively, as it will be our souls—with the attached minds, intellects, and free will—that join God, as our bodies will return to dust from which we were created [Genesis 3:19].) God holds forth the same promise of potential salvation to those willing to pay the "price of admission" while here on earth. John 14:2–3 states, "In my Father's house are many rooms; if it were not so, would I have told you that I go to prepare a place for you? And when I go and prepare a place for you, I will come again and will take you to myself, that where I am you may be also."

This postponement of merited reward of our early fathers remains part of the mystery of God. Surely, they did not suffer, except for being denied for a time (time does not exist for God; everything is always "present" to God) the honor and the grace of being in God's actual presence, the beatific vision.

Time and time again, we are reminded that God is in charge, even in those times that we perhaps wish that he wasn't. This too is another key to our understanding God.

Ephesians 5:8–14 says, "For once you were darkness, but now you are light in the Lord; walk as children of light (for the fruit of light is found in all that is good and right and true), and try to learn what is pleasing to the Lord. Take no part in the unfruitful works of darkness, but instead expose them. For it is a shame even to speak of the things that they do in secret; but when anything is exposed by the light it becomes visible, for anything that becomes visible is light. Therefore it is said, 'Awake, O sleeper, and arise from the dead, and Christ shall give you light.'"

We are to pick up where Christ left off. Mathew 27:51 says, "And behold, the curtain of the temple was torn in two, from top to bottom; and the earth shook, and the rocks were split." This speaks of the events immediately following: "Father, into your hands I commend My Spirit." And then he dies in his human body. But his immortal human soul continues to exist. Torn from the "top" is pointed out to us, to signify that it is God's work; it is God himself who has done this. Why, friends, is this so significant? It was huge and likely even needed (for man) a ladder to reach the top of it.

God is ever present and always in charge. This was an act of God's will, accomplished to teach us a lesson. The tearing of the huge veil protecting the "temple's holy of holies" is a metaphor of critical understanding. It refers to the just pierced side of Christ; the water and blood of Christ now constituted Eucharist, and importantly, it confirms the new covenant in Christ's blood, necessary for humanity's possible salvation (John 19:34).

The "holy of holies" could *only* be accessed by "the high priest" and then *only* once per year. Hebrews 6:20 states, "Where Jesus has gone as a forerunner on our behalf, having become a high priest for ever after the order of Melchiz'edek." Who offered bread and wine as a sacrifice to Abraham, and what was in the holy of holies? The spiritual presence of God, while what remains in our tabernacles—the new holy of holies—is the real body, blood, soul, and divinity of Jesus Christ, our God. Amen (which means "I believe").

The old covenant is now overridden, and the new and everlasting covenant takes its place. Jesus institutes, empowers, and perfects the Catholic priesthood implicitly through a number of Bible passages and teachings. I will share some of them here so that you can see that God is not always biblically precise and specific. At times, he allows us to search out that which would have been evident to us. This is an example of that process. And again, our conclusions must always align fully with the teachings of Christ's Catholic Church in order to be assured of our right understanding.

John 13:3–8 says, "Jesus, knowing that the Father had given all things into his hands, and that he had come from God and was going to God, rose from supper, laid aside his garments, and girded himself with a towel. Then he poured water into a basin, and began to wash the disciples' feet, and to wipe them with the towel with which he was girded. He came to Simon Peter; and Peter said to him, 'Lord, do you wash my feet?' Jesus answered him, 'What I am doing you do not know now, but afterward you will understand.' Peter said to him, 'You shall never wash my feet.' Jesus answered him, 'If I do not wash you, you have no part in me.'"

Second Timothy 2:5 states, "An athlete is not crowned unless he competes according to the rules."

Mark 10:43–45 declares, "But it shall not be so among you; but whoever would be great among you must be your servant, and whoever would be first among you must be slave of all. For the Son of man also came not to be served but to serve, and to give his life as a ransom for many."

Matthew 10:1–8 states, "And he called to him his twelve disciples and gave them authority over unclean spirits, to cast them out, and to heal every disease and every infirmity. The names of the twelve apostles are these: first, Simon, who is called Peter, and Andrew his brother; James the son of Zeb'edee, and John his brother; Philip and Bartholomew; Thomas and Matthew the tax collector; James the son of Alpheus, and Thaddaeus; Simon the Cananaean, and Judas Iscariot, who betrayed him. These twelve Jesus sent out, charging them, 'Go nowhere among the Gentiles, and enter no town of the Samaritans, but go rather to the lost sheep of the house of Israel. And preach as you go, saying, "The kingdom of heaven is at hand." *Heal the sick, raise the dead, cleanse lepers, cast out demons* [emphasis added]. You received without paying, give without pay.'"

Matthew 16:18–19 says, "And I tell you, you are Peter, and on this rock I will build my church, and the powers of death shall not prevail against it. I will give you the keys of the kingdom of heaven, and whatever you bind on earth shall be bound in heaven, and whatever you loose on earth shall be loosed in heaven."

John 17:14, 16–20 proclaims, "I have given them thy word; and the world has hated them because they are not of the world, even as I am not of the world. They are not of the world, even as I am not of the world. Sanctify them in the truth; thy word is truth. *As thou didst send me into the world, so I have sent them into the world. And for their sake I consecrate myself, that they also may be consecrated in truth* [emphasis added]. I do not pray for these only, but also for those who believe in me through their word."

Matthew 28:18–20 declares, "All authority in heaven and on earth has been given to me [you]. Go therefore and make disciples of all nations, baptizing them in the name of the Father and of the Son and of the Holy Spirit, teaching them to observe all that I have commanded *you* [emphasis added]; and lo, I am with you always, to the close of the age."

John 20:19–23 says, "On the evening of that day, the first day of the week, the doors being shut where the disciples were, for fear of the Jews, Jesus came and stood among them and said to them, 'Peace be with you.' When he had said this, he showed them his hands and his side. Then the disciples were glad when they saw the Lord. Jesus said to them again, 'Peace be with you. As the Father has sent me, even so I send you.' And when he had said this, he breathed on them, and said to them, 'Receive the Holy Spirit. If you forgive the sins of any, they are forgiven; if you retain the sins of any, they are retained.'"

Each of these passages supports, in differing manners, sacramental ordination, the Catholic priesthood.

Luke 22:19–21 says, "And he took bread, and when he had given thanks he broke it and gave it to them, saying, 'This is my body which is given for you. Do this in remembrance of me.' And likewise the cup after supper, saying, 'This is which is poured out for you is the new covenant in my blood.'"

The significance of the torn veil is profound in that it permits access to not only the spirit of Christ (like the Protestant faiths have) but also the very real presence of God, of Jesus the Christ in his now-glorified body, blood, soul, and divinity—God, not simply the spirit of God. Further, God now becomes available to *everyone* who seeks him where he can be found, not just once a year but also whenever we make the sacrificial effort to be near him. God became man, died for *all*. But only a few—dare I say, a very few—will make the effort, suffer the sacrifices, have the humility to do all that God demands for their eternal salvation, thus the parable of the "narrow gate" (Matthew 7:13–21).

Like a puzzle, God hints at who, what, and where he is and how he can be found. Some of the pieces are in this document, and others are for you to seek out for yourselves. But in closing, I will share this final clue: 1 John 4:16–18 states, "So we know and believe the love God has for us. God is love, and he who abides in love abides in God, and God abides in him. In this is love perfected with us, that we may have confidence for the day of judgment, because as he is so are we in this world. There is no fear in love, but perfect love casts out fear. For fear has to do with punishment, and he who fears is not perfected in love."

God is *love*. Every action of God is motivated by love. Everything God touches is love. God's every motive is founded in love. And we—you and me, humanity—alone have the attributes to return love to God and to be thankful for the many blessings bestowed upon us. Even the crosses God "makes for us" are motivated by love and manifested in love for us. Every single thing, every person we meet, every opportunity to sin, every good and "bad" thing is permitted by God for two and only two reasons: for the glorification of God and for the possible sanctification of us personally or someone God wants to help. Our free will permits us to choose to obey or to disobey, which is why salvation is always our choice, and we are not always conforming to God's desire for us.

Every pain is an opportunity for grace. But sometimes we are so focused "on the moment" that we overlook the future. This is something we all need to work on. "Thy will be done" here on earth "as it is in heaven." So, friend, that's the final clue. How is God's divine will done in heaven? In total and complete obedience, humility, extreme gratitude, and everlasting joy.

Genesis 1:26–27 states, "Then God said, 'Let us make man in our image, after our likeness; and let them have dominion over the fish of the sea, and over the birds of the air, and over the cattle, and over all the earth, and over every creeping thing that creeps upon the earth.' So God created man in his own image, in the image of God he created him; male and female he created them."

John 4:23–24 says, "But the hour is coming, and now is, when the true worshipers will worship the Father in spirit and truth, for such the Father seeks to worship him. God is spirit, and those who worship him must worship in spirit and truth." We see here evidence that God is "spirit and truth." We also see in Genesis, the first book, and from the first chapter of the Bible that God created man in "his own image."

Two questions loom large:

1. Just *how* does man emulate God who is a "spirit"? When God created man and choose to create them "in his own image," he did so by sharing with each and every man, from the dawn of man's creation to the very end of time, special attributes. He gives to humanity, and only to humanity, lesser versions of some of his own godly attributes, namely, a *mind* (not speaking here of our brain), an *intellect* (not meaning one's IQ), and a free will, all of which are permanently attached to *man's soul*; and each of the realities is like our God, "spiritual things." And like God, this spiritual package is eternal and can neither be killed nor die.

2. *Why* did God choose to create man? Even after the fall of Satan? Just a bit of history preceding the creation of humanity. God did not have to create man, especially after the folly and fall of Lucifer and his minions, who desired not only to be "like God" (they had this same spiritual package, as do we, of minds, intellects, and free will but with a much higher degree of use) but also to actually be god. This same treason, this same rejection of God, this very same pride-filled desire by our first parents to also "be gods," just like God, is the original sin of Adam and Eve, whom we will study in a later lesson. So here we discover just *why* humanity was created: to know, to love, to serve, to obey, and to worship God. Each of these possibilities requires us to engage the three special attributes given to us freely, much like grace, with a precise hope by God on just how they were and are to be used. It is the spiritual package all men are endowed with: a mind, intellect, and free will, all of which are permanently attached to our souls. It is these very attributes that permit us to fulfill the reason for our existence or to choose to deny God what is distinctively intended for him, namely, the salvation of our very eternal souls.

Isaiah 43:7, 21 states, "Every one who is called by my name, whom I created for my glory, whom I formed and made. The people whom I formed for myself that they might declare my praise."

Deuteronomy 30:19–20 says, "I call heaven and earth to witness against you this day, that I have set before you life and death, blessing and curse; therefore choose life, that you and your descendants may live, loving the Lord your God, obeying his voice, and cleaving to him; for that means life to you and length of days, that you may dwell in the land which the Lord swore to your fathers, to Abraham, to Isaac, and to Jacob, to give them."

We exist because God "willed" that we exist. God willed that we exist so that he could and would be recognized, honored, and worshipped as our God, as our creator, and as the one in charge of everything that he created, except in matters of free will when speaking of humanity, who could choose freely to fulfill their reason for existence or also just as freely choose not to.

In effect, they are not saying, "I love you my god," but rather proclaiming by one's thoughts and actions that they hate God. These extremes meet God's expectations; being indifferent or knowing but being uncommitted is insufficient for God's sense of justice. Revelation 3:16 states, "So, because you are lukewarm, and neither cold nor hot, I will spew you out of my mouth."

The issue then is the use of our spiritual gifts. Do we permit them to fulfill God's will, or will we actually deny God? The pivotal point is our free will. Because God is perfect, God desires that the perfect love he demonstrates for us be returned to him as "our perfect love." In order for love to be perfected, it has to be freely given. So God makes it possible to be loved perfectly by us but, in doing so, has also to make it possible for us to choose to hate him. Where we choose to spend eternity is our choice.

CHAPTER TWO

God Acts through His Church

Jesus answered, "Truly, truly, I say to you, unless one is born of water and the Spirit, he cannot enter the kingdom of God."

—John 3:5

Now the eleven disciples went to Galilee, to the mountain to which Jesus had directed them. And when they saw him they worshiped him; but some doubted. And Jesus came and said to them, "All authority in heaven and on earth has been given to me. Go therefore and make disciples of all nations, baptizing them in the name of the Father and of the Son and of the Holy Spirit, teaching them to observe all that I have commanded you; and lo, I am with you always, to the close of the age."

—Matthew 28:16–20

How and Why the Catholic Church Exists

Does the Bible really teach once saved, always saved? John 3:16–19 says, "For God so loved the world that he gave his only Son, that whoever believes in him should not [not "will not"] perish but have [attained] eternal life. For God sent the Son into the world, not to condemn the world, but that the world might be saved through him. He who believes in him is not condemned; he who does not believe [accept fully] is condemned already, because he has not believed in the name [and the words and all of the teachings] of the only Son of God. And this is the judgment, that the light has come into the world, and men loved darkness [their own human opinions rather than divine teachings] rather than the light [God's own truths], because their deeds were evil [opposed to God in their pride or lack of right understanding]."

This is how one becomes a saint. Acts 5:29 says, "But Peter and the apostles answered, 'We must obey God rather than men.'"

When we accept the teachings of Jesus Christ (as expressed, without changing the meaning), we are saying and confirming that God *is* trustworthy. (The opposite is also true.) Fr. Mitch Pacwa from EWTN

John 3:35–36 states, "The Father loves the Son, and has given all things into his hand. He who believes in the Son has eternal life [meaning, they who hear and obey]; he who does not [hear and] obey the Son shall not see life, but the wrath of God rests upon him."

My dear friends in Christ, nothing—absolutely nothing—happens without a cause, a reason. Yet despite the fact that seemingly, in my opinion, clarity of "cause" proffered by Jesus Christ in choosing to establish the Catholic Church *alone* is the normal means for humanity's path to one's own salvation, there exist in the thousands alternative paths influenced and presented as "the way, the truth, and the life" under the broad title of "Christianity" and holding "all such to be equals" despite having been "created" as simpler alternative, man-made choices to the very Son of God's own teachings yet claiming to still be a valid means and ligament alternative to what the Catholic Church teaches on the right understanding of the Bible. Can there be more than a single "truth," more than one right path to one's personal salvation?

The answer to the last questions is "perhaps" or maybe, even "yes," but then we must ask, do they converge or intersect each other at any point? And that too seems to be "yes." Let's see, as so many of these "alternatives paths to one's salvation" present themselves as "Bible churches," if in actuality investigating the Bible; can one find evidence for what their positions contain? Are there grounds for their chosen church and salvation positions with an actual biblical foundation?

Right out of the "shoot" is, of course, Matthew 16:13–19, which remains among the most disputed passages in the Bible and with good cause. Its message is unambiguously clear. Therefore, if it cannot be denied or redefined, the conversation will seemingly start and end here. But denied and redefined it is and continues to be.

By inserting additional comments that clarify what ought not, in my opinion, need clarification in these teachings, God's intent seems abundantly and indisputably clear.

Matthew 16:13–19 says, "Now when Jesus came into the district of Caesare'a Philippi, he asked his disciples, 'Who do men say that the Son of man is?' And they said, 'Some say John the Baptist, others say Eli'jah, and others Jeremiah or one of the prophets.' He said to them, 'But who do you say that I am?' Simon Peter replied, 'You are the Christ, the Son of the living God.' And Jesus answered him, 'Blessed are you, Simon Bar-Jona! For flesh and blood has not revealed this to you, but my Father who is in heaven. [Simon Peter here is already infused with heavenly knowledge by God, the Holy Spirit.] And I [God] tell you [singular], you are Peter [a new title meaning "rock"], and on this rock I [God] will build my church [singular], and the powers of death shall not prevail against it [singular]. I will give you [alone is implied here] the keys of the kingdom of heaven [all of them seem to be given to Peter], and whatever you [singular] bind on earth shall be bound in heaven, and whatever you [singular] loose on earth shall be loosed in heaven [with God's own powers and authority]."

I'll leave it up to you to decide if there is actually any "wiggle room" in this teaching for alternative positions. I personally don't see it. This then seems to put to rest, the debate of how the Catholic Church is the only Jesus-founded "church" and exists from the time of the "visitation of Jesus" to the present and onward.

We proceed now to the clear intent of Jesus, who is God, to make Peter not a mere "titular head" but a leader with authority and power, answerable directly and only to Christ, the king, which will logically be required in order to fulfill successfully the mission given with infused authority and powers of God (John 17:18–19) and at first granted to Peter alone. This assignment in Matthew chapter sixteen leads to a reasonable question, does this authority have the right to be passed on and transferred to others? This quandary seems to be the more reasonable, logical, and pertinent question to be addressed, rather than trying to senselessly attempt to redefine the meaning of our Lord's proclamation regarding Peter being the "the rock" (Ephesians 2:20), with one God, one set of faith beliefs, and one church, which is precise, specific, and clearly articulated by Jesus.

It ought to be not too surprising to discover that Simon Peter was the assumed head of the group even before our Lord's proclamation and the handing of "the keys" to him. Simon was the business head of the fishing enterprise that four of the twelve apostles were associated with, and he seemed to have possessed the personality of a leader. He was consistently the spokesperson of the group.

Matthew 10:1–4 states, "And he called to him his twelve disciples [often synonymous with *apostles*] and gave them authority over unclean spirits, to cast them out, and to heal every disease and every infirmity. The names of the twelve apostles are these: first, Simon, who is called Peter, and Andrew his brother; James the son of Zeb'edee, and John his brother; Philip and Bartholomew; Thomas and Matthew the tax collector; James the son of Alphaeus, and Thaddaeus; Simon the Cananaean, and Judas Iscariot, who betrayed him." The subtle fact that Simon is listed as "first" and Judas, the traitor, "last" gives further evidence of Peter's position and recognition as the group "leader."

Given the diversity of the selected group—fishermen, a tax collector (seen as a traitor and enemy of the peoples), doubting Thomas, a zealot (the other Simon), and the "money man" (Judas, the traitor/thief)—a strong personality is required to control, unify, and direct them. God plans for every contingency.

There is biblical evidence for a "shared leadership," with Simon as its head, which soon begins to unfold and is also found in Matthew 10, which is our next hint. Matthew 10:5–9 says, "These twelve Jesus sent out, charging them, 'Go nowhere among the Gentiles, and enter no town of the Samaritans, but go rather to the lost sheep of the house of Israel. And preach as you go, saying, "The kingdom of heaven is at hand. Heal the sick, raise the dead, and cleanse the lepers, cast out demons. You received without paying, give without pay. Take no gold, nor silver, nor copper in your belts." So now the "natural leader" was seemed to be made an equal to the other apostles in regard to powers and authority granted by Christ.

Now we share a set of teachings that are so powerful and direct that they convert the "hints" to a precise, clear directive. These are found in Matthew 18:1–7, 11–20:

> At that hour the disciples came to Jesus, saying: Who thinkest thou is the greater in the kingdom of heaven? And Jesus calling unto him a little child, set him in the midst of them, And said: Amen I say to you, unless you be converted, and become as little children [accept and become humble as Jesus], you shall not enter into the kingdom of heaven. Whosoever therefore shall humble himself as this little child, he is the greater in the kingdom of heaven. And he that shall receive one such little child in my name, receiveth me. But he that shall scandalize [teach in error] one of these little ones that believe in me, it were better for him that a millstone should be hanged about his neck, and that he should be drowned in the depth of the sea.
>
> Woe to the world because of scandals. For it must needs be that scandals [lies/heresies] come: but nevertheless woe to that man by whom the scandal cometh [causes or spreads the heresies].
>
> For the Son of man is come to save that which was lost.
>
> What think you? If a man have an hundred sheep, and one of them should go astray: doth he not leave the ninety-nine in the mountains, and go to seek that which is gone astray? And if it so be that he find it: Amen I say to you, he rejoiceth more for that, than for the ninety-nine that went not astray. Even so it is not the will of your Father, who is in heaven, that one of these little ones [anyone] should perish.
>
> But if thy brother shall offend against thee, go, and rebuke him between thee and him alone. If he shall hear thee, thou shalt gain thy brother. And if he will not hear thee, take with thee one or two more: that in the mouth of two or three witnesses every word may stand. And if he will not hear them: tell the church [singular]. And if he will not hear the church [leaders], let him be to thee as the heathen and publican. Amen I say to you [the apostles], whatsoever you shall bind upon earth, shall be bound also in heaven; and whatsoever you shall loose upon earth, shall be loosed also in heaven [the identical words used in Matthew 16:19 with Peter alone].

Luke 10:21 says, "In that same hour he rejoiced in the Holy Spirit and said, 'I thank thee, Father, Lord of heaven and earth, that thou hast hidden these things from the wise and understanding and revealed them to babes; yea, Father, for such was thy gracious will.' [God remains in charge.]"

John 14:26 declares, "But the Counselor, the Holy Spirit, whom the Father will send in my name, he will teach you all things, and bring to your remembrance all that I have said to you." John 20:22 states, "And when he had said this, he breathed on them, and said to them, 'Receive the Holy Spirit.'" This passage is addressed once again to "all remaining eleven apostles" *but* takes place well after the appointment of Simon Peter as the authoritative *head* of the Catholic Church in Christ's absence. Peter now is the known, accepted, and direct head of this new church.

One should also factor in the logical, absolute need for an organizational head, a leader foreseen as an absolute, requisite need by Jesus. To not do so would clearly indicate that Christ intended all that he came to Earth for and, in fact, did accomplish would end with the apostles' lives. That's an impossible and completely illogical conclusion, and that then becomes the motive for Christ's future actions and decisions in choosing one man to lead this new faith and church.

The writings of John ("the beloved apostle")—the youngest and the only one to survive the attempt to martyrdom, along with the eleven other apostles, and who lived to be over ninety years old—provides much further evidence of God's plan for his church (singular). John 14:16–20 says, "And I will ask the Father, and he shall give you another Paraclete, that he may abide with you for ever. The spirit of truth, whom the world cannot receive, because it seeth him not, nor knoweth him: but you [the apostles, the church] shall know him; because he shall abide with you, and shall be in you. I will not leave you orphans, I will come to you. Yet a little while: and the world seeth me no more. But you see me: because I live, and you shall live. In that day you shall know, that I am in my Father, and you in me, and I in you [another Holy Eucharist reference]."

John 17:9–11, 16–23 states, "I pray for them [the apostles]: I pray not for the world, but for them whom thou hast given me: because they are thine: And all my things are thine, and thine are mine; and I am glorified in them. And now I am not in the world, and these are in the world, and I come to thee. Holy Father, keep them in thy name whom thou has given me; that they may be one, as we also are. They are not of the world, as I also am not of the world. Sanctify them in truth. Thy word is truth.

As thou hast sent me into the world, I also have sent them into the world. And for them do I sanctify myself [only for *them*—the apostles and those who follow them], that they also may [will] be sanctified in truth. [Jesus Christ gives *himself* as the warranty of perfect truth of his church teachings on *all* matters of faith beliefs and on *all* moral issues.] And not for them only do I pray, but for them also who through their word shall believe in me; That they all may be one, as thou, Father, in me, and I in thee; that they also may be one in us; that the world may believe that thou hast sent me. And the glory which thou hast given me, I have given to them; that they may be one, as we also are one: I in them, and thou in me; that they may be made perfect in one: and the world may know that thou hast sent me, and hast loved them, as thou hast also loved me."

Then there is this exchange at the site of the now empty tomb of Christ, from John 20:16–23: "Jesus saith to her: Mary. She turning, saith to him: Rabboni (which is to say, Master). Jesus saith to her: Do not touch me, for I am not yet ascended to my Father. But go to my brethren, and say to them: I ascend to my Father and to your Father, to my God and your God. Mary Magdalen cometh, and telleth the disciples: I have seen the Lord, and these things he said to me. Now when it was late that same day, the first of the week, and the doors were shut, where the disciples were gathered together, for fear of the Jews, Jesus came and stood in the midst, and said to them: Peace be to you. And when he had said this, he shewed them his hands and his side. The disciples therefore were glad, when they saw the Lord. He said therefore to them again: Peace be to you. As the Father hath sent me, I also send you. When he had said this, he breathed on them; and he said to them: Receive ye the Holy Ghost. Whose sins you shall forgive, they are forgiven them; and whose sins you shall retain, they are retained."

At this point, I believe we have already provided sufficient evidence that explains with a clear biblical foundation the how and why today's Catholic Church exist as a command from Jesus Himself, is solely directed, and protected by God. Cf. Matthew 28:19: "Going therefore, teach ye all nations; baptizing them in the name of the Father, and of the Son, and of the Holy Ghost." But there is more, and I wish to make the case for only one God and only one set of faith beliefs under and in only one church indisputably clear under the guidance and tutelage of the Holy Spirit for *only* today's Catholic Church, having both the mandate and the ability to fully share all God's truths as Christ's specified will as clearly and powerfully as I am guided to do.

Let's now open the book called the Acts of the Apostles. This book too is authored by Saint Luke, the third Gospel author. Luke is not an apostle. Along with Saint Paul (with whom Luke traveled), he is the insider with the highest degree of education. Luke was a medical doctor and acted as a scribe for Paul. He knew personally the apostles and Paul. Therefore, his testimony is also that of a "firsthand witness."

Acts 1:1–9, 12–20 says, "The former treatise I made, O Theophilus, of all things which Jesus began to do and to teach, Until the day on which, giving commandments by the Holy Ghost to the apostles whom he had chosen, he was taken up. To whom also he shewed himself alive after his passion, by many proofs, for forty days appearing to them, and speaking of the kingdom of God. And eating together with them, he commanded them, that they should not depart from Jerusalem, but should wait for the promise of the Father, which you have heard (saith he) by my mouth. For John indeed baptized with water, but you shall be baptized with the Holy Ghost [John 20:21–22], not many days hence. They therefore who were come together, asked him, saying: Lord, wilt thou at this time restore again the kingdom to Israel? But he said to them: It is not for you to know the times or moments, which the Father hath put in his own power: But you shall receive the power of the Holy Ghost coming upon you, and you shall be witnesses unto me in Jerusalem, and in all Judea, and Samaria, and even to the uttermost part of the earth [specifically and exclusively spoken to the apostles]. And when he had said these things, while they looked on, he was raised up: and a cloud received him out of their sight. Then they returned to Jerusalem from the mount that is called Olivet, which is nigh Jerusalem, within a sabbath day's journey. And when they were come in, they went up into an upper room, where abode Peter [once again listed first] and John, James and Andrew, Philip and Thomas, Bartholomew and Matthew, James of Alpheus, and Simon Zelotes, and Jude the brother of James. All these were persevering with one mind in prayer with the women, and Mary the mother of Jesus, and with his brethren [meaning "followers"]. In those days Peter rising up in the midst of the brethren, said: (now the number of persons together was about an hundred and twenty :) Men, brethren, the scripture must needs be fulfilled, which the Holy Ghost spoke before by the mouth of David concerning Judas, who was the leader of them that apprehended Jesus: Who was numbered with us, and had obtained part of this ministry. And he indeed hath possessed a field of the reward of iniquity, and being hanged, burst asunder in the midst: and all his bowels gushed out. And it became known to all the inhabitants of Jerusalem: so that the same field was called in their tongue, Haceldama, that is to say, the field of blood. For it is written in the book of Psalms: Let their habitation become desolate, and let there be none to dwell therein. And his bishopric let another take." Succession is now firmly and biblically established, further evidence of God's plan for one God, only one set of faith beliefs, and only one church.

According to Acts 2:11–15, which follows immediately the events of the first Pentecost and Christ's promise of sending the Holy Spirit, "Jews also, and proselytes, Cretes, and Arabians: we have heard them speak in our own tongues the wonderful works of God. And they were all astonished, and wondered, saying one to another: What meaneth this? But others mocking, said: These men are full of new wine. But Peter standing up with the eleven, lifted up his voice, and spoke to them: Ye men of Judea, and all you that dwell in Jerusalem, be this known to you, and with your ears receive my words. For these are not drunk, as you suppose, seeing it is but the third hour of the day."

While there is more that could be presented as evidence, what we have shown is clear and precise and shows well the mind, heart, and will of our God for only one God, only one set of faith beliefs, and his only one church, which he alone personally founded and where Jesus gave the mission expressed in Matthew 28:19–20 directly and exclusively to his chosen apostles. "Going therefore, teach ye all nations; baptizing them in the name of the Father, and of the Son, and of the Holy Ghost. Teaching them to observe all things whatsoever I have commanded *you*: and behold I am with *you* all days, even to the consummation of the world" (emphasis added).

Where then is the authority or, for that matter, the need for competing "Bible churches"? Nowhere in the Bible is there evidence that God, neither Yahweh nor Jesus, even one time approved of, accepted, or even tolerated competing faiths. That is precisely the battle that rages on throughout the entire Old Testament: pagan faiths competing with God's one true faith.

Let's presume just for a moment that the above statement is false. It's not, but let's presume that it is. Depending on the source, there are from several hundreds to an estimated forty thousand differing Protestant faith churches, each with its own understanding of what the Bible actually says and teaches. Truth is singular and can't be anything but singular per defined issue, which on faith beliefs was already defined and declared up to 1,500 years before the Protestant Revolution and Luther's King James Bible. Which one, which single one of them is then "the one true church," and on what basis is that selection made? Only the Catholic Church can be proven to be the one Christ desired, founded, fully guides, and protects. Amen!

May God continue to bless and guide you all.

CHAPTER THREE

The "Good Book"

And the tempter came and said to him, "If you are the Son of God, command these stones to become loaves of bread." **But he answered,** *"It is written, 'Man shall not live by bread alone, but by every word that proceeds from the mouth of God.'"*

—Matthew 4:3–4

All scripture is inspired by God and profitable for teaching, for reproof, for correction, and for training in righteousness, that the man of God may be complete, equipped for every good work.

—2 Timothy 3:16–17

The Bible Is a Catholic Book

Having more than a "simple understanding" of the Catholic Bible is an essential element of defending, explaining, and understanding our Catholic faith, which is a Bible-based faith. Some key points are these. It is a fact that "the Bible" is a "Catholic book." This may come as a shock to some. This said, the Bible is a book of the Catholic Church, not the other way around as if the Catholic Church was and is completely and fully reliant on the Bible and nothing else. The analogy of a "tripod" is the common image of our Catholic faith's foundation.

Second Thessalonians 3:6 says, "Now we command you, brethren, in the name of our Lord Jesus Christ, that you keep away from any brother who is living in idleness and not in accord with the tradition that you received from us."

The Three Pillars of the Catholic Church are as follows (tripod legs):

1. Sacred Scripture. All the books of the Old Testament and the New Testament.
2. Sacred Apostolic Tradition. The living tradition of the church, the church fathers, and the sacred liturgy.
3. The Church's Magisterium. The teaching authority of the pope and all those bishops worldwide united with him.

It was Catholics who authored the entire New Testament, all twenty-seven books, under divine inspiration and collected and selected the Old Testament's forty-six books, which comprised the seventy-three books to be included as "codified," cementing the desired and "inspired" content of God's Bible with the blessing and protection of the Holy Spirit (2 Timothy 3:16–17).

The Catholic Bible was the *only* Christian Bible to exist for about one thousand years, from the time it was fully authored and later collected, somewhere in the late first century or early second century, until AD 1054, when the great eastern schism took place.

Here's a brief look at the Catholic Church's endeavors to "codify," that is, to identify and certify precisely and formally what books are in fact Holy Spirit–inspired, and to then put them into a single book, which we now call "the Bible." But I hasten to point out that the reason "it took so long" was because the early church suffered severe widespread persecution, and there were countless martyrs who offered their life in defense of this newfound faith. The persecution was so severe that it literally drove the church to practice their faith underground in the catacombs.

Let's look at the history of the codification of the Catholic Bible.

There was a constant history of faithful people from Paul's time through the Apostolic and Post Apostolic Church.

Melito, bishop of Sardis, an ancient city of Asia Minor, c. 170 AD produced the first known Christian attempt at an Old Testament canon. His list maintains the Septuagint order of books but contains only the Old Testament protocanonicals minus the Book of Esther. ["PROTOCANONICAL. A term applied to those books of the Bible, especially in the Old Testament, whose inspired character had never been questioned, e.g., by any Church Father. But the expression is misleading because it was not the Church Fathers but the Church's magisterium under the Pope that was divinely authorized to decide on the canonicity of the Scriptures" (*Father Hardon's Catholic Dictionary*).]

The Council of Laodicea, c. 360, produced a list of books similar to today's canon. *This was one of the Church's earliest decisions on a canon* [emphasis added].

Pope Damasus, 366–384, in his Decree, listed the books of today's canon [emphasis added].

The Council of Rome, 382, was the forum which prompted Pope Damasus' Decree.

Bishop Exuperius of Toulouse wrote to Pope Innocent I *in 405* requesting a list of canonical books. *Pope Innocent listed the present canon* [emphasis added].

The Council of Hippo, a local North Africa council of bishops created the list of the Old and New Testament books in [AD] 393 which is the same as the Roman Catholic list today [emphasis added].

The Council of Carthage, a local North Africa council of bishops created the same list of canonical books in 397 [emphasis added]. This is the council which many Protestant and Evangelical Christians take as the authority for the New Testament canon of books. The Old Testament canon from the same council is identical to Roman Catholic canon today. Another Council of Carthage in 419 offered the same list of canonical books.

Since the Roman Catholic Church does not define truths unless errors abound on the matter, Roman Catholic Christians look to *the Council of Florence, an ecumenical council in 1441* [emphasis added] for the first definitive list of canonical books.

The final infallible definition of canonical books for Roman Catholic Christians came from the Council of Trent in 1556 in the face of the errors of the Reformers [revolutionaries: Luther et al.] who rejected seven Old Testament books from the canon of scripture to that time.

There was no canon of scripture in the early Church; there was no Bible. The Bible is the book of the Church; she is not the Church of the Bible [emphasis added]. It was the Church—her leadership, faithful people—guided by the authority of the Spirit of Truth which discovered the books inspired by God in their writing. The Church did not *create* the canon; she *discerned* the canon. Fixed canons of the Old and New Testaments, hence the Bible, were not known much before the end of the 2nd and early 3rd century. (Catholic Biblical Apologetics)

Second Peter 1:16–21 states, "For we did not follow cleverly devised myths when we made known to you the power and coming of our Lord Jesus Christ, but we were eyewitnesses of his majesty. For when he received honor and glory from God the Father and the voice was borne to him by the Majestic Glory, 'This is my beloved Son, with whom I am well pleased,' we heard this voice borne from heaven, for we were with him on the holy mountain. And we have the prophetic word made more sure. You will do well to pay attention to this as to a lamp shining in a dark place, until the day dawns and the morning star rises in your hearts. *First of all you must understand this, that no prophecy of scripture is a matter of one's own interpretation, because no prophecy ever came by the impulse of man, but men moved by the Holy Spirit spoke from God* [emphasis added]."

Ephesians 3:9–12 says, "And to make all men see what is the plan of the mystery hidden for ages in God who created all things; that through the church [singular: *the* Catholic Church] the manifold wisdom of God might now be made known to the principalities and powers in the heavenly places. This was according to the eternal purpose which he has realized in Christ Jesus our Lord, in whom we have boldness and confidence of access through our faith in him."

Second Timothy 3:16–17 declares, "All scripture is inspired by God and profitable for teaching, for reproof, for correction, and for training in righteousness, that the man of God may be complete, equipped for every good work."

Code of Canon Law Can. 750 §1 states, "A person must believe with divine and Catholic faith all those things contained in the word of God, written or handed on, that is, in the one deposit of faith entrusted to the Church, and at the same time proposed as divinely revealed either by the solemn magisterium of the Church or by its ordinary and universal magisterium which is manifested by the common adherence of the Christian faithful under the leadership of the sacred magisterium; therefore all are bound to avoid any doctrines whatsoever contrary to them."

All non-Catholic Bibles use the Catholic Bible as their base and reference, and nearly all of what they have in their Bibles can be also found in our Bible. Of course, some changes were made to support their "new positions," *so always use the Catholic Bible when quoting verses.*

The entire original Bible (in a single language) was the Latin Vulgate, translated from Greek, Hebrew, Aramaic, and Latin around AD 350 by Saint Jerome into the first complete Bible in a single language. Latin, the official language of the Roman Catholic Church, was selected, and this was the primary complete Bible until about the year 1600.

In reaction to the Protestant Revolution, led by Luther and later by John Calvin—who were preparing their own Bible version in their common language (language of the people) of the once-Catholic Bible—the Church was forced to publish its Catholic version, also in "the common English language," so as to prevent or at least not make it necessary for "Christ's sheep" (John 10:11) to turn to the Protestant Bibles, in search of biblical literacy and understanding.

King Henry VIII separated from the Roman Catholic Church in February of 1531. His "state" religion was only practiced in England, where it was forced on the populace. However, it still exists today as the Anglican Church. While many of their practices emulate the rites of the Roman Catholic Church, there are significant differences between Catholic and Anglican faith beliefs.

The Catholic Church's policy against the
laity reading the Bible on their own

Prior to the publication of the Catholic Bible in English, the Roman Catholic Church did not want laypeople to read the Bible by themselves, fearing that it was too easy to err in self-interpretation. That fear has been validated and continues to exist today in the many thousands of protestant sects, each with their own understanding of what the Bible actually teaches (Acts 5:32). Obviously, these are not Holy Spirit–inspired understandings. The Roman Catholic Church is the only fully authorized and protected source for proper translation because that was God's plan (Matthew 28:16–20).

I strongly urge each of you to google www.drbo.org (the Douay-Rheims Bible), and when you pull it up, right click your mouse, and add an icon to your Startup page. This and the Catholic RSV (Revised Standard Version) are the Bibles I most often quote from.

A second site you may wish to add to your desktop is a Catholic commentary called Haydock's Catholic Bible Commentary (1859) found in http://haydock1859.tripod.com/. This will explain in detail nearly any verse you do not understand. It is a thoroughly Catholic site and can be trusted for accuracy. Again, google it, and right click it to add an icon to your Startup page.

With these tools, you need not memorize the entire Bible; you simply can know "what it actually teaches" and find what you're seeking by a word or phrase search. However, you must still read and gain a familiarity with the Bible to be sufficiently aware of its general content.

At minimum, you should read the entire New Testament. No hurry, but it is very important to gain an understanding of the biblical content and the flow of events.

Here is another tip on using the Bible. Protestants typically do not expect Catholics to be "Bible savvy" and are often surprised that we even own a Bible, much less read it. Saint Jerome—who translated the Bible from its original Hebrew, Aramaic, and Greek into the then-universal language of Latin, as it was at that time the language of the Roman Empire—Jerome taught that "ignorance of the Bible is ignorance of Christ." And this, my friends, is as true today as it was over a thousand years ago when he taught it.

So just how do Protestants appear to be so knowledgeable about the Bible? Truth is most aren't. More common is the practice of memorizing bits and pieces that that they can quote pretty much at will, but seldom does one find them using the entire Bible.

In truth, how is our faith spread? Is it because of us? No, it is not actually despite our efforts but nevertheless through us. Don't get hung up on what you don't know. If you're walking with God, he'll guide and assist you. That is why a solid prayer and a sacramental life is very important. Come, Holy Spirit, come! But that said, we must not be slothful; we are to read the Bible. Fifteen minutes of reading the Bible daily is a good habit to develop.

God will use you *if* you allow him but in his way and his time. It takes effort and a bit of sacrifice, but then what good doesn't?

Here are some problems that Protestants have with the Bible. For reasons beyond common sense and logic (the answer falls under the realm of the Holy Spirit withholding his Gift of right understanding), a great many Protestants do not use (or seemingly do not even accept) the entire Word of God. Much of Saint Matthew's Gospel and John chapter 6 and James chapter 2 are examples of this. Protestant principles of "once saved, always saved" and salvation by faith alone are not provable within the Bible when the entire Bible is used.

Often, when they do read these verses, they will add words or ignore words that conflict with their limited understanding. Take Matthew 16:18–19 for example: "And I tell you, you are Peter, and on this rock I will build my church [singular], and the powers of death shall not prevail against it. I will give *you* the keys of the kingdom of heaven, and whatever *you* bind on earth shall be bound in heaven, and whatever *you* loose on earth shall be loosed in heaven" (italics added).

At other times, they will simply not accept what the Bible and Jesus clearly say, despite it being in a literal sense, the "very words of God." Matthew 16:18–19 (quoted above), John 20:21–23 on sins' forgiveness God's way, 1 John 5:16–17 on "mortal sin," and John chapter 6 (the "bread of life" discourse) are all examples of this.

John 20:21–23 says, "Jesus said to them again, 'Peace be with you. As the Father has sent me, even so I send you.' And when he had said this, he breathed on them, and said to them, 'Receive the Holy Spirit. If *you* forgive the sins of any, they are forgiven; if *you* retain the sins of any, they are retained" (italics added).

First John 5:16–17 states, "If any one sees his brother committing what is not a mortal sin, he will ask, and God will give him life for those whose sin is not mortal. There is sin which is mortal; I do not say that one is to pray for that. All wrongdoing is sin, but there is sin which is not mortal." Spiritual death is the right understanding here.

All of John chapter six is unacceptable to them but, in particular, verses 46–57, which state, "'Not that any one has seen the Father except him who is from God; he has seen the Father. Truly, truly, I say to you, *he who believes has eternal life. I am the bread of life.* Your fathers ate the manna in the wilderness, and they died. This is the bread which comes down from heaven that a man may eat of it and not die. *I am the living bread which came down from heaven; if any one eats of this bread, he will live forever; and the bread which I shall give for the life of the world is my flesh.'* The Jews then disputed among themselves, saying, 'How can this man give us his flesh to eat?' So Jesus said to them, *'Truly, truly, I say to you, unless you eat the flesh of the Son of man and drink his blood, you have no life in you; he who eats my flesh and drinks my blood has eternal life, and I will raise him up at the last day. For my flesh is food indeed, and my blood is drink indeed.* He who eats my flesh and drinks my blood abides in me, and I in him" (emphasis added). This last verse expresses exactly what takes place in Catholic Holy Communion, truly a foretaste of heaven itself.

One of the most important things that I can share with you is always pray to the Holy Spirit for assistance before reading the Holy Scripture, ask for guidance and an open mind and heart, ask for and pray for *right* understanding. This itself is *not* a guarantee that God will answer your prayer immediately; however, if you are sincere in your request and persist (God *reads* hearts, as well as minds) and have *faith*, your chances will be much improved.

Early history of the Bible

The original writings from the Apostles themselves (the autographs) no longer exist.

This is due partly to the perishable material (papyrus) used by the writers, and partly to the fact that the Roman emperors decreed the destruction of the sacred books of the Christians (Edict of Diocletian, A.D. 303).

Before translating the Bible into Latin, St. Jerome had already translated into more common languages enough books to fill a library. [The Bible that Jerome translated around AD 391 is called the

Latin Vulgate and is still used today. Find it here: http://www.drbo. org/lvb/.)

In the year 383 St. Jerome revised the Latin New Testament text in accordance with some Greek manuscripts. Between the years 390 and 406 he translated the Old Testament directly from the Hebrew, and this completed work is known today as the "Old Latin Vulgate." The work had been requested by Pope Damasus, *and Copies of St. Jerome's Latin Vulgate appeared uncorrupted as late as the 11th century* [italics added].

Pope Benedict XV [not Pope Benedict XVI] wrote about St. Jerome's translation in his 1920 encyclical, **Spiritus Paraclitus** [emphasis in original], "Nor was Jerome content merely to gather up this or that teacher's words; he gathered from all quarters whatever might prove of use to him in this task. From the outset he had accumulated the best possible copies of the Bible and the best commentators on it," . . . "he corrected the Latin version of the Old Testament by the Greek; he translated afresh nearly all the books of the Old Testament from Hebrew into Latin; . . . he discussed Biblical questions with the brethren who came to him, and answered letters on Biblical questions which poured in upon him from all sides; besides all this, he was constantly refuting men who assailed Catholic doctrine and unity."

The first person known with certainty to apply the term **canon** to the Sacred Scriptures was St. Athanasius, about 350 A.D., although his private estimate of the number of canonical books differed from the books he quoted in his writings. Like him, a few other early fathers doubted some of the deutero-canonical books, but would cite them.

The Council of Carthage ([AD] 397) was the first Council to publish a list of all the inspired books of the Bible. The Council of Florence repeated the canon of the Bible, and it was restated at the Council of Trent. (No action of the Church causes a book to be inspired. The Church exercises its infallible judgment [guided by the Holy Spirit] to certify post factum that a particular book was inspired when it was written. The fact that God is its Author makes a book to be inspired. The Holy Spirit prevents the Church from erring in judging which books are inspired and included in the Bible.)

[However, God being "the author" does not mean that God actually wrote the Bible; no, it means that the Holy Spirit inspired the authors to use their own words and terms to teach and share *all* that God desired be included in them and only what God desired to be included.]

Versions of the whole or parts of the Bible in the language of the common people first appeared in Germany in the eighth century, in France and Hungary in the twelfth, and Italy, Spain, Holland, Poland and Bohemia in the thirteenth century. (Catholic Encyclopedia.)

In the 1500's in Italy, there were more than 40 vernacular editions of the Bible. France had 18 vernacular editions before 1547, and Spain began publishing editions in 1478, with full approval of the Spanish Inquisition . . . .

The area known as England was invaded and settled by Germanic tribes called "Saxons" who aligned with tribes from the area of Denmark called "Angles." In the 700's, (St. Bede the Venerable), the area was speaking a Germanic dialect. In the Middle Ages, between 1066 [and] 1377, there were different dialects depending on where you went, between the different tribes. The Normans had invaded the area, there was no written vocabulary, so Latin and Greek were most commonly used by the literate.

After 1300, the English population was still much smaller than others like the Italians or Spanish, and it was still unintelligible in a written form. After the 1500's, England became more important politically.

For centuries before the invention of printing, the only way to duplicate the text of the Bible was to copy it by hand. Copyists could have made mistakes, but, they took more care with Scripture than with any other book. Errors, while they are possible and certainly have occurred in some instances, cannot be too easily admitted or accepted as an excuse to disregard these copies. Moreover, *God in His Providence has faithfully protected His Bible from any serious corruption* [italics mine].

Even a perfectly written Bible would still need an authoritative explanation of various passages.

Chapter and verse divisions are not found in our oldest manuscripts of the Bible, and there is evidence that the early Hebrew writers did not even separate the words of the text, following a Hebrew tradition that Moses wrote the Law as one continuous word. The division into chapters was a gradual process that began in the

Middle Ages. The divisions now used were introduced by Stephen Langton (d. 1228), later archbishop of Canterbury, and are found in the Biblia Parisiensis, used at the University of Paris as early as the 13th century. (English Versions of the Bible, Rev. Hugh Pope, O.P.)

The division of Bible chapters into numbered smaller sections was introduced to facilitate scholarly reference to the individual passages. In 1528, Santes Pagnino, a Dominican, published a Bible where each chapter was divided into verses usually consisting of single sentences.

Robert Estienne, a French printer, less than thirty years later, introduced the figures that divide or "chop up" verses of the Bible. His verse divisions became standard because he also printed a Concordance based on these editions. (New Catholic Edition of the Holy Bible.) Although at times it divides a passage, the procedure has been sanctified by the Church.

In 1452, the Vulgate was the first book to be printed on the first mechanical press, invented by a Catholic - Johann Gutenberg; that particular edition is commonly known as the Gutenberg Bible. Again, the text was in Latin. (The Gutenberg Bible, Martin Davies.)

By the time of the Protestant Reformation in the 1500's, there were: 104 Latin editions of the Bible - 9 before Martin Luther's birth, and 27 before his edition. (Where We Got the Bible) About this time though, some Latin editions were defective, owing to the creativity or errors of the various publishers, so the Council of Trent intervened, choosing the "Clementine" edition as the official Latin version, authentic and approved for use in public lectures, disputations, sermons and expositions. (Canons & Decrees of the Council of Trent, TAN Publishers, page 10.) Many translators during the 1500–1900's chose the Latin Vulgate over the Greek because it was difficult to find a good Greek translation . . . .

The Latin language gradually changed. The Latin used in the Vulgate is from around 400A.D. Gradually, Latin evolved into French, Italian and Spanish. In the treaty of Verdun, (843 A.D.) the text shows the shift of vocabulary - some Latin and some Middle French. The last recorded usage of Latin being preached to the common people was around the year 800, in Italy.

However, Latin remained the universal written language in Europe for many centuries. Up to the 1400's, it was the only language to be generally used. As late as the 1660's Isaac Newton, requiring a large audience for his theories, would write his *Principlicae*

Mathematica in Latin for publication, not English (which was still obscure as a written language at the time).

From 1578 to 1593 the English College of *Douay* was temporarily housed at *Rheims. It was during this period that the Vulgate was translated into the new language called English* [italics mine]. In 1582, Queen Elizabeth ordered searchers to confiscate every copy of the New Testament newly translated into English by the College of Rheims. Priests were imprisoned for having it, and the sentence of "torture by rack" was given to those who circulated it. *The publication of the Old Testament was delayed until the Douay College had returned to England. In 1609, the College of Douay published the Old Testament English translation* [italics mine].

(Although some Catholic critics scoff at the "archaic English" used in this edition put out by these colleges, the preface of The Protestant Revised Version, or King James version (1611) credits the deliberately literal translation, and the coinage of Latin-English words for theological terms.)

Between 1609 and 1749, there were more than 23 different Catholic editions of the Bible produced, about half of which were New Testament editions, the remaining being editions of the Penitential Psalms.

Bishop Richard Challoner (1691–1781), who was previously the vice-president of the Douay College, began in 1749 the first of several revisions of the Bible from the "Old English" style into the newer English then in use. It is his work that, for the first time provided English-speaking Catholics with a portable, inexpensive and readable version of the Bible, in spite of a few inevitable defects. In all, he was responsible for 5 different editions of the New Testament, and 2 editions of the Old . . . .

Probably the next most popular Catholic Bible was the "Haydock" revision of the Challoner-Rheims Bible, which actually came about from the suggestion of Thomas Haydock, a printer and schoolmaster. His brother, Rev. George Leo Haydock, published the first edition during the years of 1811–1814, and printings continued well into 1859, after his death. Unique at the time of the Haydock editions was the inclusion of historical and chronological indexes, lists of miracles and parables, some of St. Jerome's letters added to the Addenda, and massive amounts of notes from the fathers and doctors of the Church. It was the first publication of its kind, and editions were immediately successful with several reprints.

In 1790, the first Catholic Bible was printed in the United States, (a lot of printing for America had been done in Belgium) under the encouragement of its' [*sic*] first bishop, John Carroll of Baltimore. It was based on Challoner's second edition of the Bible printed in 1764. In 1805, another version was published in the U.S., based on the Dublin "fifth edition" of Challoner, having been slightly revised under Archbishop John Troy of Dublin. (English Versions of the Bible.)

Catholic and Protestant Bibles

The Old Testament

The Protestant Old Testament omits several entire books and parts of two other books [italics mine]. To explain how this came about, it is necessary that we go back to the ancient Jewish Scriptures. The Hebrew Bible contained only the Old Testament and from its Old Testament it excluded seven entire books - *namely, Tobias, Judith, Wisdom, Ecclesiasticus, Baruch, First and Second Machabees - and parts of Esther (10:14 to 16:14) and Daniel (3:24–90; 13; 14)* [italics mine].

These books which are missing in the Jewish Bible came to the Catholic Church with the Septuagint, a pre-Christian Greek translation of the Old Testament. In the Septuagint Version they are placed among and given equal rank with the other Old Testament books as in our Catholic Bible today. Since the Hebrew is older than the Septuagint Bible, the list of books in the former is called the first canon or collection while the catalog of books in the latter is called the second canon or collection. The seven additional books are found only in the second collection and always associated with it.

Jewish opposition to the additional books of the second collection was due to the circumstances in which the Jews lived and to the spirit of the times. During the last centuries which preceded the coming of Christ the Jews - because of the captivities, persecutions and antagonisms from outside nations became more and more conservative and looked with increasing suspicion on anything that was new. Since the additional books were of comparatively recent origin and since some of them were written in Greek - the language of paganism - they naturally aroused the opposition of the Jews. The fact, too, that the early Christians used the Septuagint in their controversies with the Jews only served to confirm the latter in their opposition to this translation of the Old Testament . . . .

The Lutheran and Anglican Bibles still carry these books in the appendix or give them at least a secondary place. But many other Protestant churches reject them entirely. In 1827 the British and Foreign Bible Society decided not to print or handle Bibles that contained the additional books and not to aid financially companies that published Bibles containing them. As a result these books have practically disappeared from Protestant Bibles.

The Catholic Church has always considered these books as inspired and of the same rank as the other Old Testament books. Her attitude is based upon the following facts:

1) The Apostles and New Testament writers quoted principally the Septuagint. In fact, of the three hundred and fifty Old Testament quotations found in the New Testament, about three hundred are taken from the Septuagint.

2) Some of the New Testament writers made use of the additional books themselves, particularly of the Book of Wisdom, which seems to have been St. Paul's favorite volume. The Epistle of St. James - to take another example - shows an acquaintance with the Book of Ecclesiasticus. If the Apostles and New Testament writers used some of the additional books, did they not thereby approve the entire Septuagint collection?

3) The additional books were accepted in the Church from the beginning. The Epistle of Pope Clement, written before the end of the first century, makes use of Ecclesiasticus and Wisdom, gives an analysis of the book of Judith, and quotes from the additional sections of the book of Esther. The same is true of other early Christian writers.

4) The oldest Christian Bibles in existence (Codex Vaticanus, etc.) contain the additional books intermingled with the rest, just as we find them in the Catholic Bibles today.

5) The oldest Christian lists of Biblical books contain the additional books. In 382 Pope Damasus in a Roman Council

issued a formal list of Old and New Testament books and the list contains the same books as we have in our Bibles.

6) Finally, Christian art of the first four centuries - especially that found in the catacombs and cemeteries - furnishes among others the following illustrations from the additional books: Tobias with the fish (Tobias 6), Susanna (Daniel 13), Daniel and the dragon (Daniel 14), the angel with the three children in the fiery furnace (Daniel 3:49), Habacuc and Daniel in the lion's den (Daniel 14:35).

In conclusion, let us point out that since they follow the synagogue in their rejection of the additional books of the Old Testament, the Protestants should in all logic follow it in its rejection of the New Testament and of Christ Himself.

The Apocryphal Books [meaning those *seven* books deleted by Luther and the Protestant community based on their personal understanding of them not "being God inspired." (Go back and look at 2 Timothy 3:16–17, which they claim to accept.) The real reason had to do with making it easier to *sell* their theological views.]

The apocryphal books are divided into two groups - into the Old and the New Testament apocrypha. a) The Old Testament apocrypha supplement the inspired Old Testament books with fictitious stories about some patriarch or prophet, forged Messianic prophecies, or pious exhortations and precepts. Examples of this group are the Assumption of Moses, Apocalypse of Abraham, Ascension of Isaias, etc. b) The New Testament apocrypha strive to supplement and amplify matters either briefly mentioned in the inspired books or omitted entirely. Their favorite topics are the Infancy of Our Lord and His sojourn on earth after the Resurrection. They contain much that is silly, legendary and dis-edifying. The portrait of Our Lord contradicts in many respects that of the Gospel, and their accounts of Him contain much that is doctrinally unsound and heretical. As many as fifty Gospels, twenty- two Acts, and many Epistles and Apocalypses were known to have belonged to this group at one time.

The New Testament

> The Protestant New Testament contains the same books as the Catholic New Testament. Although Luther showed great hostility to St. James's Epistle because of its doctrine of the necessity of good works and contemptuously called it an "epistle of straw," he clearly saw that he had no more reason for excluding that book than he had for rejecting the other books of the New Testament. The differences between the Protestant and Catholic New Testament arise from changes in specific passages in various books of the New Testament. (The Catholic Encyclopedia)

At least *three* different church councils have affirmed the validity and absolute *truth* of the Catholic Bible as being literally inspired by God, and therefore, it is impossible for it to be in error.

There are a few basic and infallible rules for Bible study:

1. Never can one passage contradict, invalidate, or make void another passage. Were this possible, the Bible will be worthless as a teaching tool.
2. The Bible is *always* truthful *but not always factual*. By this, I mean that not everything in the Bible is to be taken literally.
3. The Bible is not intended to be an *accurate* history book because the two thousand years of the Old Testament were taught and passed on verbally. The message is always correct, and if there is a moral lesson, that too is always correct.
4. Because of the *many* forms of writing in the Bible, only someone *trained* and conforming to what the Catholic Church teaches may and *can* (guided by God) properly translate it.
5. As Saint Peter tells us, the Bible contains many teachings that are *very hard* to understand without instructions.

You may hear, or perhaps have already heard, that the Catholic Church prohibited layfolk to read the Bible on their own. That is true; the question is, why is that true? And here is the answer.

It was the Luther-led Protestant Revolution (he was an apostate Catholic priest) and his "rewriting" (actually, editing to meet his new faith needs is more accurate) and publication of the King James Version in German (his native tongue) that led the Catholic Church to change her long-held position of not encouraging the laity to read for themselves the Bible. Early church fathers held the view that the Bibles was (1) too complex to read and to rightly understand without having been trained to do so, and (2) what the Bible contained was too important to be left to the understanding of the untrained. Salvation itself could be at risk.

The background for this line of thought was fueled by the following facts:

1. The levels of education were insufficient for much of the laity, much less to entrust such an important "work" to them.

2. The printing press was just coming unto its own around the middle to late fifteenth century. So books prior to this were indeed rare and quite expensive, certainly a frivolous expense for most "common folk."

3. The Catholic Church understood that it was her responsibility to *teach* the Catholic faith and that permitting or encouraging the "masses" to read the Bible on their own would be, at best, counterproductive to that mission and mandate given to her by Christ himself. It was not those who "read the Word" rather those who "heard the Word," meaning those who were taught God's truth by those trained to do so, that were to be edified by it.

4. And the church even had solid biblical evidence that this is what Jesus intended for her to do. Matthew 28:18–20 says, "And Jesus came and said to them, 'All authority in heaven and on earth has been given to me. Go therefore and make disciples of all nations, baptizing them in the name of the Father and of the Son and of the Holy Spirit, teaching them to observe all that I have commanded you; and lo, I am with you always, to the close of the age.'" Acts 20:28–30 states, "Take heed to yourselves and to all the flock, in which the Holy Spirit has made you overseers [bishops in the Douay-Rheims Bible], to care for the church of God which he obtained with the blood of his own Son. I know that after my departure fierce wolves will come in among you, not sparing the flock; and from among your own selves will arise men speaking perverse things, to draw away the disciples after them." Also, 2 Corinthians 4:2–3 says, ***"We have renounced disgraceful, underhanded ways; we refuse to practice cunning or to tamper with God's word, but by the open statement of the truth we would commend ourselves to every man's conscience in the sight of God. And even if our gospel is veiled,***

it is veiled only to those who are perishing. " Romans 2:13 declares, "For it is not the hearers of the law who are righteous before God, but the doers of the law who will be justified." Mark 4:32–34 states, "'Yet when it is sown it grows up and becomes the greatest of all shrubs, and puts forth large branches, so that the birds of the air can make nests in its shade.' With many such parables he spoke the word to them, as they were able to hear it; he [Jesus] did not speak to them without a parable, but privately to his own disciples he explained everything." Mark 4:11 says, "And he said to them, 'To you [the apostles] has been given the secret of the kingdom of God, but for those outside everything is in parables.'"

5. In hindsight, history has proven that the position of the Roman Catholic Church has been a brilliant choice. One only has to look at our Protestant brethren and take note of their three-hundred-plus to thirty-thousand-plus different sets of faith beliefs (depends on who's counting, I guess) and personal understandings of the one true faith and Word of God to acknowledge that, once again, the Holy Spirit guiding her has made the difference.

CHAPTER FOUR

Meeting Truth Head-On

I am your God, and you are My people.

—Exodus 6:7

Jesus saith to them: But whom do you say that I am?

—Matthew 16:15

The Rocky Road to Truth

(Another "I *am* a Catholic" lesson)

It seems to me that one's entire life ought to be in a search mode, seeking "truth" for one thing or another, meaning, of course, the singular compulsory end reality to every defined issue. Surely, there cannot exist more than one such factual judgment to each dispute, each quandary, each question life confronts us with. After all, what is, is.

It also seems to me that because truth must be as it is, singular per defined issue, no one is able to attain the inner peace that is deep-rooted into our person, triggering a deep-seated longing in our hearts and souls without first resolving which elusive reality it is that we seek. Is there a "truth elixir"? What is now blocking my path to inner peace and joy? Inner peace is exactly what our God desires for each of us. John 14:27 says, "Peace I leave with you, my peace I give to you: not as the world giveth, do I give unto you. Let not your heart be troubled, nor let it be afraid."

Dictionary definition of "truth"

The true or actual state of a matter is as follows:
1. Conformity with fact or reality; verity (the truth of a statement).
2. A verified or indisputable fact, proposition, principle, or the like (mathematical truths).
3. The state or character of being true.
4. Actuality or actual existence.
5. An obvious or accepted fact; truism; platitude.
6. Honesty; integrity; truthfulness.
7. (Often initial capital letter) Ideal or fundamental reality apart from and transcending perceived experience.
8. Agreement with a standard or original.
9. Accuracy, as of position or adjustment.
10. (Archaic) Fidelity or constancy.

Ten definitions of just one reality testify that "truth" must be singular per defined issue in order to actually be "the truth." Discovering it for ourselves is the key to our true inner peace.

Pope Benedict XVI articulated this fact well in his first address as new pope of the Roman Catholic Church, with a clarity that is indisputable, sharing with us exactly what truth must be: "There cannot be your truth and my truth or there would be *no* truth." He also, later on, shared this: "Truth is not determined by a majority vote." And I will add that truth cannot be our own invention. Nor can it be what we want it to be just because we "want it to be."

Father Hardon shared this about truth: "Truth is the condition of grace, it is the source of grace, it is the channel of grace; it is the divinely ordained requirement of grace" ("How Infallible is the Teaching Church?").

From the difficulty of the discovery factor, the road to a singular truth can rise higher than the highest mountains, proceed down very slippery slopes, and then traverse over quicksand quagmires, seeking always rocky terrain, all in the search for that one truth that alone holds the potential to give the inner peace our hearts and souls relentlessly seek.

In this endeavor, it is possible, however, to convince ourselves that we have already found "the truth." But have we really? Might it be instead a "wolf in sheep's clothing" (Matthew 7:1)?

Jesus tells us that he and he alone is *the* way, the truth, and the life (John 14:6). The fact that each of these nouns is singular is profoundly and critically significant.

It is, to say the least, "difficult" to cull one particular factor that so often leads to a wrong or at least an incomplete understanding of the Bible, and missing the "singular tense" of the words so often and so carefully chosen by Christ and the authors of the Bible is surely one of them. This glaring error is simply too significant and too frequent of an occurrence not to point out and discuss. Second Timothy 3:16–17 says, "All scripture, inspired of God, is profitable to teach, to reprove, to correct, to instruct in justice, That the man of God may be perfect, furnished to every good work."

Here then are a few good examples of that which I speak:

Enter ye [singular] in at the narrow gate [singular]: for wide is the gate, and broad is the way [singular; meaning "obstinacy"] that leadeth to destruction, and many there are who go in thereat [meaning "at risk of their salvation"]. How narrow is the gate [singular], and strait is the way [again, singular] that leadeth to life [singular]: and few there are that find it! Beware of false prophets, who come to you [singular] in the clothing of sheep, but inwardly they [plural] are ravening wolves. (Matthew 7:13–15)

Now the eleven disciples went to Galilee, to the mountain to which Jesus had directed them. And when they saw him they worshiped him; but some doubted [pre-Pentecost]. And Jesus came and said to them, "All authority in heaven and on earth has been given to me. Go therefore and make disciples of all nations, baptizing them in the name of the Father and of the Son and of the Holy Spirit, teaching them to observe all that I have commanded *you*; and lo, I am with *you* always, to the close of the age." (Matthew 28:16–20; italics added)

My dear friends in Christ, we see here a few clear, indisputable examples of "singular" words being used that, when taken together, build "a case for truth" of always being singular per defined issue. In our effort to rightly understand what the Bible is trying to teach us, we must be aware of singular nouns, as it is important that we train ourselves to notice and to acknowledge them.

Matthew 16:15–19 states, "Jesus saith to *them* ["them" being his twelve apostles and meaning "only them"]: But whom *do you* say that I am? Simon Peter answered and said: Thou art Christ, the Son of the living God. And Jesus answering, said to him [singular]: Blessed art thou [singular], Simon Bar-Jona: because flesh and blood hath not revealed it to thee [singular], but my Father who is in heaven. And I say *to thee* [singular]: That thou art Peter; and upon *this rock* [singular; Peter] I will build *my church* [notably singular], and the gates of hell [plural, whereas the gate to heaven was and is singular presumably because of the larger influx of souls going there] shall not prevail against *it* [singular]. And I will give *to thee* [again, singular] the keys of the kingdom of heaven [all of them implied]. And whatsoever *thou* shalt bind [singular] upon earth, it shall be bound also in heaven: and whatsoever *thou* shalt loose [again, singular] upon earth, it shall be loosed also in heaven" (italics added).

Recognizing the singular tense in reference to this conversation between Jesus, who is our God, and Peter when Jesus followed Old Testament tradition of always and every time choosing just one man to lead (Aaron led *through* Moses)—such as Abraham, Moses, the judges, kings like David and Solomon, prophets like Isaiah and Jeremiah, John the Baptist, and, of course, Jesus Christ—give historical testimony that Jesus's choosing Peter was no fluke accident and not even something new and unheard of. Jesus was just following his own Old Testament tradition and now completing and perfecting it.

It's also relevant and critically important to discern correctly that Christ could not and did not expect his one God with only one set of faith beliefs (nothing else is logically possible or historically or biblically provable) through just one church, which is modeled on Old Testament historical practice, to end with Peter, as such would necessarily mean that Christianity, whose roots stem from the early Catholic Church, would not even exist today. History tells us that Wycliffe; Luther, who was an apostate Catholic priest; and Calvin, an apostate Catholic, could not and would not have had the foundation that they choose to reinvent were it not for the Catholic Church, which they willingly and with full knowledge abandoned. Read Hebrews 6:2–7 if you're curious as to what God thinks of these actions.

Further proof of Jesus having required and fully expecting succession to Peter and the apostles rests in the Bible itself by comparing *Matthew 10:1–8, especially verses 5–6, to Matthew 28:16–20, especially verse 19,* which, *if* understood correctly, mandates succession as being actually instituted by Christ himself.

Matthew 10:1–8 says, "And he called to him his twelve disciples *and gave them authority over unclean spirits, to cast them out, and to heal every disease and every infirmity.* The names of the twelve apostles are these: *first, Simon, who is called Peter,* and Andrew his brother; James the son of Zeb'edee, and John his brother; Philip and Bartholomew; Thomas and Matthew the tax collector; James the son of Alphaeus, and Thaddaeus; Simon the Cananaean, and Judas Iscariot, who betrayed him. *These twelve Jesus sent out,* charging them, '*Go nowhere among the Gentiles, and enter no town of the Samaritans,* but go rather to the lost sheep of the house of Israel. And preach as you go, saying, 'The kingdom of heaven is at hand.' *Heal the sick, raise the dead, cleanse lepers, cast out demons.* You received without paying, give without pay" (italics mine).

Matthew 28:16–20 states, "And the eleven disciples went into Galilee, unto the mountain where Jesus had appointed them [singular]. And seeing him they adored: but some doubted. And Jesus coming, spoke to them [singular], saying: All power is given to me in heaven and in earth. *Going therefore, teach ye all nations* [dear friends, please do not attempt to minimalize this command; Jesus is here commanding directly and exclusively only his apostles and their successors to *go* to teach *all* that *he* had taught to *them*]; baptizing them in the name of the Father, and of the Son, and of the Holy Ghost. Teaching them to observe all things whatsoever I have commanded *you* [indisputably singular]: and behold I am with *you* [again, singular] all days, even to the consummation of the world."

In closing, dear friends, I will share another truth, one that you may or may not yet know. God must pass final judgment upon each of us not on what we choose to believe for any reason but on what he (the Holy Spirit) has made possible for us to know through his grace and the channel he chose to use (in this instance, me) to share his "truths." Not to acknowledge this fact is to willingly choose to put one's very soul at risk. And while actually knowing God and his one true faith and church may not remove all of your stress and concerns, if you are still seeking inner peace (singular), it is a pretty good indicator that you have not yet placed God in complete charge of your life. In all things, in all decisions, put God first and then our families and only then anything and everything else. Amen!

Only "One" Proven by the Bible

(One God, One Set of Faith Beliefs, and Only One Church)

And they shall know that I the Lord their God am with them, and that they are my people the house of Israel: saith the Lord God.

—Ezekiel 34:30

I have heard the murmuring of the children of Israel: say to them: In the evening you shall eat flesh, and in the morning you shall have your fill of bread: and you shall know that I am the Lord your God.

—Exodus 16:12

Atheists, agnostics, apostates, lukewarm Catholics, Catholics who have abandoned completely their faith, and an abundance of Protestant communions seem at present to "be in charge." And perhaps they are for now. But is that God's will and desired plan or the direct result of men's deviations and gross disobedience? Time shall tell; eternity is forever, so we best be sure of what we choose to believe and accept.

From man's creation (Genesis 1:26–27), God seemed clearly to have selected only one "chosen people" as "his own." God has chosen them, which were led by Noah, Abram, Moses, David, Jacob, the judges, the kings, and the prophets; the entire Jewish nation always had one man appointed by God to lead them. In the New Testament, they were the apostles, through direct apostolic succession (commanded and demanded by Christ in Matthew 28:19–20); today's Catholic Church is the entrusted keeper of "all of the keys to God's kingdom," fulfilling that same role. The Bible itself provides indisputable evidence of this singular and stunning fact. What is important to the present discussion is simply acknowledging this reality as God's divine and perfect providential will— only one God, one set of faith beliefs, and just one "chosen people," now called by Jesus as "*my* church" in Matthew 16:18.

Having been active in the teaching arena for many years, I at times hear confusion about "the Old Testament God" as a "mean and vengeful God," compared to Jesus in the New Testament, who is most often portrayed as a "God of love and mercy." How can these divergent views be only "one and the same God?" Yet that is precisely what they are.

The reason for "both images" being correct as only one God stems from God's own attributes and his requirement for "perfect justice." Here is God's perspective: Matthew 25:29 says, "For to every one who has will more be given, and he will have abundance; but from him who has not, even what he has will be taken away." This refers to God's grace and our correct understanding. "Divine judgment" is not based on what we know or choose only to accept and believe. Satan, the father of lies, is a powerful adversary to what must be singular truths. Rather, it will be as "perfect fairness and justice" dictates, based on what God makes possible for us to know and understand. This, dear friends, is a point of critical comprehension, if we hope to merit heaven.

Yahweh's task was significantly different than Christ's on many levels: education standards, city stability, nomadic lifestyles, availability of writing material; awareness of God as their sovereign and only God took a long time to be grasped and accepted. It was the normal "ups and downs" of the inevitable educational process, with obedience competing with frequent severe, blatant disobedience requiring reward and punishment that was swift and highly notable. By the time of the incarnation, many cities had been established, resulting in far greater stabilization and better education; trade was broader and more sophisticated, and systems of governance were better and more firmly established. At last, God's chosen people were sufficiently prepared for the often-predicted Messiah (Isaiah 9:1–7).

Second Esdras 7:19 –25, 28–29 says, "And he said to me, 'You are not a better judge than God, or wiser than the Most High! Let many perish who are now living, rather than that the law of God which is set before them be disregarded! For God strictly commanded those who came into the world, when they came, what they should do to live, and what they should observe to avoid punishment. Nevertheless they were not obedient, and spoke against him; they devised for themselves vain thoughts, and proposed to themselves wicked frauds; they even declared that the Most High does not exist, and they ignored his ways! They scorned his law, and denied his covenants; they have been unfaithful to his statutes, and have not performed his works. 'Therefore, Ezra, empty things are for the empty, and full things are for the full. For my son the Messiah shall be revealed with those who are with him, and those who remain shall rejoice four hundred years. And after these years my son the Messiah shall die, and all who draw human breath." Note that *four hundred years* means a very long time, not literally four hundred years.

Second Esdras 12:32 states, "This is the Messiah whom the Most High has kept until the end of days, who will arise from the posterity of David, and will come and speak to them; he will denounce them for their ungodliness and for their wickedness, and will cast up before them their contemptuous dealings."

John 1:41 says, "He first found his brother Simon, and said to him, 'We have found the Messiah' (which means Christ)." John 4:25 declares, "The woman said to him, 'I know that Messiah is coming (he who is called Christ); when he comes, he will show us all things." First Corinthians 8:6 states, "Yet for us there is *one God*, the Father, from whom are all things and for whom we exist, *and one Lord, Jesus Christ*, through whom are all things and through whom we exist" (italics mine).

So for all time, the concept of only one God has been pressed, taught, expected, and mostly accepted, although at times with great suffering, pain, and difficulty. This belief is the first commandment.

The premise for a single set of faith beliefs is founded on and flows directly from this first reality of *only one God*. Because all of Christianity agrees on only one God, it follows that the one God can have only one set of faith beliefs. Even Almighty God can do nothing more.

This then leads us to the foundational issue, one that is widely disputed, widely and incorrectly understood, and seldom accepted outside of the Catholic Church, which is that God desired exactly what he established—"only one church," which is also the same as one God's will and the reality of history and biblical teaching.

I will proceed by sharing various passages from the Douay-Rheims Bible because I am a Catholic. However, I think one will find little or no differences in the selected passages in the King James Bible. So the issue then is not what the Bible says, rather what the actual teaching really is saying. And yes, I intend to prove that this exclusive right, this mandate belongs only to today's Catholic Church. Indeed, that is the precise challenge that lies before us.

There are two infallible rules for *right* understanding of the Bible. The first one is "Never ever may, can, or does one verse, passage, or teaching make void, invalidate, override, or contradict, when rightly understood, another part of the Bible." The reason is obvious. Were there even the slightest possibility (there's none), then the Bible would be worthless to learn or teach the faith of Jesus Christ and the blessed Trinity. Amen!

The second one is "If your understanding does not align fully with what the Catholic Church teaches (as the only holders of all 'the keys' to heaven's gate [Matthew 16:18–19]), you need to change it to come in line with what God wants you to know," his truth.

Argument No. 1

Matthew 4:18–22 says, "As he [Jesus] walked by the Sea of Galilee, he saw two brothers, Simon who is called Peter and Andrew his brother, casting a net into the sea; for they were fishermen. And he said to them, *'Follow me, and I will make you fishers of men.'* Immediately they left their nets and followed him. And going on from there he saw two other brothers, James the son of Zeb'edee and John his brother, in the boat with Zeb'edee their father, mending their nets, and he called them. Immediately they left the boat and their father, and followed him."

John 15:16 states, "You did not *choose me, but I chose you* and appointed you that you should go and bear fruit and that your fruit should abide; so that whatever you ask the Father in my name, he may give it to you." This is important as it relates to the seven sacraments instituted by Christ.

The evident meaning of these two passages is that "God is in charge." It is God who selects those he wants for service. Yes, everyone is to have a role in evangelization but only when given the opportunity to do so by God and then limited to the opportunity he has given to us. This is not something one just assumes, which is the condition of some hidden (to me at least) "as a right" found in all the Protestant communions. And yes, I fully agree that anyone "with me" can't be, at the same time, be "against me." Yet that is clearly the case of the Protestant faiths. The Catholic Church has a two-thousand-year history, dating back to Christ, Peter, and the apostles. No other religion has both the total truth and the fullness of that truth that God desires to share and, indeed, demands the right to share with each of us.

Matthew 12:30 says, "He that is not with me, is against me: and he that gathereth not with me, scattereth." Highly significant is the extensive use of the "singular tense" found as a common thread in these passages. And that, dear friend, is a very important point.

Explanation

First, notice that Simon (Peter) is the first apostle selected by Christ. With God, coincidence, happenstance, or luck simply does not exist. Words have meanings, and the economy of words is made more critical because of the cost and availability of writing materials at the time of the Bible authorship. Second, already, Christ has made evident that his choosing is with a specific purpose in mind and, at least to this point, limited to those he has already chosen. Third, God remains and must remain in charge. God's "job" is to call whom he chooses; our task is to accept and obey them. I don't exclude here papal succession, which Christ himself instituted.

Argument No. 2

Matthew 10:1–8 says, "And [Jesus] having called his twelve disciples together, he gave them power over unclean spirits, to cast them out, and to heal all manner of diseases, and all manner of infirmities. And the names of the *twelve apostles* are these: The *first, Simon who is called Peter*, and Andrew his brother, James the son of Zebedee, and John his brother, Philip and Bartholomew, Thomas and Matthew the publican, and James the son of Alpheus, and Thaddeus, Simon the Cananean, and Judas Iscariot, who also betrayed him. These twelve Jesus sent: commanding them, saying: Go ye not into the way of the Gentiles, and into the city of the Samaritans enter ye not. But go ye rather to the lost sheep of the house of Israel. And going, preach, saying: The kingdom of heaven is at hand. Heal the sick, raise the dead, cleanse the lepers, cast out devils" (italics mine).

Explanation

First, no greater evidence exists than what is evident in the fact that Christ clearly extends and transfers, in a limited manner (evidenced also in John 17:18, 20:21), his own godly powers and authority to this select group of twelve men, whom he called "his apostles." Second, in the beginning, Christ attempts to fulfill the Old Testament promises to his one chosen people. Because of their hardness of hearts, Christ later extends this call to *all* of humanity, thus making necessary the succession of these powers and authority. Third, the message they are to share is nothing less than an affirmation that the long-awaited Messiah is now in their midst. Fourth, Christ understands that in order for his ministry to be completed, he must delegate and empower those he has chosen with godly attributes because the task, the challenge given to them can only be accomplished through, with, and by God himself.

Argument No. 3

Matthew 16:15–19 states, "Jesus saith to them: But whom do you say that I am? Simon Peter answered and said: *Thou art Christ, the Son of the living God*. And Jesus answering, said to him: Blessed art *thou*, Simon Bar-Jona: because flesh and blood hath not revealed it to thee, but my Father who is in heaven. And I say to thee: That thou art Peter; and upon this rock I will build my church [singular], and the gates of hell shall not prevail against it. And I will give to thee the keys of the kingdom of heaven. And whatsoever thou shalt bind upon earth, it shall be bound also in heaven: and whatsoever thou shalt loose upon earth, it shall be loosed also in heaven" (italics mine).

Explanation

The reason this is among the most widely disputed teachings in the entire Bible is that there is no grounds biblically, morally, or theologically for any religion other than Catholicism. First, here, Jesus is asking the apostles as a group a question. But it is Peter alone, divinely inspired, who replies on behalf of all of them, a clear indication that already some degree of his leadership is evident. Second, Jesus confirms Peter in the Holy Spirit by clarifying that he was speaking through and on behalf of God (the Father through the Holy Spirit). It's a divinely inspired proclamation. Third, Jesus now changes the name of "Simon" to "Peter," which is the framework for the present tradition of popes' new-name practice. Whenever God changes the name of a person, it is indicative of great grace and greater expectations of God for that person (Abram to Abraham, for example). Fourth, it is no accident that "Peter alone" is mentioned. Just as there was a high priest heading the hierarchy of the Jews, so too will there be only one in charge and empowered in this new "church" founded on the new covenant, which overrides the one in existence up to that moment (Jeremiah 31:31, Luke 22:20, Hebrews 8:8, 13). Fifth, highly significant are the next words of Christ:

"I [God] will build [he alone is the architect] my church [singular; the one and only one desired, wanted, or needed to accomplish Christ's mandated mission]." The term "church" is first used here by Christ to clarify and make exceedingly clear that what he is doing is founding, that is, establishing a new, separate, different, and overriding religion (faith). God's choice of location is no accident and indeed is a critical part of right understanding. Caesarea Philippi (verse 13) was the site of the area's largest pagan temple; so clearly implied here is the task of Peter to overcome this pagan faith's practice and supplant it with God's own truth. There were pagan temples and Jewish synagogues in existence at the time but *no* "church." Sixth, how the handing of the keys essential for entry into heaven itself by God directly to Peter is ignored, overlooked, and by intent denied is astounding. How can anyone honestly doubt the resolve of God to do this? Seventh, the terms carefully chosen by Christ, when rightly understood in the context of "binding and loosing," are very common rabbinic terms of power and freedom of governance, fully enforceable at law. Sites were then often walled and fortified as was Jerusalem itself, with real gates, real doors, and a real "gatekeeper" who unlocked them in the morning for commerce and locked them at night for security. This "holder of the keys" was most often the prime minister or vicar, who answered directly to and only to the king. This is the precise role Christ envisioned and implemented through the selection of Peter. Protestant leaders understand that they must neuter this teaching in order to justify their own church's faith.

Argument No. 4

Matthew 18:16–18 says, "And if he will not hear thee, take with thee one or two more: that in the mouth of two or three witnesses every word may stand. And if he will not hear them: tell the church [singular]. And if he will not hear the church, let him be to thee as the heathen and publican. Amen I say to you, whatsoever you shall bind upon earth, shall be bound also in heaven; and whatsoever you shall loose upon earth, shall be loosed also in heaven."

Explanation

First, affirmation of Christ's intent for a totally new religion and form of governance is here cited to make clear the above passages. Disputes that had, in the past, been taken to the high priest or Sanhedrin are now to be taken to Peter and the other apostles or "the church" (singular). Second, the powers and authority granted to Peter *alone* is now extended through Peter to include all the apostles (Matthew 18:18).

Argument No. 5 (Postresurrection)

Matthew 28:16, 18–20 "And the eleven [remaining] disciples went into Galilee, unto the mountain where Jesus had appointed them. And Jesus coming, spoke to them, saying: All power is given to me in heaven and in earth. Going therefore, teach *ye* all nations; baptizing them in the name of the Father, and of the Son, and of the Holy Ghost. Teaching them to observe all things whatsoever I have commanded *you*: and behold I [Jesus personally] am with *you* all days, even to the consummation of the world" (italics mine).

Explanation

First, this conversation is also critical to right understanding. Here, Jesus is addressing only the remaining apostles, Judas having hanged himself in despair. This fulfills the predeath promise of Jesus to afterward meet them (the apostles) in Galilee (Matthew 26–32). Second, we see evidence of God's own powers and authority being passed on, in a limited manner, by absolute necessity to these very (and initially exclusively to them) apostles. Third, *to all nations* means "the entire world." By absolute necessity then, in order to fulfill this command issued by our perfect God, succession of powers and authority *had* to continue beyond the lives and deaths of the apostles. Certainly, Christ did not intend for this new religion to end with the demise of the apostles, who are foundational with Christ as the cornerstone of a new covenant but not its competition. If not, the fulfillment of the mandate *is impossible*, and God's plan and will will be left uncompleted, an untenable position. Fourth, the form Christ desires the sacrament of baptism to take is clearly articulated as Christ institutes this first of his seven sacraments. Highly notable is that it does *not* exclude infant baptism, for it is God's desire that "all men" participate in his salvation (conditionally). Babies too have souls (1 Timothy 2:4). Fifth, take note again of the fact that Christ is addressing directly and exclusively only his apostles and issues directly to them alone the command to teach all nations. (See also Ephesians 2:20, 3:9–10,

4:1–7.) Sixth, this final promise (postresurrection) affirms Christ's real presence in the Eucharist, another sacrament instituted by Christ. The promise here specifies himself to remain "with them," not only the Holy Spirit as separately promised elsewhere (John 14:16–17).

Argument No. 6

Having established only one God, faith, and church, we now proceed to *the evidence for the long-accepted practice of succession.*

First, let's look from the perspective of the apostles: Acts 1:24–26 says, "And praying, they said: Thou, Lord, who knowest the hearts of all men, shew whether of these two thou hast chosen, To take the place of this ministry and apostleship, from which Judas hath by transgression fallen, that he might go to his own place. And they gave them lots, and the lot fell upon Matthias, and he was numbered with the eleven apostles." Second, let's take from the hands of God directly: Acts 26:14 states, "And when we were all fallen down on the ground, I heard a voice speaking to me in the Hebrew tongue: Saul, Saul, why persecutest thou me? It is hard for thee to kick against the goad."

Explanation

Here is evidence of both Peter's and the apostles' recognition of the absolute need for succession number two and also God's continued direct involvement in the choosing of these men.

Argument No. 7

It deals with the God's protected and guided authority of his one church. John 14:16–17 "And I [Jesus] will ask the [my] Father, and he shall give you another Paraclete [person in the blessed Trinity, the Holy Spirit], that he may abide with you for ever. The spirit of truth, whom the world cannot receive, because it seeth him not, nor knoweth him: but you shall know him; because he shall abide with you, and shall be in you."

Explanation

First, this conversation takes place between Jesus, in *both* his humanity and his divinity, and his Father and is expressly on behalf of only his apostles. Second, Christ makes evident that "truth" is a "singular thing." Third, this "truth warranty" is never-ending. Fourth, the world seems "naturally" to "kick against the goad of God's singular truth[s]." This is a direct effect of lost grace and willing complicity in falsehoods not fully known or understood because of the lack of grace. Fifth, the apostles and those whom chosen shall be protected from teaching in error on all matters of faith and morals because the Holy Spirit will guide, protect, lead, *and* even reside in them.

Argument No. 8

John 20:19–23 says, "Now when it was late that same day, the first of the week, and the doors were shut, where the disciples were gathered together, for fear of the Jews, Jesus came and stood in the midst, and said to them: Peace be to you. And when he had said this, he shewed them his hands and his side. He said therefore to them again: Peace be to you. *As the Father hath sent me, I also send you.* When he had said this, he breathed on them; and he said to them: Receive ye the Holy Ghost. *Whose sins you shall forgive*, they are forgiven them; and whose sins you shall retain, and they are retained."

Explanation

First, twice in these brief passages, Jesus tells them (and us), "Peace be with you." Thus we can know that is God's desire for us, to have peaceful hearts founded on belief, obedience, and right and a full understanding of him. Second, using precise terms, Christ once again passes his godly powers and authority onto his apostles and *through* them, by absolute necessity, to their successors. "As the Father hath sent me, I [God] also send you," said Jesus, addressing once again only Peter and the other apostles. Third, here, Christ fulfills his promise to the apostles made earlier in John 14 and sends the Holy Spirit to actually reside within the apostles. Fourth, yes, now that the apostles are empowered as was Christ himself, now that they are "filled with the Holy Spirit," *Jesus further empowers and commands them in his name with his authority* to determine whose sins shall be forgiven and whose shall not. Christ remains the one who does the actual forgiving but *only* after being given the essential permission of his priest to do so. It is the priest again as the *persona Christi* (person of Christ), just like in transubstantiation, where the priest is transformed and *performs as Christ himself.* Once again, we witness Christ's institution of another sacrament—the sacrament of confession, the only *known* forgiveness of sin. FYI, priests were used for this function in the Old Testament too but not with the same degree of authority and power. (See Leviticus 5:13, 6:7.)

Argument No. 9

It seems reasonable that some might ask, were these teachings understood, accepted, and applied in the early church? It seems prudent to reference the "last apostle," Paul, to see what he taught and what divinely inspired teaching has been handed on to us.

Paul's testimony speaks for itself. Amen!

1. 1 Corinthians 1:12: "Now this I say, that every one of you saith: I indeed am of Paul; and I am of Apollo; and I am of Cephas; and I of Christ."
2. 1 Corinthians 15:5: "And that he [the risen Christ] was seen by Cephas; and after that by the eleven."
3. Ephesians 5:23: "Christ is the head of the church [singular], his body [singular]."
4. Ephesians 2:19–20: "Now therefore you are no more strangers and foreigners; but you are fellow citizens with the saints, and the domestics of God, Built upon the foundation of the apostles and prophets, Jesus Christ himself being the chief corner stone."
5. Romans 13:1–2: "Let every person be subject to the governing authorities. For there is no authority except from God, and *those that exist have been instituted by God.* Therefore he who resists the authorities resists what God has appointed, and those who resist will incur judgment" (italics added).
6. Romans 16:17–19: "I appeal to you, brethren, to take note of those who create dissensions and difficulties, in opposition to the doctrine which you have been taught; avoid them. For such persons do not serve our Lord Christ, but their own appetites, and by fair and flattering words they deceive the hearts of the simple-minded. For while your obedience is known to all, so that I rejoice over you, I would have you wise as to what is good and guileless as to what is evil."
7. 1 Timothy 3:15: "If I am delayed, you may know how one ought to behave in the household of God, which is the church [singular]

of the living God, the *pillar* and bulwark of *the truth*" (italics added).

8. Romans 15:4–6: "That by steadfastness and by the encouragement of the scriptures we might have hope. May the God of steadfastness and encouragement grant you to live in such harmony with one another, *in accord with Christ Jesus, that together you may with one voice glorify the God and Father of our Lord Jesus Christ*" (italics added).

9. 2 Corinthians 9:13: "Under the test of this service, you will glorify God by your obedience in acknowledging the gospel [singular] of Christ."

10. Ephesians 4:1–7: "I therefore, a prisoner for the Lord, beg you to lead a life worthy of the calling to which you have been called, with all lowliness and meekness, with patience, forbearing one another in love, eager to maintain the unity of the Spirit in the bond of peace. There is one body [which means one church] and one Spirit, just as you were called to the one hope that belongs to your call, one Lord, one faith [only one set of beliefs], one baptism, one God and Father of us all, who is above all and through all and in all. But grace was given to each of us according to the measure of Christ's gift."

11. 2 Timothy 4:1–4 "I charge *you* in the presence of God and of Christ Jesus who is to judge the living and the dead, and by his appearing and his kingdom: preach the word, be urgent in season and out of season, convince, rebuke, and exhort, be unfailing in patience and in teaching. For the time is coming when people will not endure sound teaching, but having itching ears they will accumulate for themselves teachers to suit their own likings, and will turn away from listening to the truth and wander into myths" (italics added).

12. Ephesians 3:9–11: "And to make all men see what is the plan of the mystery hidden for ages in God who created all things; that through *the church* [singular] the manifold wisdom of God might now be made known to the principalities and powers in the heavenly places. This was according to the eternal purpose which he has realized in Christ Jesus our Lord" (italics added).

John 10:16 says, "And I have other sheep, that are not of this fold; I must bring them also, and they will heed my voice. *So there shall be one flock, one shepherd*" (italics added).

Acts 20:28 states, "Take heed to yourselves and to all the flock, in which the *Holy Spirit has made you* overseers, to care *for the church of God* [singular] which he obtained with the blood of his own Son" (*overseers* is *bishops* in Douay-Rheims Bible; textual change in the King James and some other Bible versions as well; italics added).

May God please grant us his wisdom and understanding and make it possible for *all* to come to *his truth*.

Summation

Luke 10:16 says, "He who hears you hears me, and he who rejects you rejects me, and he who rejects me rejects him who sent me." Matthew 7:21, 24–27 states, "Not everyone that saith to me, Lord, Lord, shall enter into the kingdom of heaven: but [only] he that doth the will of my Father who is in heaven, he shall enter into the kingdom of heaven. Every one therefore that heareth these my words, and doth them, shall be likened to a wise man that built his house upon a rock, And the rain fell, and the floods came, and the winds blew, and they beat upon that house, and it fell not, for it was founded on a rock. And every one that heareth these my words, and doth them not, shall be like a foolish man that built his house upon the sand, And the rain fell, and the floods came, and the winds blew, and they beat upon that house, and it fell, and great was the fall thereof." Amen!

God, in his perfect wisdom, chose only "one," knowing full well man's distinctive tendency to sin because of the effects of original sin, termed concupiscence. Desiring to increase man's effort to merit salvation, he knew in giving just one true option that it ought to be less difficult for mankind to discern right from wrong. Sirach 15:18 says, "Before man is life and death, good and evil, that which he shall choose will be given him."

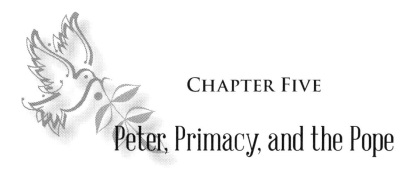

CHAPTER FIVE

Peter, Primacy, and the Pope

And I say to thee: That thou art Peter; and upon this rock I will build my church, and the gates of hell shall not prevail against it. And I will give to thee the keys of the kingdom of heaven [**perhaps the most debated and misunderstood passage in the Bible**].

—Matthew 16:18–19

Keys to the Kingdom Explained

This topic is among the most debated topics in the entire New Testament and for "good cause." If we Catholics are able to prove what the Bible says as actually being divine will (and we can), then all other faiths will seem to have no, or at least extremely shaky, grounds to find and to prove their beliefs. This really is a battle of "right versus wrong." And sadly, it simply is not explained and told often enough to stem the tide of the "floodgates" of apostates, leaving the Catholic Church, for other faiths, often seen as being "as good" and better suited to their own wants and beliefs.

The debate centers of the biblical term for "rock" as found in Matthew 16:15–20, which we will cover in detail. But for now, I would like to set our foundation by explaining two other words found in that same teaching and one additional fact.

While it is true that much of the New Testament was written in the Greek language, the language of the intellectuals, Jesus himself spoke a far more common language, the language of the poor, the marginalized, and the undereducated—the masses. The language Jesus spoke was Aramaic. And this fact will provide a significant evidence in support of our case.

Matthew 16:19 says, "I will give you the keys of the kingdom of heaven, and whatever you bind on earth shall be bound in heaven, and whatever you loose on earth shall be loosed in heaven." We begin the defense of the Bible teaching by first addressing verse 19 and the terms Jesus unerringly chose to use. The two terms I like to highlight are the terms "to bind" and "to loose." To objectively define these two terms, we will reference *Strong's Concordance* of the Greek and Hebrew lexicon, which is an independent, non-Catholic source.

"Bind" in Hebrew

2280 chabash, *khaw-bash'*; a primitive root; to stop, to rule: govern
3256 yacar, *yaw-sar'*; a primitive root; to chastise, to instruct: correct, reform, reprove, teach

"Bind" in Greek

No relevant use of this word

"Loose" in Hebrew

7368 rachaq, *raw-khak'*; a primitive root; to widen, recede or remove (literally or figuratively)
8271 shre', *sher-ay'*; (Aramaic) to free, separate; to unravel

"Loose" in Greek

142 air*ó, ah'-ee-ro*; to take up or away; to expiate sin; remove
630 apolu*ó, ap-ol-oo'-o*; relieve, release, dismiss, pardon, divorce, to let go

At the time and place these very precisely chosen words were spoken by Jesus, who being God cannot err, nor could the apostles have been keenly aware of exactly what Jesus was saying and precisely why he was saying it.

What Jesus did here was exactly what he was set out to do. This was a direct transfer of power based upon a local tradition of kings who ruled walled-in cites, sharing their power and authority, thus freeing themselves to a more leisurely lifestyle. This act was so common that its conveyance was actually covered and protected in Jewish laws of the time, which might explain why no questions were asked and why no later debates or disputes ensued on the issue of leadership.

I marvel at the wisdom of God. The terms of sheer brilliance that God chose were not merely picturesque; they were also shockingly clear, explosively appropriate, and precisely descriptive so that the apostles (and any other Jews who might have overheard) would hear and then correctly apply the message being shared by Christ. What Jesus was saying and doing here was choosing Peter to be his vicar, his prime minister. Leaving nothing to "chance" (a term that simply cannot coexist with God), even the location Christ chose to make this appointment—and to be sure, an appointment is exactly what it was—also has great significance to all of us and, in fact, may well be the undergirding of this entire teaching that is so often debated by competing faiths. The location Christ chose was carefully selected to add weight, meaning, and emphasis to the message and the very motive Christ had for doing what he was so unerringly intent on accomplishing.

The location was Caesarea Philippi, located on the coast and was a very large and active shipping location. As a result of its ideal location, it was common that pagans from around the globe, at some time, made port there. And flowing from that reality, this location was home to the area's largest pagan shrine. It was purposefully selected by Jesus to make the point that what he was doing was preparing to battle Satan on "Satan's home turf." This new church and the faith of that church [both singular] were and are meant to be the alternative God gives men, which was so well articulated in the Old Testament in Sirach 15:18: "Before man is life and death, good and evil, that which he shall choose shall be given to him."

Many large cities at that time were actually walled-in cites, with real gates that were closed and locked at night and then reopened again in the morning for trade and business. Jerusalem was such a city to the present day. The holder of these keys was a "vicar" or "prime minister," chosen by the king of that city and answerable to and only to that king. This carrier of the "keys" was fully empowered to run that city's day-to-day business in the name of the king, with the power and authority of that king, and everyone knew it. And this, dear friends, is exactly, specifically, and fully what God intended in choosing Peter to hold this critical but also, in an absolute sense, essential role from God's perspective, knowing full well that he was soon to die and that in order for his one God, one faith in and through his newly established one church to flourish in his absence, there would have to be a top-down organization and someone to man it.

This really ought not to be the surprise that certain others would like to pretend it to be. God, throughout the entirety of the Bible, has, with utter consistency, chosen just one man to be his spokesman, his teacher to guide, to chide, to teach, and to preach on his behalf—men like Abram (later Abraham, who like Simon Peter had his name changed by God), Moses, the judges and kings like David and Solomon, the prophets like Isaiah and Jeremiah, and John the Baptist, the last prophet and the one man chosen to introduce Jesus as the long-awaited Messiah. Just as the kings of the various walled-in cities shared their power and authority by choosing one man to be granted the authority of his keys, answerable only to the king (Jesus is "Christ the King" [Matthew 2:2]), so do Christ chose Peter as his one chosen man, following what had already been a long-established practice and tradition; this one man was often seemingly unqualified for the task so that there would be no doubt as to whom to credit for its success—God, not Peter and not Peter's necessary successors but God. There is no room at all to doubt what I just shared.

John 17:18–19 says, "As thou has sent me [Jesus praying in his human nature to God the Father on behalf of his apostles, whom he will shortly leave but not abandon], I [God] also have sent them into the world. And for them do I sanctify myself, that they also may be sanctified in truth." No other church or faith can make the claim that Jesus Christ makes himself the personal warranty for all of their faith beliefs and moral teachings, except his Catholic Church, and be able to sustain it. Jesus Christ offers himself to God the Father as evidence of our blessed Lord's intent and desire to establish one God with one Faith and in and through one and just one church, his Catholic Church, which alone will be guided, inspired, and protected to share the fullness of his truths.

Now let's look at the entirety of the passage in question, dissect it, and see if there is any, even the slightest bit of, wiggle room for other man-made, competing faiths and churches in it that might be used as a justification for their competing faith beliefs. I mean no lack of charity here; but the entire basis for the Catholic Church and what we teach, preach, and practice is at stake. There is charity in the truth that is shared here.

When Pope Benedict XVI was elected, from the balcony of Saint Peter's, he shared this irrefutable wisdom: "There cannot be your truth and my truth, or there would be no truth." Amen!

Matthew 16:15–19 says, "He said to them [directly and exclusively], 'But who do you say that I am? *Simon Peter replied*, 'You are the Christ, the Son of the living God.' And Jesus answered him, 'Blessed are *you*, Simon Bar-Jona! For flesh and blood has not revealed this to you, but my Father who is in heaven. And I tell *you*, you are Peter, and on this rock [you] I will build my church [singular], and the powers of death shall not prevail against it. I will give *you* the keys of the kingdom of heaven, and whatever *you* bind on earth shall be bound in heaven, and whatever *you* loose on earth shall be loosed in heaven" (italics added).

Nothing in this teachings hints of it being metaphorical or anything other than literal in a correct translation. Taken literally, this passage means precisely what it says, and what it says is exactly what Christ intended to accomplish. Jesus, as king of the heavenly kingdom, chose to make Peter his vicar, his prime minister, the keeper of all the keys to heaven's gate. This was the norm for kings of walled-in cites, so Jesus, who earlier had taught us about the "narrow gate" into heaven (Matthew 7:13–14), was making this analogy for our sake. There were no clarifications asked or needed.

God has blessed me with a most wonderful friend. She is a convert from the Anglican faith, has expertise in church history, and is an attorney. From time to time, I share without pinpointing her identity. Just to make sure that I am being clear and on the right track, I asked for her view on this issue. Her comments below follow, a discussion on this very topic that I was having with a possible convert. I have her permission to share it.

Here are a few thoughts from a friend who also is a catechist:

That was a great reply! Now she'll be armed against Protestant claims that *petra* and *petros* are different words. They were in Attic Greek, centuries before Christ; but in Koine Greek, they were the same word with feminine/masculine endings. And of course, Protestant skeptics overlook the evidence of Peter's title in Aramaic altogether.

A small interesting point about the transfiguration and Simon's appointment as first pope. It happened at the headwaters of the Jordan, at the site of an older temple of the pagan Hellenistic god Pan and the later white marble temple Herod built to Caesar Augustus. There, a site that had been dedicated to false gods—imaginary and human—is supplanted by the creation of the one, holy, apostolic, *and* visible church. Here, where the headwaters of the Jordan arise in a great fountain, on the mountain of Caesarea Phillipi, Jesus establishes the new order. I find that a thrilling image. Where there had been superstition, fear, and slavery, Jesus creates mother church to guide and preserve us. And he gives us Peter, "the Rock," our Holy Father, to stand upon that high place to inspire and lead us. She is a visible church, created to stand high upon a mountaintop, led by a human. This is another rebuttal of Protestant theology that the church is an invisible entity. The church is a visible, human institution, not some airy-fairy "spiritual" idea. One can go to that mountain today and stand where Peter stood and watch the waters of baptism well up out of the ground. Jesus gave us physical touchstones to confirm our faith: water, bread, wine, a pope.

Catholic Church Authority: The Bible's Testimony

Luke 10:16 says, "He who hears you hears me, and he who rejects you rejects me, and he who rejects me rejects him who sent me."

John 21:15–19 states, "When they had finished breakfast, Jesus said to Simon Peter, 'Simon, son of John, do you love me more than these?' He said to him, 'Yes, Lord; you know that I love you.' He said to him, *'Feed my lambs.'* A second time he said to him, 'Simon, son of John, do you love me?' He said to him, 'Yes, Lord; you know that I love you.' He said to him, *'Tend my sheep.'* He said to him the third time, 'Simon, son of John, do you love me?' Peter was grieved because he said to him the third time, 'Do you love me?' And he said to him, 'Lord, you know everything; you know that I love you.' Jesus said to him, *'Feed my sheep.* Truly, truly, I say to you, when you were young, you girded yourself and walked where you would; but when you are old, you will stretch out your hands, and another will gird you and carry you where you do not wish to go.' (This he said to show by what death he was to glorify God.) And after this he said to him, 'Follow me'" (italics added).

Ephesians 4:1–7 declares, "I therefore, a prisoner for the Lord, beg you to lead a life worthy of the calling to which you have been called, with all lowliness and meekness, with patience, forbearing one another in love, eager to maintain the unity of the Spirit in the bond of peace. There is one body [which means one church] and one Spirit, just as you were called to the one hope that belongs to your call, one Lord, one faith [only one set of true beliefs], one baptism, one God and Father of us all, who is above all and through all and in all. But grace was given to each of us according to the measure of Christ's gift."

Matthew 28:19–20 says, "Go therefore and make disciples of all nations, baptizing them in the name of the Father and of the Son and of the Holy Spirit, teaching them to observe all that I have commanded you; *and lo, I am with you always, to the close of the age"* (italics added).

Matthew 7:21–23 states, "Not every one who says to me, 'Lord, Lord,' shall enter the kingdom of heaven, but he who does the will of my Father who is in heaven. On that day many will say to me, 'Lord, Lord, did we not prophesy in your name, and cast out demons in your name, and do many mighty works in your name?' And then will I declare to them, 'I never knew you; depart from me, you evildoers.'"

Second Peter 2:1–3 says, "But false prophets also arose among the people, just as there will be false teachers among you, who will secretly bring in destructive heresies, even denying the Master who bought them, bringing upon themselves swift destruction. And many will follow their licentiousness, and because of them the way of truth will be reviled. And in their greed they will exploit you with false words; from of old their condemnation has not been idle, and their destruction has not been asleep."

Ephesians 4:4–7 states, "There is one body [one church] and one Spirit [one set of beliefs], just as you were called to the one hope that belongs to your call, one Lord [one God], one faith [one set of doctrine and dogma], one baptism [by water in the Trinity], one God and Father of us all, who is above all and through all and in all. But grace was given to each of us according to the measure of Christ's gift."

Ephesians 3:9–11 says, "And to make all men see what is the plan of the mystery hidden for ages in God who created all things; that through the church [singular] the manifold wisdom of God might now be made known to the principalities and powers in the heavenly places. This was according to the eternal purpose which he has realized in Christ Jesus our Lord."

Colossians 1:18 states, "He is the head of the body [singular], the church [singular]; he is the beginning, the first-born from the dead, that in everything he might be pre-eminent. For in him all the fulness of God was pleased to dwell."

Acts 20:28 declares, "Take heed to yourselves and to all the flock, in which the Holy Spirit has made you overseers, to care for the church of God [singular]."

First Corinthians 12:12–13 states, "For just as the body [singular] is one and has many members, and all the members of the body [singular], though many, are one body [singular], so it is with Christ. For by one Spirit we were all baptized into one body—Jews or Greeks, slaves or free—and all were made to drink of one Spirit."

The keys are prima facie evidence of papal succession. Here is another peek at Matthew 16:19: "And I will give to thee the keys," a critical point to comprehend involving papal succession. It is absurd to think that the new faith and one church just founded by Christ was meant to end with the demise of Peter. The keys to heaven's access remain with his successors. In Matthew 28:19–20, it says, "Going therefore, teach *ye* all nations; baptizing them in the name of the Father, and of the Son, and of the Holy Ghost. Teaching them to observe all things whatsoever I have commanded [and taught] *you*: and behold I am with *you* all days, even to the consummation of the world" (italics added).

For anyone seeking more information, here is a site and explanation by Dr. Scott Hahn: http://www.catholic-pages.com/pope/hahn.asp.

CHAPTER SIX

Prayer and Its Necessity in Our Lives

Seek ye the Lord, while he may be found: call upon him, while he is near. Let the wicked forsake his way, and the unjust man his thoughts, and let him return to the Lord, and he will have mercy on him, and to our God: for he is bountiful to forgive. For my thoughts are not your thoughts: nor your ways, saith the Lord. For as the heavens are exalted above the earth, so are my ways exalted above your ways, my thoughts above your thoughts.

—Isaiah 55:6–9

And when ye pray, you shall not be as the hypocrites, that love to stand and pray in the synagogues and the corners of the streets, that they may be seen by men: Amen I say to you, they have received their reward.

—Matthew 6:5

Lesson No. 1

Pray Always

The only thing necessary for the triumph of evil is for good men to do nothing.

—Edmund Burke

Those who pray will be saved, *and those who do not will be damned!*
—Saint Alphonsus Liguori

Prayer is the key *that opens the heart of God.*
—Fr. Bill Casey, CPM

Prayer is a sacred, often private, always willful and personal intercourse with our Lord and Savior Jesus Christ, who himself tells us, "All that the Father gives me will come to me; and him who comes to me I will not cast out. For I have come down from heaven, not to do my own will, but the will of him who sent me" (John 6:37–38). "All things have been delivered to me by my Father; and no one knows the Son except the Father, and no one knows the Father except the Son and any one to whom the Son chooses to reveal him. Come to me, all who labor and are heavy laden, and I will give you rest" (Matthew 11:27–28). Prayer is the lifting of our minds and hearts to God in thanksgiving, petition, intercession, or adoration.

Prayer is absolutely essential to our salvation. Jesus, his apostles, and every acknowledged saint were people of prayer, and so must we be if we are going to get to heaven. I will quote extensively from both the Holy Scripture and *Catechism of the Catholic Church*, the magisterium's document for teaching and learning our faith. Even when I do not quote directly these two documents, their message is uppermost in my mind and in my heart.

Similar to love, prayer is an act of the will. We must desire to pray in order for our prayers to be acceptable to God. However, willingness is only the first step in praying. Prayer presupposes effort, desire, discipline, and openness to the Holy Spirit, our constant partner in prayer. Proper—that is, effective—prayer enjoins the mind, the heart, and the will into a single unified act. Each element aids in the perfection of our prayers. Prayer is consummation of man's covenant relationship with our creator. Prayer from the mind, heart, and will is further perfected through humility; being ever mindful that God knows all and has an active role in our current circumstances, it is well to begin our prayers by acknowledging God's active presence in our lives.

Saint Teresa of Avila, a doctor of the church, was a person of constant prayer. She asserted that the foundation to all prayer consists not in thinking much but in loving much. "It must be recognized that not everyone has by nature the imagination capable of meditating, whereas all souls are capable of love." "True sacrifice; the surrendering of our will, our wants and desires, to His, is imperative. It is just as imperative in prayer as in daily activity" (Stephen N. Filippo, *How to Pray According to St. Teresa of Avila*).

Prayer produces three marvelous effects:
1. It detaches us from creatures.
2. It unites us entirely with God.
3. It gradually transforms us into (the image and likeness of) God. (A. Tanquerey, *Spiritually*)

The roots of prayer?

God has made man in his image and likeness (cf. James 3:9); we therefore are complex beings, capable of expressing prayer verbally, silently, with gestures, and with songs. But always, it is the heart of man that leads prayer. Desire for prayer stems from our heart, takes its form from our mind, and is put into action by our wills. The depot of prayer is our soul, wherein resides the Holy Spirit of God when we are in the state of grace, who is constantly working to gain entrance to our souls, through confession and contrition, when we are not in the state of grace.

One cannot pray if one does not know Jesus Christ, and one prays best who has a deep personal relationship with our Lord and Savior, as he is the only way to the Father. (Cf. Matthew 11:27–28.) This statement does not preclude the worth of intercessory prayer, which we shall discuss later. Frequent reception of the sacraments—especially the Holy Eucharist, where Jesus is clothed in humility, which is a "perfect prayer" (because it is Christ himself)—and frequent reading of the Holy Scripture are the best and surest ways to develop a personal relationship with our God.

Pope John XXIII canonized Saint Peter Julian Eymard, founder of the Blessed Sacrament Fathers and Brothers, on December 9, 1962. Here are a few of his thoughts on the topic of prayer from his book *Holy Communion*. "Prayer is the distinguishing characteristic of the Catholic religion; it is the sign of a soul's holiness; indeed it is its holiness. It makes (one) holy and is the first sign of holiness (p. 233). . . . Just as the natural life depends on nourishment, so the supernatural life is absolutely dependent on prayer. Though you should be obliged to give up everything else, penance, religious labors, even Communion, never give up prayer! It belongs to the very state of life that sanctifies them all . . . . If we do not pray, neither the saints nor God Himself will bring us forward on the road of sanctity (p. 237)."

"Parents have the first responsibility for the education of their children in the faith, prayer, and all the virtues particularly, daily family prayer is the first witness of the Church's living memory as awakened patiently by the Holy Spirit. The Christian family is the first place of education in prayer. Based on the sacrament of marriage, the family is the 'domestic church' where God's children learn to pray 'as the Church' and to persevere in prayer" (CCC 2252, 2685). As is so often the case, the best way to teach someone to pray is to be a person of prayer yourself. Jesus was such a person and, by his personal example, prompted the apostles to request Jesus to "teach us to pray." (Cf. Luke 11:1.) Jesus, as the "God-man" had no absolute need to pray, as his dual human and divine nature was always one with the Father; still, he found it comforting and beneficial. Christ prayed before he selected the twelve apostles, he prayed that the apostles would not be tempted, and he prayed before his passion and death, to identify but a few of the times mentioned in the Bible. (Cf. Luke 6:12, 9:18, and 22:41–44.)

The apostles took what they learned from Jesus and put it into practice. "Then they returned to Jerusalem from the mount called Olivet, which is near Jerusalem, a sabbath's day journey away; and when they had entered, they went up to the upper room, where they were staying, Peter and John and James and Andrew, Philip and Thomas, Bartholomew and Matthew, James the son of Alphaeus and Simon the Zealot and Judas the son of James. All these with one accord devoted themselves to prayer, together with the women and Mary the mother of Jesus, and with his brothers" (Acts 1:12–14). "Pick out from among you seven men of good repute, full of the Spirit and of wisdom, who we may appoint to this duty. But we will devote ourselves to prayer and to the ministry of the word"

(Acts 6:3–4). The apostles, in turn, taught the disciples to pray. "And they devoted themselves to the apostles' teaching and fellowship, to the breaking of bread and the prayers" (Acts 2:42).

Types of prayer

God, who is all-knowing, has no need to be told what we want or need and in no way benefits from our prayers. Prayers are essential precisely because we and those for whom we pray are the beneficiaries. Prayer is both the natural and the supernatural response to all of man's needs.

Prayer is always prayer of the church; it is a communion with the Holy Trinity.

Music and song as prayer

Praise the Lord! For it is good to sing praises to our God; for he is gracious, and a song of praise is seemly.

—Psalm 147:1

"Song and music fulfill their function as signs in a manner all the more significant when they are more closely connected . . . with the liturgical action" (SC 112 no. 3). Why? Because song is an act held in common with the community of believers and presented to God as a single offering from all of us, perfected by the Holy Spirit and heart filled in nature. The act of singing is a common communion with one another and our God. It is a sign of unity, faith, hope, and love. Music and song cause a special fellowship of the communion of saints. They develop a unity and joy-filled communion that makes it easier for us to focus and lift our minds, hearts, and wills to the Almighty. It doesn't depend on how loud or how well we sing, only that we participate. I have heard it said, "Those who sing pray twice," and my heart tells me it is so.

Vocal prayer

The common message of prayer is often "Maranatha! Come, Lord Jesus!" This is the common plea and desire of our hearts in song; vocally and silently, we beckon God to come.

Vocal prayer is essential. We have a need to express vocally, at times, our prayers. It is as though by verbalizing our prayers, we somehow are closer to union with God. Vocal prayer allows our bodies, along with our minds and hearts, to praise God. The effort to vocalize and the act of actually hearing ourselves speak to our Lord seem to more intimately bind us to him and him to us. "Pray constantly" (1 Thessalonians 5:17). It is always possible to pray. It is even a vital necessity. "Prayer and Christian life are inseparable" (CCC 2757). "The Holy Spirit who teaches the Church and recalls to her all that Jesus said also instructs her in the life of prayer, inspiring new expressions of the same basic forms of prayer: petition, intercession, thanksgiving, and praise" (CCC 2644).

"*The Eucharist contains and expresses all forms of prayer*: it is 'the pure offering' of the whole Body of Christ to the glory of God's name and, according to the traditions of East and West, it is the 'sacrifice of praise'" (CCC 2643; italics added).

Prayers of petition

Often, the most common type, nature, and purpose of our prayers are to ask God for something or to do something for us or for someone or something we care about. God promises an answer, but keep in mind that God can say "yes," "no," and "not now," depending on whether it is against his will and not for our spiritual well-being. This is a good time to state that all prayers that conform to the divine will of God and that are somehow for our greater good, that is, in some mysterious way will aid us in getting to heaven, are answered favorably. They likely will not be answered in the exact form or in the precise timetable that we have in mind, as the most perfect petition is always not our will but God's will and in his time. "For the eyes of the Lord are upon the righteous, and his ears are open to their prayer" (1 Peter 3:12).

Prayers of petition that benefit others are more pleasing to God than prayers that benefit only ourselves, unless we are asking for special graces to aid in our state of life. "Is any among you sick? Let him call for the elders of the church, and let them pray over him, anointing him with oil in the name of the Lord; and the prayer of faith will save the sick man, and the Lord will raise him up" (James 5:14–15).

A most desired and required personal prayer of petition is asking for forgiveness. God in justice is serious that we will be forgiven in direct relationship with how we forgive each other. Forgiveness cannot be selective; it must be all-inclusive. "So if you are offering your gift at the altar, and there remember that your brother has something against you, leave your gift there before the altar and go; first be reconciled to your brother, and then come and offer your gift" (Matthew 5:23–24).

Intercessory prayers

Prayers of intercession can take several forms. We can and should pray for others, especially our pope, pastors, and our families, as well as the poor souls in purgatory, who can gain a quicker access to heaven through our prayers. This doctrine was made official at the Councils of Trent and Florence. "Through indulgences the faithful can obtain the remission of temporal punishment resulting from sin for themselves and also for the souls in Purgatory" (CCC 1498).

As members of the mystical body and communion of saints, God finds much good in our prayers for others. We can and should also pray "through," not "to," the holy saints, especially Mary, the first and most perfect tabernacle of our Lord and Savior Jesus Christ. Our prayers through Mary and the saints are prayers of veneration, not prayers of adoration, which are reserved for God alone. The church recommends that we also pray through the holy and blessed saints, who share a most intimate union and communion with Almighty God and desire the same grace for us. "Prayer of intercession consists in asking on behalf of another. It knows no boundaries and extends to one's enemies" (CCC 2647). We too are intercessors when we lift our minds and hearts to God to benefit someone or some cause, like ending abortion or like a family member or friend that we care about. After all, we too are saints in training.

Prayers of thanksgiving

God is our creator, and all the circumstances of our lives are attributable to his divine providence. We are saying that everything is either caused by God or permitted by God; therefore, in justice, we must give thanks to God for all that we have (or don't have). It is good to ponder this reality, as it should keep us humble. Often, God is saying "no" to our request, while at times an unwanted cross is also a hidden blessing. No one here on earth is capable of understanding the mind and will of God, yet we are able to comprehend that all things that are good and even much of what we consider as "bad" (not evil, which can only come from Satan), such as serious illness, is permitted by God and intended for our sanctification. We are created to "know, love, and serve" God in this world so that we can be happy with him in the next. Thanking God while we are able is just, proper, and necessary. A loving heart is a thankful heart, and God desires that we have loving hearts. "Enter his gates with thanksgiving, and his courts with praise! Give thanks to him, bless his name!" (Psalm 100:4).

Prayers of praise

"Praise is the form of prayer which recognizes most immediately that God is God. It lauds God for his own sake and gives him glory, quite beyond what he does, but simply because He Is. It shares in the blessed happiness of the pure of heart who love God in faith before seeing him in glory. By praise, the Spirit is joined to our spirits to bear witness that we are children of God, testifying to the only Son in whom we are adopted and by whom we glorify the Father. Praise embraces the other forms of prayer and carries them toward him who is its source and goal: the 'one God, the Father, from whom are all things and for whom we exist" (CCC 2639). "Rejoice in the Lord always; again I will say, Rejoice. Let all men know your forbearance. The Lord is at hand. Have no anxiety about anything, but in everything by prayer and supplication with thanksgiving let your requests be made known to God. And the peace of God, which passes all understanding, will keep your hearts and your minds in Christ Jesus" (Philippians 4:4-7).

Silent prayer

If we are to take seriously Christ's desire that we "pray constantly" (1 Thessalonians 5:17), we must learn to meditate and contemplate God privately within our minds and hearts. We need to develop the practice of constant awareness of God in our minds and not limit his holy presence to our hearts. It is good to pray throughout the day, but often, we are in no position to vocalize these prayers. God understands, yet lack of opportunity for vocal prayer is no excuse for not praying at all. These prayers need not be long or complex, only heartfelt and sincere. Simply saying, "Thanks, Lord," or "Help me, Lord," or praying the Angelus or the Lord's Prayer can be easily accomplished in our busy lives and can bring many graces and blessings. Yet there are times when we need to be in closer communion with our God, and it is these times that meditation or contemplative prayer are desirable, even necessary.

Meditation on God

Meditation can take several forms. In its less formal application, it is simply carrying on a person-to-person conversation with our Lord, and it may be vocalized or internalized. We speak to Jesus through his Holy Spirit, the "comforter" and "enlightener," who is always in our midst. Christ is our best friend, and we need hold nothing back from him. It's OK to be angry, to let God know that we are hurting, that we are disappointed, even if the object of the hurt, anger, or disappointment is God himself. Speak to God as you would a trusted friend, and then pray for discernment, which is a gift from the Holy Spirit, which allows us to either understand God's will or at least be resigned to his holy will for us. Meditation is a form of prayer that should be a regular part of every Christian's walk with the Lord. I repeat, prayer is for our benefit and for those whom we pray and intercede for. "Meditation engages thought, imagination, emotion, and desire. This mobilization of faculties is necessary in order to deepen our convictions of faith, prompt the conversion of our heart, and strengthen our will to follow Christ" (CCC 2708). Learning and putting into practice meditation techniques is something that we owe to ourselves. If we truly wish to develop a personal relationship with our God, this is the vehicle that best assures that the opportunity becomes a reality. If you can't or don't talk to God on a regular and daily basis, you very likely do not yet have a personal relationship with your Savior.

Formalized meditation

The focus of more formal, that is, planned meditation, centers around our Savior Jesus Christ and his stay on earth, especially his passion and death. Perhaps an example will aid us in understanding this topic, but keep in mind that this is a personal intercourse between you and your creator, and one needs always to be open to the prompting of the Holy Spirit, who both teaches us to pray and, in a very real sense, is also the object of our prayers. This dialogue, directed by the Holy Spirit, might be compared to lovers in the act of love, telling each other what they like or do not care for. Similarly, once one becomes familiar with how to meditate, there is less interaction on how and more discourse on the act of love itself. Here's an example to assist you.

We begin to meditate upon a scene of the passion. For example, we begin with the binding of our Lord to the column to be scourged. The mind sets to work to seek the reasons, which include to inflict greater pain, embarrassment, and distress, which our Lord silently suffered when he was being whipped. We take this thought and consider it carefully and as fully as we are enabled to do so by the Holy Spirit. Then move on to the next and so on. This is a most excellent and safe road until the Lord leads us to other methods, which are supernatural; it is well to reflect here for a time and to think of the pains that he bore there, why he bore them, who he is who bore them, and with what love he suffered them.

What we are saying when we are praying

The Lord's Prayer is the embodiment of how we Christians are to live our lives. It is a common prayer of all Christians, not only we Catholics. It is the short version of our Lord's sermon on the mount (cf. Matthew 5, Luke 6:20–46) and includes both the corporal and spiritual works of mercy in its message and commands.

Until the Middle Ages, about AD 1500, the Lord's Prayer was always prayed in the "mother tongue" of the Roman Church, which is Latin. In Latin, it is termed the Paternoster. We need to recall that this is the prayer that our Lord taught us to pray, and theologians often call it the "perfect prayer," and indeed, it is that. The Our Father is a complete compendium of our faith and how we are to (no option here) live it. It is not a prayer that our blessed, perfect, holy Lord prayed for himself, as he has no need of forgiveness, being the manifestation of perfect and complete forgiveness; and having forgiven us for nailing him to the cross by our sins, he still prayed for us: "And Jesus said, 'Father, forgive them; for they know not what they do'" (Luke 23:34).

"He was praying in a certain place, and when he ceased, one of his disciples said to him, 'Lord, teach us to pray, as John taught his disciples.' And he said to them, 'When you pray, say: "Father, hallowed be thy name. Thy kingdom come. Give us each day our daily bread; and forgive us our sins, for we ourselves forgive every one who is indebted to us; and lead us not into temptation"'" (Luke 11:1–4).

"Our Father who art in heaven"

It invites us to recognize that God is and God desires to be our father, Abba, daddy; as such we owe him (our triune Godhead) complete respect, love, fidelity, and obedience. We acknowledge his proper place is heaven, and our life's goal is to join him there. We also acknowledge his triune nature and the presence of Jesus and the Holy Spirit, the second and third members of the Trinity, who mysteriously reside here on earth and at the same time also reside in heaven, as is his holy will. "For my thoughts are not your thoughts, neither are your ways my ways, says the Lord. For as the heavens are higher than the earth, so are my ways higher than your ways and my thoughts than your thoughts" (Isaiah 55:8–9). We are to seek first the kingdom of God, and in doing so, all things will be given to us that God sees as beneficial to our salvation.

Practice of this petition in our life: We are gravely obligated to know, live, and share our faith; for building the kingdom is a shared responsibility of all Christians.

"Hallowed be thy name"

"When we say 'hallowed be thy name,' we ask that it should be hallowed in us who are in him; but also in others whom God's grace still awaits, that we may obey the precept that obliges us to pray for everyone, even our enemies. That is why we do not say expressly 'hallowed be thy name "in us,"' for we ask that it be so in all men" (CCC 2814). We state our belief in a single but triune Godhead and acknowledge that all salvation is through the only church that Jesus founded, the Roman Catholic Church, and that knowing Jesus is essential to salvation.

Practice of this petition in our life: We must cooperate fully with all of God's graces for us. "Only faith reproduces faith. Only believers reproduce other believers" (Fr. John A. Hardon, *The Catholic Catechist Manual*). We must do everything in our power to protect the holy name of God from profane use, correcting and praying for those who have this bad habit.

"Thy will be done on earth as it is in heaven"

In this petition, God shows his sense of humor. He gives us the most powerful force on earth, man's free will, and then asks that we give it back to him. We are saying that it is our heart's desire to put his holy will first every time and all the time. But first we must be able to discern his will, and in order to do that, we must have a personal relationship with the Holy Spirit. How is God's will done in heaven? His angels accomplish it consistently, constantly, perfectly, unselfishly, lovingly, obediently, zealously, and absolutely willingly; and we are to imitate their perfect example, which is only possible with God's grace.

Practice of this petition in our life: We ask God for what is humanly impossible, to give complete control of our most precious and prized gift, our free will, back to him. Why? Because it is through our sacrificial efforts and example that others will be led to do the same, and saving souls for Christ is to be our life's goal. We begin by saving our own, knowing that we can leave no greater heritage to those we love.

"Give us this day our daily bread"

This is a heartfelt plea for salvation with a dual nature. "Save our souls, Lord, and while you're at it, save our temples, our bodies." God created both our bodies and our souls and therefore has a "vested interest" in redeeming both. To do so requires the "bread for life," which is the manna in the wilderness, and the "bread of life," which is Jesus Christ himself in Holy Communion. Man needs both and desires both but often is not willing to cooperate, that is to say, to sacrifice as necessary to obtain both. One is available in many places and the other, "the bread of life," only in his Catholic Church and the Eastern Churches.

Catholics have a grave obligation to share this good news. We naturally seek nourishment for the body and ask for God's provident care, love, and guidance to assist us in this endeavor, which he does according to what he deems best for our spiritual well-being.

God permits abject poverty to afford those with means the opportunity to work in the vineyard of the Lord and care for them. "Give to him who begs from you, and do not refuse him who would borrow from you" (Matthew 5:42).

Just as the body needs bread for nourishment, so too the soul needs the "bread of life"—the body, blood, soul, and divinity of Jesus in Holy Communion.

When we ask or pray, "Give us this day our daily bread," we are really asking God to give us "tomorrow's bread today," meaning, "Lord, give us the bread of salvation," his very self as our spiritual nourishment. There is no greater source of grace available to us.

Practice of this petition in our life: The obligation to share all of our gifts is a grave one. Everything we have comes from God's divine providence. Each of us is called to evangelize, utilizing the gifts and talents God has bestowed upon us whenever he gives us the opportunity to do so.

Everything we "own" and everything we love, including our families, are simply on loan from God. We are to take what we need for sustenance and security and then share the balance. This also means we are to share both time and talent in the vineyard of the Lord. "Give, and it will be given to you; good measure, pressed down, shaken together, running over, will be put into your lap. For the measure you give will be the measure you get back" (Luke 6:38).

"Forgive us our trespasses as we forgive those who trespass against us"

It seems inconceivable to me that mankind can pray this petition with a sincere heart and full understanding. In pleading with God to forgive us as we forgive others, we are saying, "God, only forgive me to the degree that I forgive all others for everything they have or may have ever done to me. If I don't forgive them, don't bother forgiving me. And if I only forgive what I choose to forgive, please treat me the same way. Forgive me only for that which you choose to forgive me." It's darn near enough to get one to stop praying the Lord's Prayer. Included in this forgiveness is forgiveness of self. (I personally find this far more difficult than forgiving others.) None of us are perfect, yet that is what we are called to be (Matthew 5:48). It is humanly impossible to live this petition without the constant supernatural grace of God through the Holy Spirit.

Practice of this petition in our life: If we are to even come close to fulfilling what we are asking God in this petition, we must—absolutely must—lead a sacramental life, as they are the primary channels of God's supernatural grace and the essential means of our salvation. The blessed sacraments, in turn, must be fortified through an active, willed, and heart-filled prayer life that allows God to hear what he desires and respond to our pleas. A strong prayer life naturally leads us to the sacraments, which in turn lead us to a closer personal relationship with our blessed Savior.

"Lead us not into temptation"

This is not in the strict sense, a request not to be tempted. Concupiscence, resulting from the common inherited sin from Adam, demands in justice that we prove our love, faithfulness, and willingness to endure trials for our blessed Lord. What we are asking for is the ability to discern these evils, that they not exceed our natural ability to withstand them and aid us in not exposing ourselves to "the near occasion of sin." We are asking God to protect us from all evil that he sees will not be beneficial to our spiritual well-being because we lack either the necessary spiritual strength or the generosity to profit from the suffering God may choose to send us.

Practice of this petition in our life: In order for God to protect us, we must offer our free will to him in prayer. This returning to God what is rightly his is perhaps the most difficult act that man can do for his God. Just as Jesus told the Father, "Thy will be done" (Matthew 26:42), and thereby received the necessary graces to accomplish his passion and death, so too we receive the necessary graces for every possible challenge to our holiness when we say, pray, and mean, "Thy will be done. Thank you, Lord!"

"Deliver us from evil"

This petition is most fittingly the final one, as it deals with our final judgment. Here, we are asking God to save us from eternal damnation. All of us are sinners to varying degrees. Sins are always a willful act, or they are not sins. It is faith, knowing that we are unworthy but relying on the promise of God that allows us to beg for merciful forgiveness (Ephesians 1:7–8) and thus, God willing, to attain heaven. That should motivate all of our thoughts and actions. In so praying, it is good, even necessary, that we be ever mindful that it is God who chooses to forgive us but in divine justice, only to the degree that we forgive others and ourselves.

Practice of this petition in our life: We should live being ever mindful that someday we shall all die. We should wish to die being mindful that when we die—in fact, the very instant that we die—we will be judged justly by our Almighty and all-just Savior, Jesus Christ. Therefore, we should know, live, and share our faith; we should lead by example; and in this secular, new age, ungodly time, we must be willing to "recover the zeal and the spirit of the first century Christians . . . Unless we are willing to do what they did and to pay the price that they paid, the future of our country, the days of America are numbered" (Fr. John A. Hardon, SJ [my occasional mentor and friend, may he rest in peace]).

Our souls are at great risk. There is, has been, and always will be a high price to pay for heaven. Whoever said that "nothing in life is free" is correct. God gave us free will so we could decide for ourselves to go to hell or go to heaven. It's our decision, but know that it will take an active spiritual prayer life to return to God our free will, which is necessary to maximize the supernatural graces he wishes to bestow on us. We can do none of the things we need to do to get to heaven without the grace of God. Come, Holy Spirit, come!

"Then, after the Lord's Prayer is over we say 'Amen,' which means 'So be it,' thus ratifying with our 'Amen' what is contained in the prayer that God has taught us" (Saint Cyril of Jerusalem, CCC 2856).

A concise reflection on the meaning of prayer

Prayer has been described as "the voluntary response to the awareness of God's presence. This response may be an acknowledgment of God's Greatness and a person's total dependence on Him [adoration], or gratitude for His benefits to oneself or others [thanksgiving], or sorrow for sins committed and begging for mercy [expiation], or asking for graces needed [petition], or affection for God, who is all good [love]." Listen to how some of the saints describe prayer:

"True prayer," wrote Saint Augustine, "is nothing but love."

"Prayer," said Saint John Vianney (patron saint of all priest), "is the inner bath of love into which the soul plunges itself."

"Everyone of us needs a half-hour of prayer each day," remarked Saint Francis de Sales, "except those who are too busy—then they need one hour a day."

Saint John Damascene gave a classic definition of prayer: "Prayer is the raising of the mind and heart to God or the requesting of good things from God."

Finally, Saint Alphonsus Liguori saw prayer as a relationship based on God's unconditional love for us. "Consider that no one, friend, father, mother, sister, or brother loves you more than your God." Amen.

Patrick Miron

The key to finding *true* "joy" according to Mother Teresa of Calcutta

J = Jesus first in everything
O = Others next
Y = Yourself always last

Catholics and the "New" Old Creed

Knowing what we're saying when we're praying the creed, which is a summary of Catholic beliefs, is an essential step in actually knowing our Catholic faith.

The Nicene Creed dates back to AD 325 and the Council of Nicaea. It is used at all masses on Sundays and solemnities (although the shorter older Apostles' Creed will also be an option with the new missal). Our creeds are a summary and a brief catechism of our Catholic beliefs.

The following is the complete new English text of the Nicene Creed, with its changes in italics:

I believe in one God, the Father almighty, maker of heaven and earth, of all things visible and invisible. I believe in one Lord Jesus Christ, the Only *Begotten* Son of God, born of the Father *before all ages*. God from God, Light from Light, true God from true God, begotten, not made, *consubstantial* with the Father; through him all things were made. For us men and for our salvation he came down from heaven, *and by* the Holy Spirit was *incarnate* of the Virgin Mary, and became man. For our sake he was crucified under Pontius Pilate, he *suffered death* and was buried, *and rose again on the third day* in *accordance with* the Scriptures. He ascended into heaven and is seated at the right hand of the Father. He will come again in glory to judge the living and the dead and his kingdom will have no end. *I believe* in the Holy Spirit, the Lord, the giver of life, *who* proceeds from the Father and the Son, *who* with the Father and the Son is adored and glorified, *who* has spoken through the prophets. I believe in one, holy, catholic and apostolic Church. *I confess* one Baptism for the forgiveness of sins *and I look forward to* the resurrection of the dead and the life of the world to come. Amen.

"I believe in one God" (Triune)

Always, both in tradition and in fact, have Yahweh, Jesus Christ, Peter, and his successors proclaimed this single truth. "We" has been changed to "I," stressing the fact that it is "me" proclaiming "my" personal beliefs. "I *do* believe."

OT: "Do not afflict your countrymen, but let every one fear his God: because *I am the Lord your God*" (Leviticus 25:17).

NT: "And Jesus answered him: The first commandment of all is, Hear, O Israel: *the Lord thy God is one God*" (Mark 12:29).

God's brilliance is evident in many clear ways. One perhaps overlooked is the fact of just "one God"—one only, which makes clear who is in charge and who's in control without even a possibility of argument or debate. Nothing is accidental or coincidental with God. Everything, from the least significant to the most momentous, is part of God's "divine providence," which is too often forgotten or laid aside.

"The Father almighty"

Few who really know God doubt this unlimited power and authority at least in a conscious manner. I suspect, however, in a less conscious manner, doubts do arise. Most often, when our prayers are not answered immediately and in the exact manner we have requested, a thought creeps in that maybe God "can't" do it. Frankly, this isn't even a possibility but not for completely obvious reasons. Let's make clear that *God can do any good thing.* And therein is the answer. What we think is "good" for us might well not be. God alone know this and responds accordingly. Answers to our prayers can be "yes," "no," or "not now." God will always do what *he* knows to be best for our spiritual benefit.

OT: "And after he began to be ninety and nine years old, the Lord appeared to him [Abram]: and said unto him: I am the Almighty God: walk before me, and be perfect" (Genesis 17:1).

NT: "And I will receive you; and I will be a Father to you; and you shall be my sons and daughters, saith the Lord Almighty" (2 Corinthians 6:18).

"Maker of heaven and earth"

OT: "Thus saith the Lord thy redeemer, and thy maker, from the womb: I am the Lord, that make all things, that alone stretch out the heavens, that establish the earth, and there is none with me" (Isaiah 44:24).

NT: "Who having heard it, with one accord lifted up their voice to God, and said: Lord, thou art he that didst make heaven and earth, the sea, and all things that are in them" (Acts 4:24).

There is a "new atheism" following in the form of age-old Gnosticism that preaches and believes "I do know more, I do know better, for I am my own god. Don't even attempt to set other gods or God before me." It is a heady, vibrant, prideful, and growing mind-set, which is heavily promoted duplicitously in the media and in our public schools and at times ignored or not identified by parents and even parts of the church. Its foundation differs little from new age theology with its focus on self— me, me, me—so it's an easy "sell." Because "me" takes up nearly all of one's mind and will, there is no room left for God. It's not so much a direct conscious denial of God, as it is a single-minded focus on self. Little thought, if any, is given to the vast realities of creation, through which all men could (and should) discover God and the majesty of his handiwork, which exists for this very purpose.

"Of all things visible and invisible"

This budding "new atheism" can be defeated. This evil is not invincible. It has been my experience that atheists concoct numerous and various explanations for how the universe and even humanity "came to exist," often through some theory of "evolution," without acknowledging that "evolution" can't just happen on its own, that there absolutely had and has to be a "first cause," which they then must ignore because they are unable to explain this fact away. We choose to call this *first cause* "our God."

Of the *billions* of things in the universe, there are two "invisible things" that stick out for their uniqueness, majesty, and necessity. They are the so-called natural laws and man himself, who alone is able to reflect God's "moral laws."

"Man himself?" you say. "Man's not invisible." Actually, what makes man the top of the "command chain," what makes man individually unique, and what makes man alone able to emulate our God is provable to be invisible. They are like God himself, "spiritual realities."

Only man can create something new out of existing things, like a rocket to send men to the moon and back or the Sears Tower or music and art. Only man can know good and evil (and then choose to deny either or both). Only man can rationalize. Only man can freely choose to love and/or to hate. Because only man can, it therefore becomes man's very reason to exist, to first know of God, then through grace to be enabled to actually know God. It is a fact that the entire universe exist for this very reason and this reason alone.

Isaiah 43:7, 21 says, "Every one who is called by my name, whom I created for my glory, whom I formed and made. The people whom I formed for myself that they might declare my praise."

In order to accomplish these things, man is given exclusive gifts, exclusive attributes of a mind, intellect, free will, and soul. And like our God, these are "spiritual and invisible" realities (John 4:23–24), and it is these "spiritual realities" that fulfill Genesis 1:26–27, where God announces that he will create man "in his own image."

Take for example your "free will." What is its size, shape, weight, and color? We don't know because, while its existence is a verifiable reality, our mind, intellect, and free will—each a component of our eternal soul—are "spiritual realities" and like, God, are eternal.

OT: "In the beginning God created heaven, and earth. And the earth was void and empty, and darkness was upon the face of the deep; and the spirit of God moved over the waters. And God said: Be light made. And light was made. And God saw the light that it was good; and he divided the light from the darkness. And he called the light Day, and the darkness Night; and there was evening and morning one day" (Genesis 1:1–5; see the entire first chapter).

NT: "By faith we understand that the world was framed by the word of God; that from invisible things visible things might be made" (Hebrews 11:3).

"I believe in one Lord Jesus Christ"

What we are commanded to believe here, what we profess as "truth" is that Jesus Christ is both "true man and true God," a man like us in every way except sin.

OT: "For a CHILD IS BORN to us, and a son is given to us, and the government is upon his shoulder: and his name shall be called, Wonderful, Counsellor, God the Mighty, the Father of the world to come, the Prince of Peace" (Isaiah 9:6; about seven hundred years before Christ's birth).

NT: "And they that were in the boat came and adored him, saying: Indeed thou art the Son of God" (Matthew 14:33).

There is much evidence in the Bible and in secular history that proves that Jesus did exist. There is also evidence that Jesus is God. But no amount of evidence can or will convince an obstinate, self-absorbed intellect of this fact. It is God's choice, God's providence that permits one to actually "discover God's existence." Everyone has the ability to at least know of "a god" and then, through endless creation and grace offered and accepted, to actually discover for themselves the reality of the one we call "our God."

OT: "And you shall say to him, 'The Lord, the God of the Hebrews, sent me to you, saying, "Let my people go, that they may serve me in the wilderness; and behold, you have not yet obeyed"'" (Exodus 7:16).

NT: "For God so loved the world, as to give his only begotten Son; that whosoever believeth in him, may not perish, but may have life everlasting" (John 3:16).

"Born of the Father before all ages [of the same one nature and essence]. God from God, Light from Light, true God from true God, begotten, not made [always existed], consubstantial with the Father"

Consubstantial means "of the same substance."

OT: "Who hath wrought and done these things, calling the generations from the beginning? I the Lord, I am the first and the last" (Isaiah 41:4).

NT: "I am the Alpha and the Omega, the first and the last, the beginning and the end" (Revelations 22:13).

Again, we profess only one God, but now the *blessed Trinity* is being exposed as "coequal and coeternal," three persons having but one nature and each owning this one nature in its entirety.

Matthew 3:13–17 says, "Then cometh Jesus from Galilee to the Jordan, unto John, to be baptized by him. But John stayed him, saying: I ought to be baptized by thee, and comest thou to me? And Jesus [the Son] answering, said to him: Suffer it to be so now [permit it]. For so it becometh us to fulfill all justice. Then he suffered him. And Jesus being baptized, forthwith came out of the water: and lo, the heavens were opened to him: and he saw the Spirit of God [the Holy Spirit] descending as a dove, and coming upon him. And behold a voice [The Father] from heaven, saying: this is my beloved Son, in whom I am well pleased." Three in one.

Matthew 28:19 states, "Going therefore, teach ye all nations; baptizing them in the *name of the Father, and of the Son, and of the Holy Ghost* [italics added]."

The Trinity according to the *Catechism of the Catholic Church* is as follows:

234 The mystery of the Most Holy Trinity is the central mystery of Christian faith and life. It is the mystery of God in himself. It is therefore the source of all the other mysteries of faith, the light that enlightens them. It is the most fundamental and essential teaching in the "hierarchy of the truths of faith." The whole history of salvation is identical with the history of the way and the means by which the one true God, Father, Son and Holy Spirit, reveals himself to men "and reconciles and unites with himself those who turn away from sin."

237 The Trinity is a mystery of faith in the strict sense, one of the "mysteries that are hidden in God, which can never be known unless they are revealed by God." To be sure, God has left traces of his Trinitarian being in his work of creation and in his Revelation throughout the Old Testament. But his inmost Being as Holy Trinity is a mystery that is inaccessible to reason alone or even to Israel's faith before the Incarnation of God's Son and the sending of the Holy Spirit.

253 *The Trinity is One* [italics in original]. We do not confess three Gods, but one God in three persons, the *"consubstantial Trinity"* [italics mine]. The divine persons do not share the one divinity among themselves *but each of them is God whole and entire* [italics mine]: "The Father is that which the Son is, the Son that which the Father is, the Father and the Son that which the Holy Spirit is, i.e. by nature one God." In the words of the Fourth Lateran Council (1215), "Each of the persons is that supreme reality, viz., the divine substance, essence or nature."

"Through him all things were made"

OT: "And God saw all the things that he had made, and they were very good. And the evening and morning were the sixth day" (Genesis 1:31).

NT: "All things were made by him: and without him was made nothing that was made" (John 1:3).

"For us men and for our salvation [conditionally]"

OT: "The Lord is my strength and my praise, and he is become salvation to me: he is my God and I will glorify him: the God of my father, and I will exalt him" (Exodus 15:2).

NT: "And hath raised up an horn of salvation to us, in the house of David his servant" (Luke 1:69). "To give knowledge of salvation to his people, unto the remission of their sins" (Luke 1:77). "Neither is there salvation in any other. For there is no other name under heaven given to men, whereby we must be saved" (Acts 4:12).

Implied here is the absolute necessity that we merit our salvation in the precise and specific manner ordained and demanded by Christ himself. That is *why* there is but one God, one faith, and one church and only one holder of the keys to heaven here on earth (Matthew 16:18–19), and that is the Christ-founded Catholic Church.

"He came down from heaven"

OT: "For a CHILD IS BORN to us, and a son is given to us, and the government is upon his shoulder: and his name shall be called, Wonderful, Counsellor, God the Mighty, the Father of the world to come, the Prince of Peace" (Isaiah 9:6).

NT: "I came forth from the Father, and am come into the world: again I leave the world, and I go to the Father" (John 16:28).

"And by the Holy Spirit was incarnate of the Virgin Mary, and became man"

OT: "Therefore the Lord himself shall give you a sign. Behold a virgin shall conceive, and bear a son, and his name shall be called Emmanuel [meaning 'God with *us*']" (Isaiah 7:14).

NT: "And in the sixth month, the angel Gabriel was sent from God into a city of Galilee, called Nazareth, To a virgin espoused to a man whose name was Joseph, of the house of David; and the virgin's name was Mary. And the angel being come in, said unto her: Hail, full of grace, the Lord is with thee: blessed art thou among women. Who having heard, was troubled at his saying, and thought with herself what manner of salutation this should be. And the angel said to her: Fear not, Mary, for thou hast found grace with God. Behold thou shalt conceive in thy womb, and shalt bring forth a son; and thou shalt call his name Jesus. He shall be great, and shall be called the Son of the most High; and the Lord God shall give unto him the throne of David his father; and he shall reign in the house of Jacob for ever. And of his kingdom there shall be no end. And Mary said to the angel: How shall this be done, because I know not man? ["I'm a virgin."] And the angel answering, said to her: *The Holy Ghost shall come upon thee, and the power of the most High shall overshadow thee. And therefore also the Holy which shall be born of thee shall be called the Son of God*" (Luke 1:26–35).

This was prophesied about seven hundred years before it was fulfilled.

"For our sake he was crucified under Pontius Pilate"

OT: "And the Lord was pleased to bruise him in infirmity: if he shall lay down his life for sin, he shall see a long-lived seed, and the will of the Lord shall be prosperous in his hand. Because his soul hath laboured, he shall see and be filled: by his knowledge shall this my just servant justify many, and he shall bear their iniquities. Therefore will I distribute to him very many, and he shall divide the spoils of the strong, because he hath delivered his soul unto death, and was reputed with the wicked: and he hath borne the sins of many, and hath prayed for the transgressors" (Isaiah 53:10–12).

NT: "And after they had crucified him, they divided his garments" (Matthew 27:35).

"He suffered death and was buried"

To be clear, it was the humanity of Christ that was killed and buried, not his divinity, which is eternal. But *both* the divinity and the humanity of Christ suffered and endured every pain, every abuse, and every humiliation for us—his humanity in his flesh and his divinity in his spirit.

OT: "He poured out his soul to death, and was numbered with the transgressors" (Isaiah 53:12).

NT: "Jesus therefore, when he had taken the vinegar, said: It is consummated. And bowing his head, he gave up the ghost [died]" (John 19:30).

"And rose again on the third day in accordance with the Scriptures"

OT: "Thy dead men shall live, my slain shall rise again: awake, and give praise, ye that dwell in the dust: for thy dew is the dew of the light: and the land of the giants thou shalt pull down into ruin. Go, my people, enter into thy chambers, shut thy doors upon thee, hide thyself a little for a moment, until the indignation pass away. For behold the Lord will come out of his place, to visit the iniquity of the inhabitant of the earth against him: and the earth shall disclose her blood, and shall cover her slain no more" (Isaiah 26:19–21).

NT: "For as Jonas was in the whale's belly three days and three nights: so shall the Son of man be in the heart of the earth three days and three nights" (Matthew 12:40). "Jesus saith to her: Woman, why weepest thou? whom seekest thou? She, thinking it was the gardener, saith to him: Sir, if thou hast taken him hence, tell me where thou hast laid him, and I will take him away. Jesus saith to her: Mary. She turning, saith to him: Rabboni (which is to say, Master). Jesus saith to her: Do not touch me, for I am not yet ascended to my Father. But go to my brethren, and say to them: I ascend to my Father and to your Father, to my God and your God [in his now-glorified body]" (John 20:15–17).

The church teaches that it is the resurrection, not the birth of Christ, that is our primary cause for a joy-filled celebration. It is because Christ in his humanity did arise from the dead that we too can hope, pray, and obey so that we too might participate in Christ's eternal glory.

> Belief in the resurrection of the dead has been an essential element of the Christian faith from its beginnings. "The confidence of Christians is the resurrection of the dead; believing this we live."
>
> > How can some of you say that there is no resurrection of the dead? But if there is no resurrection of the dead, then Christ has not been raised; if Christ has not been raised, then our preaching is in vain and your faith is in vain . . . . But in fact Christ has been raised from the dead, the first fruits of those who have fallen asleep. (CCC 991)

**"He ascended into heaven and is seated at
the right hand of the Father"**

Matthew 25:33–34 says, "And he shall set the sheep on his right hand [destination: heaven], but the goats on his left [destination: hell].

Then shall the king say to them that shall be on his right hand: Come, ye blessed of my Father, possess you the kingdom prepared for you from the foundation of the world."

Mark 16:19 states, "And the Lord Jesus, after he had spoken to them, was taken up into heaven, and sitteth on the right hand of God."

Hidden in the events surrounding this unexpected event of the ascension of Christ in his now-glorified body, blood, soul, and divinity—his complete and perfect humanity united with his always present divinity—were a number of extremely important lessons for the apostles and, through them, to us in the present times.

NT: "And no man hath ascended into heaven, but he that descended from heaven, the Son of man who is in heaven" (John 3:13).

The term "ascended" means under his own power, by his own will united in the Trinity. (FYI: Mary was "assumed," meaning drawn up to heaven by her son, not of her own power.)

The Six Lessons of the Resurrection

"They therefore who were come together, asked him, saying: Lord, wilt thou at this time restore again the kingdom to Israel? But he said to them: It is not for you to know the times or moments, which the Father hath put in his own power" (Acts 1:6–7).

Lesson 1: A final warning: Be ready. Be always prepared, for you know not the hour of his return.

"But you shall receive the power of the Holy Ghost coming upon you, and you shall be witnesses unto me in Jerusalem, and in all Judea, and Samaria, and even to the uttermost part of the earth" (Acts 1:8).

Lesson 2: *Fulfilled in John 20:21–22,* this was for them the sacrament of confirmation, which he leaves also for us. It's not just an indelible anointing but also the grace to know, to love, to obey, and to serve him and all others. Compare the mission expressed in Matthew 28:19–20 to go and teach the "whole world" *all* that he taught them. And the *mandate* extends to each and every one of us, who also are to teach, as God has prepared us too, each using the gifts of the Holy Spirit given to us for the good of our families *and* of "the church."

"And when he had said these things, while they looked on, he was raised up: and a cloud received him out of their sight. *And while they were beholding him going up to heaven,* behold two men stood by them in white garments. Who also said: Ye men of Galilee, why stand you looking up to heaven?" (Acts 1:9–11).

Lesson 3: Go! Get to work, and fulfill the mission and the mandate given to you.

"This Jesus who is taken up from you into heaven, shall so come [again], as you have seen him going into heaven" (Acts 1:11).

Lesson 4: Revelation 22:12 says, "Behold, I come quickly; and my reward is with me, to render to every man according to his works."

"In those days *Peter rising up in the midst* of the brethren, said: (now the number of persons together was about an hundred and twenty) Men, brethren, the scripture must needs be fulfilled, which the Holy Ghost spoke before by the mouth of David concerning Judas, who was the leader of them that apprehended Jesus: Who was numbered with us, and had obtained part of this ministry. And he indeed hath possessed a field of the reward of iniquity, and being hanged, burst asunder in the midst. For it is written in the book of Psalms [Psalm 68:26]: Let their habitation become desolate, and let there be none to dwell therein. And his bishopric let another take. Wherefore of these men who have companied with us all the time that the Lord Jesus came in and went out among us, Beginning from the baptism of John, until the day wherein he was taken up from us, one of these must be made a witness with us of his resurrection. And they appointed two, Joseph, called Barsabas, who was surnamed Justus, and Matthias" (Acts 1:15–18, 20–23).

Lesson 5: Peter, the recognized leader of the apostles, calls for a replacement for Judas the traitor and thus establishes the sacred tradition of succession, made necessary by Christ's *new* command to *now* go into the entire world (Matthew 28:19–20) and thus mandating succession in order to fulfill the mission.

"And praying, they said: Thou, Lord, who knowest the hearts of all men, shew whether of these two thou hast chosen, To take the place of this ministry and apostleship, from which Judas hath by transgression fallen, that he might go to his own place" (Acts 1:24–25).

Lesson 6: It is mortal men, guided by the Holy Spirit, who initiate the selection of popes, bishops, and even priests and religious; *but* specifically here, it references future popes: "You did not choose me, but I chose you and appointed you that you should go and bear fruit and that your fruit should abide; so that whatever you ask the Father in my name, he may give it to you" (John 15:16).

It is and remains God himself, the Holy Spirit, who makes the selection through mortal men of our popes—promised in John 14:16–17, fulfilled in John 20:21–22, and assured in Matthew 16:18–19 with the keys and the promise that "the gates of hell shall *never* prevail." And in John 17:15–19, Jesus Christ commits himself in person as the warranty of this truth and of the men he chooses as being *unable* to error when teaching on all matters to be believed in faith and also on all moral matters.

"He will come again in glory to judge the living and the dead"

OT: "Now is an end come upon thee, and I will send my wrath upon thee, and I will judge thee according to thy ways: and I will set all thy abominations against thee" (Ezekiel 7:3).

NT: "And he shall send his angels with a trumpet, and a great voice: and they shall gather together his elect from the four winds, from the farthest parts of the heavens to the utmost bounds of them. And from the fig tree learn a parable: When the branch thereof is now tender, and the leaves come forth, you know that summer is nigh. So you also, when you shall see all these things, know ye that it is nigh, even at the doors. Amen I say to you, that this generation shall not pass, till all these things be done. Heaven and earth shall pass, but my words shall not pass. But of that day and hour no one knoweth, not the angels of heaven, but the Father alone" (Matthew 24:31–36).

Several explanations seem prudent here. "That this generation" means the Jewish nation shall not cease to exist, *not* those in existence at the time of the proclamation. "But of that day and hour no one knoweth," not even Christ? This is an issue of Christ's two natures. Christ in his human nature could not "naturally" know of it, but because both his human and divine natures were inseparable, Christ *had* to know in his enlightened human nature and, of course, in his divine nature as part of the Trinity. (Within the Trinity, what one knows they *all* know.)

Revelation 20:12 says, "And I saw the dead, great and small, standing in the presence of the throne, and the books were opened; and another book was opened, which is the book of life; and the dead were judged by those things which were written in the books, according to their works."

Revelation 22:12 states, "Behold, I come quickly; and my reward is with me, to render to every man according to his works."

"And his kingdom will have no end"

OT: "For to us a child is born, to us a son is given; and the government will be upon his shoulders, and his name will be called 'Wonderful Counselor, Mighty God, Everlasting Father, Prince of Peace.' *Of the increase of his government and of peace there will be no end*, upon the throne of David, and over his kingdom, to establish it, and to uphold it with justice and with righteousness from this time forth and for evermore. The zeal of the Lord of hosts will do this" (Isaiah 9:6–7; italics added).

NT: "Behold thou shalt conceive in thy womb, and shalt bring forth a son; and thou shalt call his name Jesus. He shall be great, and shall be called the Son of the most High; and the Lord God shall give unto him the throne of David his father; and he shall reign in the house of Jacob for ever. And of his kingdom there shall be no end. And Mary said to the angel: How shall this be done, because I know not man? And the angel answering, said to her: The Holy Ghost shall come upon thee, and the power of the most High shall overshadow thee. And therefore also the Holy which shall be born of thee shall be called the Son of God" (Luke 1:31–35).

Eternity is what is in front of us. Sirach 15:18 says, "Before man is life and death, good and evil, that which he shall choose shall be given him." *We* decide which.

"I believe in the Holy Spirit, the Lord, the giver of life, who proceeds from the Father and the Son"

We covered the Trinity in an earlier segment. I see no need to repeat the information on the most blessed Trinity here. The only part not previously addressed is "proceed from." This is a primary issue keeping much of the Eastern Church in schism from us.

The Roman Catholic Church's infallible teaching is that it is by and through "the love" of the Father for the Son and the love of the Son for the Father that makes the Holy Spirit present and part of the Trinity of one God, each of them coequal and coeternal. This too is a part of the divine mystery that is God and beyond comprehension in this life.

"I believe in one, holy, catholic and apostolic Church"

One

"And having called his twelve disciples together, he gave *them* power over unclean spirits, to cast them out, and to heal all manner of diseases, and all manner of infirmities. And the names of the twelve apostles are these: The first, Simon who is called Peter, and Andrew his brother, James the son of Zebedee, and John his brother, Philip and Bartholomew, Thomas and Matthew the publican, and James the son of Alpheus, and Thaddeus, Simon the Cananean, and Judas Iscariot, who also betrayed him. These twelve Jesus sent: commanding them, saying: Go ye not into the way of the Gentiles, and into the city of the Samaritans enter ye not. But go ye rather to the lost sheep of the house of Israel. And going, preach, saying: The kingdom of heaven is at hand. Heal the sick, raise the dead, cleanse the lepers, cast out devils: freely have you received, freely give" (Matthew 10:1–8; italics added). The command is changed in Matthew 28:18–20 to "Go therefore and make disciples of all nations, . . . teaching them to observe all that I have commanded you."

"Simon Peter answered and said: Thou art Christ, the Son of the living God. And Jesus answering, said to him: Blessed art thou, Simon Bar-Jona: because flesh and blood hath not revealed it to thee, but my Father who is in heaven. And I say to thee: That thou art Peter; and upon this rock I will build my church, and the gates of hell shall not prevail against it. And I will give to thee the keys of the kingdom of heaven. And whatsoever thou shalt bind upon earth, it shall be bound also in heaven: and whatsoever thou shalt loose upon earth, it shall be loosed also in heaven" (Matthew 16:16–19).

Once again, further clarification of God's proclamation seems unwarranted.

Lesson 1: Here is an example so that we can know how God chooses to work. Peter's acknowledgment of Christ as "the Son of God" was something Peter had failed to grasp from self-observation or self-knowledge but a startling revelation he announced by knowledge infused from God the Father *into* Peter, who then spoke *as God wanted him* to speak or what God wanted him to announce. We have here for *our* benefit an example of how papal infallibility works.

Lesson 2: The indisputable evidence of Jesus speaking directly to Peter is astoundingly clear. "Thou," "I", "thee," "my," "upon this rock,"

"I," "it," "*the* keys," "*the* kingdom," "thou shalt bind," and "thou shalt loose" are *all* singular, so no one can logically dispute that Christ intended to establish a new faith; the term "church" instituted here by Christ is to differentiate both a new set of faith beliefs and a new type of place for worship. Pagans had temples, the Jews had synagogues, and Christians were to have "churches."

Lesson 3: Ignored by their absolute necessity by all competing faiths is the *fact* that God himself gives to and through Peter alone the role of the head of this new institution. Christ founded only "one" new faith and in only "one" church; the *only* keys to heaven's access are in the hands that Christ intended them to be for man's possible salvation—today's Catholic Church.

Lesson 4: The terms "binding" and "loosing" used by our perfect, unerring God were well-known and common terms of the time. They reference unlimited, unfettered governance of this new church, founded on the faith beliefs that Christ personally taught to Peter and the other apostles (Matthew 28:19–20).

Christ knew that he would soon be sacrificed for our sins—our redemption and possible salvation. Matthew 28:21–25 speaks directly to this known reality. Thus, a successor had to either be chosen and empowered or risk not fulfilling the mandate Christ himself was given from the Father, an impossibility for God. Cities at the time, including Jerusalem itself, were "walled in." They actually had gates, and the gates really had keys. The "keeper of the keys" had unlimited day-to-day authority of governance and answered *only* to the King. *This* is the precise role Christ envisioned for Peter, and *this* is what was clearly understood by *all* who heard of it, which explains why there was no debate or dissension among the twelve on this matter.

Holy

This term applies directly and exclusively to "the church" and only applies to its members when they strive to be holy and accomplish it through grace. We can sin; the church cannot, yet she (mother church) is a living entity.

The church is and *must* be "holy" because she is alter Christus, another form of Christ. Christ is so much "in the church" that we can understand a sense of "Christ actually being the church." "For I am the

Lord your God: be holy because I am holy" (Leviticus 11:44). "Because it is written: You shall be holy, for I am holy" (1 Peter 1:16).

Catholic

The church is "catholic," a term defined as "universal," because she is, and she "is required to be worldwide" (Matthew 28:28–20).

Apostolic

This is following the command in Matthew 28:19–20, once again given by Christ personally, directly, and exclusively to Peter and through Peter to the other apostles, from whom we inherit by absolute necessity the same powers and authority and mandate to *go*.

Compare Matthew 10:1, 8 with Matthew 28:19–20. "Going therefore, teach ye all nations [this new and last-minute command, in effect, has Jesus instituting papal succession]; baptizing them in the name of the Father, and of the Son, and of the Holy Ghost. Teaching them to observe all things whatsoever I have commanded you: and behold I am with you all days, even to the consummation of the world" (Matthew 28:19–20). "And having called his twelve disciples together, he gave them power over unclean spirits, to cast them out, and to heal all manner of diseases, and all manner of infirmities. Heal the sick, raise the dead, cleanse the lepers, cast out devils" (Matthew 10:1, 8).

John 17:18 says, "As thou hast sent me into the world, I also have sent them into the world." This means exactly what it says: with a portion of God's own powers and authority.

John 20:21–22 states, "He said therefore to them again: Peace be to you. As the Father hath sent me, I also send you. When he had said this, he breathed on them; and he said to them: Receive ye the Holy Ghost."

"I confess one Baptism for the forgiveness of sins"

"Going therefore, teach *ye all nations*; baptizing them in the name of the Father, and of the Son, and of the Holy Ghost [with water]" (Matthew 28:19; italics added).

"And I look forward to the resurrection of the dead and the life of the world to come"

OT: "I call heaven and earth to witness this day, that I have set before you life and death, blessing and cursing. Choose therefore life, that both thou and thy seed may live" (Deuteronomy 30:19).

NT: "And Paul knowing that the one part were Sadducees, and the other Pharisees, cried out in the council: Men, brethren, I am a Pharisee, the son of Pharisees: concerning the hope and resurrection of the dead I am called in question. And when he had so said, there arose a dissension between the Pharisees and the Sadducees; and the multitude was divided. For the Sadducees say that there is no resurrection, neither angel, nor spirit: but the Pharisees confess both" (Acts 23:6–8). "And coming out of the tombs after his resurrection, [Jesus] came into the holy city, and appeared to many" (Matthew 27:53).

Because Christ did rise from "the dead," we too can look forward to eternal life, an eternity that we ourselves can choose. So choose wisely. Amen.

It's important that, when we pray, we know what we are praying and what we are saying and agreeing to. This is God's expectation for each of us. It is my prayer that this will help you understand what we claim to believe in our creed.

May God continue to guide us, and may Mary lead us to her Son Jesus. Amen!

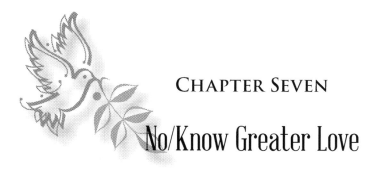

CHAPTER SEVEN

No/Know Greater Love

Greater love has no man than this, that a man lay down his life for his friends.

—John 15:13

For since, in the wisdom of God, the world did not know God through wisdom, it pleased God through the folly of what we preach to save those who believe. For Jews demand signs and Greeks seek wisdom, but we preach Christ crucified, a stumbling block to Jews and folly to Gentiles, *but to those who are called, both Jews and Greeks, Christ the power of God and the wisdom of God. For the foolishness of God is wiser than men, and the weakness of God is stronger than men.*

—1 Corinthians 1:21–26

The Stations of the Cross

"This is my commandment, that you love one another as I have loved you. Greater love has no man than this, that a man lay down his life for his friends. You are my friends if you do what I command you. No longer do I call you servants, for the servant does not know what his master is doing; but I have called you friends, for all that I have heard from my Father I have made known to you" (John 15:12–15).

The mob was more surprised than Jesus. He knew their sinister plan and was prepared, even eager, for it. Still, he must have looked both majestic in his cooperative attitude of unresisting compliance and frightful in appearance, as he was heaving, covered with sweated blood, and so deprived of rest. He reminded them that they had many opportunities to seize him and asked, "Why now?" The answer was apparent. *His hour was now at hand.* "'But all this has taken place that the scriptures of the prophets might be fulfilled.' Then all the disciples forsook him and fled" (Matthew 26:56).

Both pleasure and pain are greatly enhanced by anticipation, foreknowledge, and comprehension of what is to take place. Similarly, it is far easier to love someone who loves or will love you in return. What Jesus was to endure out of love for us involved totally his mind, his body, and his soul; and there was not a single sinner whom Jesus did not love. Love is not an emotion; it is a conscious decision, a continuous act of the will that permits one to love someone, even without "liking" that person or approving of his or her actions. Love always requires sacrifice, and love always requires a conscious decision. *If you can't forgive, you can't love.* Christ forgives and loves us.

We take Jesus to a confrontation with his accusers. It was the religious leaders of the time that stirred up, provoked, led, and insisted that "it is better for one man to die" than for us to suffer. Why? First, because they rejected the grace offered that would permit them to recognize God as goodness. Second, Jesus was a threat, both real and imagined, to their authority; his evident power was unlimited and theirs very limited. Third was one of Satan's favorite tools—jealousy. Jesus was actually liked and respected, even loved by some, while they, for the most part, were simply feared.

The First Station: Jesus Is Condemned to Die

"For as by one man's disobedience many were made sinners, so by one man's obedience many will be made righteous" (Romans 5:19).

"Now the chief priests and the whole council sought testimony against Jesus to put him to death; but they found none. The high priest asked him, 'Are you the Christ, the Son of the Blessed?' And Jesus said, 'I am; and you will see the Son of man seated at the right hand of Power, and coming with the clouds of heaven.' And the high priest tore his garments, and said, 'Why do we still need witnesses? You have heard his blasphemy. What is your decision?' And they all condemned him as deserving death. And some began to spit on him, and to cover his face, and to strike him, saying to him, 'Prophesy!' And the guards received him with blows" (Mark 14:55, 61–65).

The Jewish nation was in captivity, subservient to the ruling Roman Empire. Officials lacked the power to pronounce and execute a death mandate. It was the judgment of the Roman protectorate, Pilate, who had the legal power to kill, and he had to be persuaded to issue a "guilty, go ahead and crucify him" verdict. Pilate had heard of Jesus and did not see him as a threat to either himself or Rome. He reckoned correctly that jealously was the motive of the Jewish leaders, but he simply didn't wish to make a decision in opposition to their wishes for fear of a possible Jewish revolt. Pilate knew well the power to sway the masses that the religious leaders had.

Pilate's wife had warned him not to get involved, as she had a dream about Jesus. The Romans had very little respect for life, were active abortionists, and used gruesome killings to maintain fearful but orderly governance. "Pilate asked him, 'Are you the King of the Jews?' And he answered him, 'You have said so'" (Mark 15:2). "Pilate saw that he was gaining nothing, but rather that a riot was beginning, he took water and washed his hands before the crowd, saying, 'I am innocent of this man's blood; see to it yourselves.' And all the people answered, 'His blood be on us and on our children!' Then he released for them Barab'bas [a justly convicted criminal], and having scourged Jesus, delivered him to be crucified" (Matthew 27:24–26).

The Crowning of Thorns

A key to being a successful politician is to make as few public decisions as possible, not to procrastinate but to delegate. The job gets done, you can take the credit if it goes well, and you have someone to blame if it doesn't. Pilate was brilliant in passing Jesus on to Herod, who was governor of Galilee. Herod was anxious to see Jesus perform his magic, but Herod was so steeped in sin that he could not discern simple magic from a miracle, a trick from an act of love. Jesus doesn't do "tricks"; he performs miracles when they can have a soul-changing affect. He seeks not to impress but to save. Curiosity would not be quenched.

Disappointed but grateful for the opportunity and recognition from Pilate, Herod joined with the rest of us sinners and issued Jesus a purple "goodwill" cloak, a sign of royalty, and a crown of long very sharp thorns, which were pounded into the head of Jesus, just to make sure that the self-proclaimed king was appropriately attired. It's so easy to have a laugh at someone else's expense. We too thought it was funny. Like a lamb being led to slaughter, Jesus humbly and meekly did not resist. It was the Passover; he was the unblemished sacrificial lamb. Love gives his all to all.

The Scouring at the Pillar

Scourging was common treatment before a crucifixion for three reasons. This was a "spectators' sport." The Romans were a barbaric people, and crucifixion was so common that—while they wished it to be as painful, as gruesome, and therefore as memorial as possible—they frankly got bored with the spectacles and desired to, for their own benefit, shorten the death process. But this was a special case—a person of notoriety, a celebrity, well-thought-of by many in the subservient Jewish community, which was a community that looked down with notable disdain on the low-life Romans, especially the legionnaires. This required a demonstration of the "superior cruelty" of the torturers, who were eager to prove their reputation was rightly earned.

We watched as the sadistic huge muscular legionnaire prepared his victim. The preparation was as much mental as physical. The victim's wrist was tied to a high whipping post that would support his weight, even if the victim passed out, as was often the case. The chained victim's body was exposed to all sides, stripped naked.

To instill fear, they would, in the most graphic and vulgar terms, inform the victim what to expect: the ripped flesh torn off in hunks, the biting and burning feel of the whip, and the enjoyment they derived from slowly afflicting as much pain as possible. They would lay the whip made of leather—with chunks of sharp bone, steel balls, and hooks attached—on the back of the victim; and its weight would scratch and cut them. Then confronting the victim, they would jeer and taunt them into begging for mercy, a mercy that never materialized. It was a moment of sheer joy for them to look the victim in the eye and see enough fear to cause them to pass out. Normally, forty lashes less one were administered. Care was taken not to kill the victim and thus spoil "the main event," the crucifixion.

When the torturer confronted Jesus, he saw a look of pity, not fear. Jesus humbly looked him straight in the eyes, forgiveness written on his holy, innocent face. This so infuriated the torturer that he discarded the "legal whip" and got one that had longer lashes that would wrap around the body and tear more flesh. *Jesus was beaten by not one but two torturers, who completely spent themselves while making sure that every inch of Christ's innocent, holy body was torn front and back. The number of blows administered was not counted. It was likely that they far exceeded the legal limit.* The beating was so severe as to make the innocent Lamb of God unrecognizable. Yet love desired to go on, to give more, and to endure more.

The Second Station: Jesus Carries His Cross

"We see Jesus, who for a little while was made lower than the angels, crowned with glory and honor because of the suffering of death, so that by the grace of God he might taste death for every one" (Hebrews 2:9).

The weight of the cross was far more than the natural weight of the wood. It was loaded with our sins, our guilt, and his loneliness. With every step, with every curse, with every insult, and with every unjust blow, Christ became weaker and the load more difficult to bear.

Love keeps giving, and true love knows no bounds.

The Third Station: Jesus Falls the First Time

As we follow along the road to Calvary, trying not to miss any of the gory details out of morbid curiosity, Jesus did not see a stone in the road, stumbled and fell for the first time. The fall made us laugh and jeer and brought blows from the legionnaires. Christ had a rope tied about his waist so as not to escape. He was cruelly dragged to his feet and ordered to again pick up his heavy cross.

Love never gives up.

The Fourth Station: Jesus Meets His Mother

"But I have calmed and quieted my soul, like a child quieted at its mother's breast; like a child that is quieted is my soul" (Psalm 131:2).

Those of us who were there likely missed it. But when Jesus and his mother, Mary, met, with the first contact of their eyes, there was at least an attempt to smile, not a happy smile but more of with a knowing understanding that this must be done.

"Thy will be done on earth" so that heaven might at least be a possibility for some. And that was the painful point where Jesus, the Son of God, with Mary—the first and most perfect tabernacle, full of grace, God's most perfect human being—would endure pain and grief that neither words nor a picture can paint. It was so deep and so intense as to be unable to be comprehended by mortal man, yet only a fraction of humanity would respond to God's graces and accept the crosses necessary for our salvation. "Many are called, but few are chosen" (Matthew 22:14).

The meeting lasted a few brief minutes, and it just barely gave Jesus the adrenaline boost his bruised and battered body needed to carry on. It was only time to say, "I love you," to acknowledge each other's pain and, without words, to communicate the fervent desire to endure each other's cross.

Resigned to the will of the Father, with hearts seemingly ripped from their bodies by an evil invisible force, forgiveness seems unimaginable. But forgiveness is an issue of love; and perfect love can, perfect love does, perfect love must forgive. Mother and son are perfect lovers.

The Fifth Station: Simon, the Cyrene, Son of Rufes, Is Compelled to Help

"Before those who stood by thou wast my helper" (Sirach 51:2).

With heavy, labored breath, Christ was still resigned, obedient, and desiring to serve and to save. He was grateful for the assistance, no matter the level of reluctance of this Simon. Divine providence hinted again at the importance of Simon (the soon-to-be pope) by choosing yet another "Simon" to aid Jesus.

We were in the crowd; it could have been us selected. We were. We are and will be Christ's Simon today and every day to everyone, for everyone we meet is a Christ, and everyone we meet is in need of assistance in carrying his or her cross. *This is a second step to our conversion.*

Having said good-bye to his mother, Jesus was noticeably more tired and weaker, but love never gives up.

The Sixth Station: Blessed Veronica Wipes the Face of Jesus

"For kindness to a father will not be forgotten, and against your sins it will be credited to you" (Sirach 3:14).

This incident of Blessed Veronica is both puzzlement and embarrassment to us men, as we can't understand why the legionnaires have allowed these acts of pity and mercy, and we are embarrassed that a woman is showing greater courage than the men present. Women are often more ardent lovers, more focused and committed. Certainly, they are more willing to take the risk for the object of their love. Pride is often the greatest impediment to men's being more complete, more passionate, more giving lovers.

Christ the man shows us that perfect love is doable, and the price that must be paid is self-sacrifice. Veronica displays great courage and empathy, and the rewards are immediately evident in the rebirth of energy and confidence of our blessed Lord and the creation of the world's first "Polaroid" remembrance of the passion. No gift is sought, but love given usually gets love in return.

The Seventh Station: Christ Falls a Second Time

"And the Lord turned and looked at Peter. And Peter remembered the word of the Lord, how he had said to him, 'Before the cock crows today, you will deny me three times.' And he went out and wept bitterly" (Luke 22:61–62).

All lovers know that it is more enjoyable to make up than to break up. But not all lovers are willing to say, "I'm sorry." The line that says that "love means never having to say you're sorry" is a lie. It is the act of forgiveness and the act of asking for forgiveness that build character, strengthen relationships, and are foundational to true love.

Peter's true repentance and sorrow made the second fall less painful. Adam's sin wrought in us concupiscence, the natural tendency to sin, further aided by our free will. There is a price for sinning. ("The wages of sin is death" [Romans 6:23].)It's the price Christ paid and a price we have to pay. Those who claim that simple believing will lead to salvation need to read the second chapter of James. There is more joy in heaven over one repentant sinner than a hundred perfect souls. It is God's redeeming mercy and love that saves us, but it requires cooperation out of free will on our part.

The Eighth Station: Jesus Meets the Holy Women

"They will console you, when you see their ways and their doings" (Ezekiel 14:23).

Again, it is women—this time mothers, who are empathic, courageous, nurturing, and loving—that challenge the Roman legionnaires for access to the Christ. They are concerned about the souls of their sons, husbands, and brothers who are participating in this killing of the holy innocent. They grieve for Jesus and for their men. A mother's sixth sense can usually "feel" goodness or evil in a man. They sense the presence of evil's influence over us and know in their hearts that Jesus is an innocent man. Filled with pity and outrage at the injustice being perpetrated against Jesus, the kindly women know that someone sometime will have to repay justice for this insane brutality. They are concerned about the meek and humble Jesus and their men who will have innocent blood on their hands. They weep for and with Jesus and have their worst fears confirmed, that there will be, must be a retribution and repayment for this atrocity.

At times, true love must be tough love to be truthful love. Throughout history, actions, both good and evil, have drawn consequences. Free will is not a free ride. Love is a destination requiring active participation, usually gained by giving. Divine justice demands a just response. These women know Jesus as good but, time and time again, refuse to recognize him as God. Thus, Christ reminds them and gives them yet another opportunity at salvation. "Weep not over me; but weep for yourselves, and for your children" (Luke 23:27). Do they hear? Do we?

The Ninth Station: Jesus Falls a Third Time

It's not the failing or falling that causes damnation; it's one's prideful neglect of repentance. It is simply the decision not to get back up, not to seek forgiveness.

The Judas-like leaders of the synagogue in Jerusalem were politically astute. Desiring to be seen as just, not as vengeful, with great diplomacy and even greater hypocrisy, they forewent the pleasure of following every step of the way, depriving themselves of the joyful sight of every blow, every insult, every profanity, every fall. Hypocrites indeed and in deeds, they went ahead toward the "finish line" so as not to miss the really good and cruel stuff. "You will know them by their fruits." They witnessed with concealed joy the third fall, and their hearts skipped a beat. "Don't let him die yet!" They desired blood vengeance, and the excruciating crucifixion was longed for, waited for, like lovers anticipating the wedding night's embrace.

The kangaroo court judges and we other sinners watched as the totally spent Christ was plastered to the rough earth that he created, unable to move, much less continue on his own. Simon now eagerly lifted the sin-loaded cross, for he had seen goodness up close and personal and was now able to recognize godliness. Simon was converted, and so were some of us. Nearly everyone in attendance had witnessed other crucifixions. No one had ever seen such meekness, such humility, even a cooperative attitude. It reminded one of a Paschal Lamb being led to slaughter without complaint. But this wasn't a dumb lamb; this was an intelligent human being.

This is our God; this is true love.

The Tenth Station: Jesus Is Stripped of His Garments

"And many spread their garments on the road, and others spread leafy branches which they had cut from the fields. And those who went before and those who followed cried out, 'Hosanna! Blessed is he who comes in the name of the Lord!'" (Mark 11:8–9).

In order for us to better understand the motive and effect of the "stripping," we might consider a man who has spent a twelve- to fifteen-hour day in the very hot summer sun putting on a new roof. He too is exhausted and spent from the heat and physical exertion. Nearing the end of the job, he misses the head of the roofing nail and slams his thumb.

Instantly, he is revitalized as the pain has a shocking, awakening effect on his body. Adrenaline is now flowing rapidly and freely, and the traffic cop brain is sending urgent messages of pain throughout his entire body. Like a bucket of ice water in the face of a sleeping man, he is instantly awake and alert.

The rapelike attack of Jesus has the same effects. The tearing off of all his garments glued to his wounded, bloodied body, as flesh was savagely, cruelly torn off in chucks, reopens old wounds and creates some new ones. Instantly, the flow of adrenaline and blood is reestablished; and once again, the numbed body comes alive with raw nerve endings. Jesus is again fully awake, fully alive, nerve endings ripe for further abuse. Bleeding profusely from ripped-open wounds, the sadistic premeditated wake-up call works exactly as planned. Now he is ready for the main show. Love desires to give even more. Is concupiscence, fear, or hypocrisy the culprit? Do we or can we blame someone other than ourselves for choosing to serve Satan rather than God? "Hosanna! Blessed is he who comes in the name of the Lord!" How soon, how easily we forget. Love understands and forgives us.

The Eleventh Station: Jesus Is Nailed to the Cross

"And the flesh of the sacrifice of his peace offerings for thanksgiving shall be eaten on the day of his offering" (Leviticus 7:15).

"The sacrifice of a righteous man is acceptable, and the memory of it will not be forgotten" (Sirach 35:7).

It was maniacal, sadistic genius that devised the forty-five-degree angle of the foot-nailing platform. If it had been flat, it would have been far easier for the victims to breathe, as they had to regularly push up from their legs in order to get air into their lungs. It would have taken longer for the victims to die, but it would not cause pain equal to the actual nailing every time they needed air in their lungs. The forty-five-degree foot angle meant that each time they used their legs to raise themselves, their body weight would enlarge the nail holes, sending excruciating, heart-pumping, and bloodcurdling pain to every nerve ending in the body. And the hanging bodies needed air in the lungs to stay alive, or they would suffocate. The victim could choose between indefinable, intense pain and choking to death. Some choice. It made for great spectator involvement. Betting on the time of death was common.

As for the nailing, because of the intense pain, if a victim had thoughts about fighting back, here was where it happened. The Romans were stunned when Jesus, like a king assuming his throne, meekly lay on the cross, stretched out his arms, and allowed himself to be nailed to his throne. A legionnaire sat on his chest, while two others knelt on each arm and held tight the wrist, palm up. The guard doing the nailing would press the large nail into the flesh, pause an instant to allow the victim to comprehend what was about to take place, and with a single hammer blow pound the nail through the flesh into the wood. They would allow for some of the pain to subside before proceeding to maximize the pain. "Let them beg for mercy." They always did, regularly mixed with profanities. But only muffled moans came from the Jews' king. No shrieking, no profanities, no cries for mercy, just heart-wrenching, soul-searching, involuntary moans. The Romans were suitably impressed.

Love conquers all.

The Twelfth Station: The Son of God Dies for Our Salvation

"For if we have been united with him in a death like his, we shall certainly be united with him in a resurrection like his" (Romans 6:5).

What is the asking price for the sacrifice of the Son of God? It is no less than our sacrifice of our very lives and surrender of our free will to do his will. This is to be accomplished by discerning God's will for our vocation and in every instance, with divine assistance, making God's will our avocation. We are to know, love, and serve God in this life, that we may be happy with him in the next. We are to actively teach others to do the same.

From the throne of the cross, Christ spoke seven words. Much has been written about them. It will be our task to relate each to its message of love.

The first word: "Father, forgive *them*, they know not what they are doing" (Luke 23:24; italics added).

And just who did Jesus mean by "them"? Caiphas, the high priest, and his kangaroo court of unjust judges; Pilate; the politically astute, gutless-wonder, disappointed, deprived-of-magic Herod; the Roman executioners? Or how about the apostles, especially Peter, who deserted him; the mob who profaned, hit, spit at, and mocked him; or you and me?

All of the above are included. A God does not suffer and die for a limited, carefully selected few. No. All—each and every human person, man, woman, and child—have to be included in the possibility of salvation, and even then, the price paid seems too high.

Christ was too kind, too gentle; we knew what we were doing. "Father, forgive them" was a shared directive, not a request. God's heart must love, and God's heart must forgive; so must ours. They have. Have we?

The second word: "'Jesus, remember me when you come to your kingdom.' And he said to him, 'Truly, I say to you, today you will be with me in Paradise.'" (Luke 23:42–43).

Some folks "are born lucky"; the really fortunate ones die lucky.

A dying man without hope asked a dying man who had no need of hope for the gift of eternal life, and it was granted. Bishop Sheen commented that "like a thief, he stole paradise." Many of us knew of someone who repented, converted, and was saved in the final hours of life. Many more of us knew of many more who were not.

The request "remember me when you return to paradise" acknowledges kingship, begs forgiveness, and is a plea to be loved. Love speaks to the thief, as he will speak to us, if we too ask love with repentant hearts to take us with him to paradise.

The third word: "When Jesus saw his mother, and the disciple whom he loved standing near, he said to his mother, 'Woman, behold, your son!' Then he said to the disciple, 'Behold, your mother!'" (John 19:26–27).

Jesus gave us two mothers: his mother, Mary, and his bride, his church. We are to learn from, listen to, and obey both. Moments before, he has granted the request of a repentant sinner, and now he specifically, almost by name, includes you and me in his forgiveness while still hanging from what appears to be his cross but what really is his royal throne. A king without a single earthly possession gives what he has, a mother's love and a mother's care and concern for the well-being of her children. Christ is thinking that even those who cannot understand the depths of his love will understand a mother's love. "Take the love of my mother for yourself."

The fourth word: "My God, my God, why hast thou forsaken me?" (Matthew 27:46).

The despair was total, abject, and complete in every way—in a word, "perfect." Was Christ in despair for himself? He was fully, completely a human being but a divine person, retaining only his divine will and intellect that would not interfere with the perfection of this sacrifice.

Christ, for an instant, felt separated from all love, divine and human. But then, as now, our minds and our bodies seem to play tricks on us. While separated for a while from the love of unity with the Trinity, Jesus was never without the love of God. The pain was the realization that he did not have our love. You and I didn't love him enough to accept his total, complete gift of love.

With God, time does not exist, then is now, future is present, and everything is known. But it is not too late; only death separates us from the possibility of forgiveness and perfect love. What's more amazing is that God neither needs nor benefits from our love; we cannot exist without his.

The fifth word: "I thirst" (John 19:28).

Was this a strange request? Jesus had neither food nor drink from the time of the Passover supper, where he forewent the final cup of the Seder traditional meal. No doubt, he was and had been for what must have seemed like eternity, dying of thirst. One can thirst for many things. It can be a drink of liquid, to squelch a parched throat. One can thirst for knowledge, for adventure, for love, and even for death itself. It is clear that what Jesus sought was more than a simple and much needed and desired taste of wine.

Christ is the Savior and was always aware of his role of redeemer. King David in the Old Testament had foretold of the passion and thirst of the Savior, and every word of the prophecy was to be completed. Physical thirst was part of what the Christ desired, but as it dealt, albeit in a small way, with his personal comfort, it was more necessary and important for the fulfillment of the Holy Scripture than satisfying his personal thirst. We gave our creator and savior vinegar and gall; how could we be so generous? What Jesus was saying, with a necessary economy of words, is that, even this close to death, he desired to do more for us, desired to love us more.

The sixth word: "It is finished" (John 19:30).

Jesus knew he had accomplished the mission. Jesus literally gave all, gave everything, held nothing in reserve, made the most complete, the most perfect sacrifice possible, even for the God-man. A lesson taught with the personal example of extreme suffering would now have to serve as sufficient incentive to countless souls desiring to get to heaven. The price of admission was both paid and set.

Now the question is, will it be sufficient for you and for me? Are we willing to pay the price? "Take up thy cross, and follow me." Love beckons; will we respond?

The seventh word: "Then Jesus, crying with a loud voice, said, 'Father, into thy hands I commit my spirit!' And having said this he breathed his last" (Luke 23:46).

And he said it not in a shy way but in nearly a shout of joy. Like kings before him, Jesus was saying, "I came, I saw, and I conquered." The difference was not in its truth but in the promised permanence of its reality. "I will build my church, and the powers of death shall not prevail against it" (Matthew 16:18).

The Thirtieth Station: Christ Is Taken Down from the Cross and Placed in His Mother's Arms

Mother, you joined your son in his crucifixion, knowing that both as God and as man he is perfect holiness, completely without sin or error. All he did was love and teach others to love. This, his only crime, caused him and you such soul-wrenching pain, and despite his merciful forgiveness, his total and completely joined sacrifice will not be sufficient to redeem all mankind. I marvel at his love, compassion, and obedience and the God-given power of our free will. "Pray for us sinners now and at the hour of our death."

The Fourteenth Station: Jesus Is Laid in the Tomb

God is spirit and has no need of a tomb. It is God as man, divinity and humanity joined, that is buried. The human body remains in the tomb for three days, while the soul of Christ, his divinity, descends into the land of the "just judged" (Limbo) to release them into heaven. The divinity of Christ remains with both his dead human body and with his human soul. Their just reward has been waiting salvation's call, and the time of justice is at hand. Christ has also, in a show of divine justice, visited hell to demonstrate that there is and must be a price paid for willful rejection of the Almighty—eternal damnation.

Christ died and was buried as a man and on the third day arose, body and soul (as the God-man), to prove and substantiate all that he taught and all that was foretold. It was sublime evidence of truth and perfect love from perfect love.

"Greater love has no man than this, that a man lay down his life for his friends" (John 15:13).

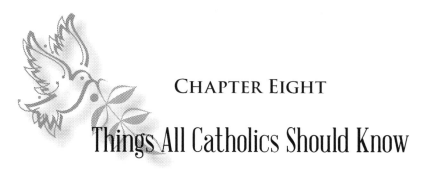

CHAPTER EIGHT

Things All Catholics Should Know

And I say to thee*: That thou art Peter; and upon this rock I will build my church, and the gates of hell shall not prevail against it. And I will give to* thee *[all] the keys to the kingdom of heaven. And whatsoever* thou *shalt bind upon earth, it shall be bound also in heaven: and whatsoever* thou *shalt loose upon earth, it shall also be loosed in heaven.*
—Matthew 16:18–19; emphasis added

Take heed to yourselves, and to the whole flock, wherein the Holy Ghost hath placed you bishops, *to rule the church of God [singular], which he hath purchased with his own blood. I know that, after my departure, ravening wolves will enter in among you, not sparing the flock. And of your own selves shall arise men speaking perverse things, to draw away disciples after them.*
—Acts 20:28–30; emphasis added

The Four Identifying Marks of the Catholic Church

Our Catholic Church: Exploring the Meaning of "Church"

It is common these days to hear the Catholic laity referred to as "the church." The biblical reference for this is from 1 Peter 2:5: "And like living stones be yourselves built into a spiritual house, to be a holy priesthood, to offer spiritual sacrifices acceptable to God through Jesus Christ."

Some, however, have taken this passage too literally and have used this message as a platform to usurp power and positions rightly reserved to the ordained clergy. The church and therefore "we" are better served by understanding that we are "the mystical body" (spirit of the church) and "the church militant" (defenders of the church and our faith). We represent our faith by our visible practice of it and our visible godly commitment by knowing our faith, living it, and defending it in truth and charity when called to do so. If a non-Catholic or a non-Christian came into our church, would they even suspect that Christ is present? We are either part of the problem or part of the solution.

In truth, "we are the church" *only* when we represent her holiness and her goodness and manifest her charity.

"The mystery of faith!" With these words, spoken immediately after the words of consecration, the priest proclaims the mystery being celebrated and expresses his wonder before the substantial change of bread and wine into the body and blood of the Lord Jesus, a reality which surpasses all human understanding. The Eucharist is a "mystery of faith" par excellence: "the sum and summary of our faith." The Church's faith is essentially a Eucharistic faith, and it is with the Risen Lord which takes place in the sacraments: "faith is expressed in the rite, while the rite reinforces and strengthens faith." For this reason, the Sacrament of the Altar is always at the heart of the Church's life: "thanks to the Eucharist, the Church is reborn ever anew!" The livelier the Eucharistic faith of the People of God, the deeper is its sharing in ecclesial life in steadfast commitment to the mission entrusted by Christ to his disciples. The Church's very history bears witness to this. Every great reform has in some way been linked to the rediscovery of belief in the Lord's Eucharistic presence among his people. (Pope Benedict XVI, *Sacramentum Caritatis*, "The Church's Eucharistic Faith")

Precisely because of this reality, Catholics, similar to the apostles, are personally called by God and are given a mission and the grace to fulfill it. "Seek, and you shall find" (Matthew 7:7). "And he said to them, 'Take heed what you hear; the measure you give will be the measure you get, and still more will be given you. For to him who has will more be given; and from him who has not, even what he has will be taken away'" (Mark 4:24–25).

My comments will include a few quotes from *Adoremus Bulletin* of March 2011, from an article entitled "Sacred Architecture: Encountering the Beauty and Mystery of God" by His Eminence, Cardinal Justin Rigali, currently archbishop of Philadelphia; in addition, he is a member of several Roman Curia departments, including the Congregation for Divine Worship and the Discipline of the Sacraments.

I'd like to begin with a quote intended for "the church building" but very much in line with our first category, "church." "The mystery which we gather to reflect upon today is at once timely and timeless. Timely, as Aime'-Georges Martimort has noted, 'In our day the faithful have greater difficulty in achieving prayerful recollection and a sense of God's presence.' At the root of this difficulty is a crisis, a contemporary crisis that surrounds the sacred."

While the reference is specifically applied to "church buildings," I think it is far more than just church architecture that is greatly influenced in the realm of all that touches us and the practice of our Catholic faith. "Secular humanism," founded on pride, ("I know more, and/or I know better") is manifested in many evil ways, proving that Satan is real, is present, and is effective in turning a great many away from God. The faithful are under constant attack. In the past fifty years, "fallen-away Catholics" have blossomed into the second largest "religious" group in America.

Leviticus 11:44 says, "For I am the Lord your God; consecrate yourselves therefore, and be holy, for I am holy." Matthew 5:48 states, "Be perfect, as your heavenly Father is perfect."

In these passages, we are taught the entire "spiritual message" of the entire Bible.

1. "I *am* God." There is no other (Exodus 34:14).
2. "Dedicate yourself to me."

3. "Be holy because I am holy." This is impossible without confronting God and also without permitting God to confront us.

Few, if any, of us have not heard about the necessity of having a "personal relationship with God." Are you aware that God desires this far more than the most ardent believer? This fact is proven by our being a creation of God "in God's image" (Genesis 1:26). To this end, God gives us (and only humanity) the attributes necessary to accomplish emulating God—a mind, an intellect, and a free will; each of these is intricately and permanently connected to our souls. We are able to love or hate, which no other creation of God can do. Isaiah 43:7–8 says "'Every one who is called by my name, whom I created for my glory, whom I formed and made.' Bring forth the people who are blind, yet have eyes, who are deaf, yet have ears!" Isaiah 43:21 states "The people whom I formed for myself that they might declare my praise."

Our Catholic Catechism: *Catechism of the Catholic Church* (CCC)

1844 By charity, we love God above all things and our neighbor as ourselves for love of God. Charity, the form of all the virtues, "binds everything together in perfect harmony" (Col 3:14).

2658 "Hope does not disappoint us, because God's love has been poured into our hearts by the Holy Spirit who has been given to us." Prayer, formed by the liturgical life, draws everything into the love by which we are loved in Christ and which enables us to respond to him by loving as he has loved us. Love is the source of prayer; whoever draws from it reaches the summit of prayer. In the words of the Cure of Ars [the patron of all priest]:

I love you, O my God, and my only desire is to love you until the last breath of my life. I love you, O my infinitely lovable God, and I would rather die loving you, than live without loving you. I love you, Lord, and the only grace I ask is to love you eternally . . . . My God, if my tongue cannot say in every moment that I love you, I want my heart to repeat it to you as often as I draw breath.

In an absolute sense, each of us must confront God, both on his terms and in a manner suitable to who we are, what we are, and where we are. What this means is that, as a first step, we must do a "self-inventory" of our spiritual status. Where am I now? What areas can I improve in? What do I need to do to grow closer to my God? The second step is to "write a plan of action." *Start small*; when you have accomplished your goal, then set another one—one attainable goal at a time. Take it seriously, and *work* at it. It will be a mistake to commit to something you can't or will not do for a very long time. The key is to *be successful* and accomplish the goals you set for yourself. If you fail, ask God for more help, and try again. Small goals build success, and success builds spiritual character. Romans 5:1–5 says, "Therefore, since we are justified by faith, we have peace with God through our Lord Jesus Christ. Through him we have obtained access to this grace in which we stand, and we rejoice in our hope of sharing the glory of God. More than that, we rejoice in our sufferings, knowing that suffering produces endurance, and endurance produces character, and character produces hope, and hope does not disappoint us, because God's love has been poured into our hearts through the Holy Spirit which has been given to us." Putting it in writing tends to cement the obligation.

Not only must we confront our God but we also must confront ourselves. This self-evaluation *must* be candid, frank, and sincere if we are to benefit from the experience and grow closer to our God. *Small* steps will get us there much quicker than jumping around. Expect no improvement, no spiritual growth without prayer and without occasional personal sacrifices. When you hear of Catholics being referred to as "the church," think about this as "what we ought to be perceived as being by the example of our lives. We are to be the "light on the hillside for all to see."

It is always best to "meet God where God is." Spend some time in adoration on a committed basis. God is also where "we are" when we are in the state of grace. A more regular use of the sacraments will be a *great* benefit to one's spiritual growth—regular confession, daily mass if possible (even once a week), and adoration of Jesus in the blessed sacrament. A disciplined prayer life is also critical. One of my favorite saints Saint Peter Julian Eymard has this to share about prayer: "Prayer is the distinguishing characteristic of the Catholic religion; it is the sign of the soul's holiness; indeed it is its holiness. It both makes holy and is the first evidence of holiness. When you see someone living a life of prayer, you may say: 'There goes a saint!'"

One additional thing we all might be mindful of is what kind and how much light our personal living witness is giving to those who know that we are Catholic and those who might guess that we love Jesus by the way we live our life and our faith. Matthew 5:15 says, "Nor do men light a lamp and put it under a bushel, but on a stand, and it gives light to all in the house." Matthew 6:22 declares, "The eye is the lamp of the body. So, if your eye is sound, your whole body will be full of light."

What and where we are currently is of far less importance than where we choose to be and are willing to pay the price necessary to attain. Psalm 17:13 states, "Arise, O Lord! confront them, overthrow them! Deliver my life from the wicked by thy sword [grace]."

Our Catholic Church is known and distinguished by "four marks," four independent but related characteristics: (1) she is "one," (2) she is "holy," (3) she is "catholic," and (4) she is "apostolic." What do these characteristics actually mean?

> The Church is ultimately one, holy, catholic, and apostolic in her deepest and ultimate identity, because it is in her that "the Kingdom of heaven," the "Reign of God," already exists and will be fulfilled at the end of time. The kingdom has come in the person of Christ and grows mysteriously in the hearts of those incorporated into him, until its full eschatological manifestation. Then all those he has redeemed and made "holy and blameless before him in love," will be gathered together as the one People of God, the "Bride of the Lamb," "the holy city Jerusalem coming down out of heaven from God, having the glory of God." For "the wall of the city had twelve foundations, and on them the twelve names of the twelve apostles of the Lamb." (CCC 865)

"One." Nowhere in the entire Word of God, the Bible, can we find a desire by Yahweh or Jesus Christ for belief in more than one God (Triune), one faith (set of beliefs to be held and followed), and only one organization (temple in the Old Testament and church in the New Testament). Matthew 16:18–19 says, "And I [Jesus] tell you, you are Peter, and on this rock I will build my church [singular], and the powers of death shall not prevail against it. I will give you [have now been given you] the keys of the kingdom of heaven [*all* access to heaven], and whatever you bind on earth shall be bound in heaven, and whatever you loose on earth shall be loosed in heaven [the power to make, enforce, or void laws and commands and teach with authority]."

"Holy." We speak here of the church herself as a separate and living entity. The church cannot sin, although her members can. She is the bride of Christ and, like Christ, is both perfect and holy. *Perfect* means whenever she teaches on matters of faith beliefs and or morals, she is literally incapable of error. John 14:16–17 states, "And I will pray the Father, and *he will give you another Counselor, to be with you for ever* (italics added), even the Spirit of truth, whom the world cannot receive, because it neither sees him nor knows him; you know him, for he dwells with you, and will be in you." John 17:15, 17–19 says, "I [Jesus] do not pray that thou shouldst take them out of the world, but that thou shouldst keep them from the evil one. Sanctify them in the truth; thy word is truth. As thou didst send me into the world, so I have sent them into the world. And for their sake I consecrate myself, that they also may be consecrated in truth."

Later, Christ would use these identical words to initiate the founding of the Catholic Church. Note the transfer of godly power and authority. Then note that Christ literally gave *himself* as warranty for her truths. No other religion, faith, or church is directly founded by God (Jesus Christ himself) except for his Catholic Church. Others, such as our Orthodox brethren and fellow Christians, are later grafted on to the "vine." Nor has any other faith or church been promised the Holy Spirit as guardian and protector of the fullness of her truths, except the Catholic Church (John 17:20).

"Catholic." The church as we know it today was first termed "the Way." How and why the name "the Way" came into use? Matthew 22:16 says, "And they sent their disciples to him, along with the Hero'dians, saying, 'Teacher, we know that you are true, and teach *the way* of God truthfully, and care for no man; for you do not regard the position of men." Mark 1:3 also states, "The voice of one crying in the wilderness: Prepare *the way* of the Lord, make his paths straight." John 14:6 says, "Jesus said to him, 'I am *the way*, and the truth, and the life; no one comes to the Father, but by me." Acts 24:14 states, "But this I admit to you, that according to *the Way*, which they call a sect, I worship the God of our fathers, believing everything laid down by the law or written in the prophets."

Then we were called "Christians." Acts 11:26 states, "And when he had found him, he brought him to Antioch. For a whole year they met with the church, and taught a large company of people; and in Antioch the disciples were for the first time called Christians." This was around

AD 80 to AD 90, then in AD 110, the term "Catholic" was first used by Saint Ignatius of Antioch.

The word *catholic* means "universal" and is necessary because of the mandate Jesus gave to the apostles. Matthew 28:19–20 says, "Go therefore and make disciples of all nations, baptizing them in the name of the Father and of the Son and of the Holy Spirit, teaching them to observe all that I have commanded you; and lo, I am with you always, to the close of the age."

"Apostolic."

The Church is apostolic because she is founded on the apostles, in three ways:

- She was and remains built on "the foundation of the Apostles," the witnesses chosen and sent on mission by Christ himself;

- With the help of the Spirit dwelling in her, the Church keeps and hands on the teaching, the "good deposit," the salutary words she has heard from the apostles;

- She continues to be taught, sanctified, and guided by the apostles until Christ's return, through their successors in pastoral office: the college of bishops, "assisted by priests, in union with the successor of Peter, the Church's supreme pastor":

> You are the eternal Shepherd
> who never leaves his flock untended.
> Through the apostles
> you watch over us and protect us always.
> You made them shepherds of the flock
> to share in the work of your Son . . . . (CCC 857)

Lesson No. 2

The Catholic Church as Teacher

God's only active and fully correct voice here on earth is today's Catholic Church, who alone is commanded in Matthew 28:16–20 to go and teach Christ's faith beliefs and moral teachings. God will be with her until the end of time.

That Jesus chooses to share in a limited yet essential manner a portion of his own godly powers and authority is indisputable. Matthew 10:1–4 says, *"And he called to him his twelve disciples and gave them authority over unclean spirits, to cast them out, and to heal every disease and every infirmity. The names of the twelve apostles are these: first, Simon, who is called Peter, and Andrew his brother; James the son of Zeb'edee, and John his brother; Philip and Bartholomew; Thomas and Matthew the tax collector; James the son of Alphaeus, and Thaddaeus; Simon the Cananaean, and Judas Iscariot, who betrayed him"* (italics added).

Therefore, when we read John 17:18–19 ("As thou didst send me into the world, so I have sent them into the world. And for their sake I consecrate myself, that they also may be consecrated in truth.") and again John 20:21 ("Jesus said to them again, 'Peace be with you. As the Father has sent me, even so I send you.'"), we ought not to have even the slightest doubt about the literacy and intent of Jesus as God to share with his apostles directly and exclusively some extraordinary powers and authority. These godly gifts are also given, of course, to Peter's successors as I will shortly demonstrate.

Two critical points overlooked, denied, or simply not correctly understood need to be pointed out and clarified, as they are sufficiently clear and precise so as to remove any and all doubt about Catholicism's exclusive claims to be the only church, with the only set of faith beliefs in their entirety, to be taught by Jesus Christ, guarded by Jesus Christ, and desired by Jesus Christ, as well as the Holy Spirit. These two points are as follows:

1. "As my heavenly Father sent me into the world [Luke 1:26–36], that the world might better know him through me, I now send my apostles and through them my church [Matthew 28:18–20], who alone have me." Jesus is the warranty of their unerring teachings on faith and morals (John 17:18–19). "My faith beliefs

can only be fully transmitted through Peter and his successors, with whom I share my godly powers and authority alone and exclusively. Therefore, all that I desire for you to know, to accept, and to live in order to merit your salvation can only be conveyed through my Catholic Church. For the fullness of my truth is mine to share in the manner in which I wish to share it." The Eastern Churches do have the seven sacraments validly, but only our Catholic Church has them both validly and licitly.

2. "I, God, choose only one church [Matthew 16:18] to have the fullness of my faith and moral beliefs, knowing that by giving only one right choice, humanity might be more inclined not to miss, not to doubt the wisdom of 'one.'"

Know that the Bible is a Catholic book, that it was the early Catholic Church that "gave birth" to it. It was the early fathers who, inspired by the Holy Spirit, selected the testimony and history of the "chosen people" (Exodus 6:7) to be included, and this assembled the Old Testament. And it was the early fathers who actually authored, inspired by the Holy Spirit (2 Timothy 3:16–17), the entire New Testament.

Therefore, it is completely logical that the ones who made the Bible possible, having been assuredly guided by Christ (John 17:19) and the Holy Spirit (John 14:26), are the only ones fully qualified and guided (Matthew 28:18–20) to know, to understand, and therefore to alone teach correctly what the Bible is saying and teaching in its fullness.

Recognizing this reality, most parishes today offer some sort of Bible study, very often led by a priest, deacon, or religious. It is time well spent, so you may wish to check it out.

One can be assured that if one's understanding of the Bible does not fully align with the Catholic understanding and teaching, such an understanding is simply wrong.

One of the really positive things to come out of Vatican II was the bishops' request to the "bark of Peter" to formulate and issue a catechism. This was accomplished first in 1962 and revised slightly for ease of reading in 1964. This catechism, while available to anyone, was intended primarily for our bishops, priests, and those involved in lay catechesis. More recently, 2006, a far more "user-friendly" catechism has been issued by the USCCB (United States Conference of Catholic Bishops) entitled *United States Catholic Catechism for Adults*, available at their website, http://www.usccb.org/, and it is easier to read and follow.

The founder of the Marian Catechist Lay Apostolate, the late father John A. Hardon, SJ, was often heard to say, "You can't share what you yourself don't have." Father was among the more notable and highly regarded theologians of the twentieth century and an extraordinary teacher and catechist. This advice was the motivation behind this book.

Parents have the first responsibility to teach their children. CCC 2223 says, "Parents have the first responsibility for the education of their children. They bear witness to this responsibility first by creating a home with tenderness, forgiveness, respect, fidelity, and disinterested service rule. The home is well suited for education in the [seven] virtues. This requires an apprenticeship in self-denial, sound judgment, and self-mastery—the preconditions of all true freedom. Parents should teach their children to subordinate the 'material and instinctual dimensions to interior spiritual ones.' Parents have a grave responsibility to give good example to their children. By knowing how to acknowledge their own failings to their children, parents will be better able to guide and correct them."

This is a grave and very serious responsibility. If circumstances permit it, sending one's offspring to a Catholic school is highly recommended. If circumstances prohibit this, then it is imperative that your kids attend your parish's religious K-12 education programs. This is not a substitute for you not to demonstrate our Catholic faith at home by family prayer, ensuring that mass is attended at least on Sundays and holy days and that if someone were to come to your home, they could convict you of being Catholic. It goes without saying that you must live fully as "lights on the hillside" (Matthew 5:14–16). We are to lead by our personal examples and live our lives visibly for all, especially and critically important your other family members, to emulate.

We sin both by what we do in error and by what we fail to do as sins of omission. Matthew 18:6, 10, 14 says, "But whoever causes one of these **little ones** who believe in me to sin, it would be better for him to have a great millstone fastened round his neck and to be drowned in the depth of the sea. See that you do not despise one of these **little ones**; for I tell you that in heaven their angels always behold the face of my Father who is in heaven. So it is not the will of my Father who is in heaven that one of these **little ones** should perish." We can't teach and we can't share what we ourselves don't know, don't understand, and don't model.

In closing, I will add that one of the really great ways to share our faith with our families is to have an active ministry role in the parish

Patrick Miron

community. There are many such opportunities available. Check with your pastor or DRE (director of religious education) in your parish for opportunities to allow "your light" to be a bit more visible. Each of us is called to know, to live, to share, and when necessary to defend our Catholic faith.

The Seven Capital Sins and Their Offsetting Virtues

When the church teaches about "deadly sins," she is addressing what we call "mortal sins" (1 John 5:16–17). These grievous acts are so serious that they separate us from the unity with our God, until such time as they are confessed and forgiven (John 20:19–23).

"Mortal sin destroys charity in the heart of man by a grave violation of God's law; it turns man away from God, who is his ultimate end and his beatitude, by preferring an inferior good to him" (CCC 1855).

The seven capital sins are often divided into two categories: "spiritual sins" and "corporal" or bodily sins.

1. **Pride** (spiritual sin)

   It has been said that "pride is the root of all evil" and with good cause. It is pride that caused the formerly good angel Lucifer to attack God's sovereignty and desire to also be "god." It is pride that led Eve and Adam to the same sin for the same reason. And it is pride today that permits countless numbers of souls to think that they know more or that they know better than God and God's one true church. New Agers proudly proclaim that "I *am* a god." Many more don't recognize that by their actions and life's choices they are effectively making the very same choice, that very same "meism" god in preference to God.

2. **Envy** (spiritual sin)

   "The green-eyed monster!" One of the most evident realities of the existence of "concupiscence" (the "natural" tendency toward sin) residing within each of us is this propensity to always want, always desire more not based on need but on want. Often, it is because a neighbor, a coworker, or a sibling has more of this or that (maybe both) than we do. It is an inordinate desire to have what we don't, shouldn't, or can't have.

3. **Wrath** (spiritual sin affected by body)

   Wrath is the work of Satan within us or at the least attacking us. I say this because the access that Satan has "over us" is through our emotions. "Wrath" flows from an inner state of unhappiness, an inner state of unrest, which stems from not allowing God to run our lives; rather, we choose to think that we can, that we are capable of doing this always by ourselves. We can't. And therefore, we get frustrated and take it out on those around us, trying to make others as miserable as we are.

4. **Accidie or Sloth** (corporal sin)

Sloth is laziness or quickness to pass the buck when there is a need that requires an effort. *Father Hardon's Catholic Dictionary* says, "Sloth or laziness as [*sic*] a state of mind that finds the practice of virtue troublesome. It is not so much a repugnance of conviction as of indifference to God and to the practice of one's religion." This is most evident in all parishes where an estimated 10–15 percent of the parish members do 100 percent of the work, the ministries that need to be filled, and the remaining 85–90 percent of God's flock seemingly don't lift a finger to assist them. Our talents are gifts from God, given to us to be shared and used to nourish, sustain, and grow his church. Once again, we see "meism" raise its ugly head.

5. **Avarice or Greed** (corporal sin)

If "envy" is Satan's "right hand," then "avarice" is Satan's "left hand." These two are a one-two punch to our soul's mortal health. This sin is the sin of wanting "more" in an extreme manner, just for the sake of "having more," and a willingness to "do anything" to accomplish this end.

6. **Gluttony** (corporal sin)

"Yummy, yummy, good for the tummy" may be true (but very often is not), but it is always bad for our spiritual life. Here's what we're missing. Mark 4:24 says, "And he said to them: Take heed what you hear. In what measure you shall mete, it shall be measured to you again, and more shall be given to you."

Man's unique package of spiritual realities, those things by which we emulate our God—our minds, intellects, and free will—fulfills Genesis 1:26–27, which proclaims that all of us are made into the image of our God. We are able to choose right or wrong, good or evil. The choices God permits us ("permits" being the critical word here) are an ever-flowing gift from God.

God expects each of to take control of our inordinate desires. Food and drink are for bodily nourishment. And yes, it can be enjoyable but is not to be excessive. Here, we are called to recognize and separate our "needs" from our "wants." We need to keep this in mind.

7. **Lust** (corporal sin)

I'm always a bit amused when I read that "lust" is listed as the last of the seven capital sins. Be assured it is not the "least." When I read this list, the first thing that comes to my mind is Matthew 19:30: "And many that are first, shall be last: and the last shall be first." I don't see lust knocking pride out of first place because lust is tied into pride. Father Hardon in his *Stations of the Cross* says, "And I will turn away my eyes so that I don't see vanity." And "vanity," my dear friends, is the fertilizer for lust.

Lust, in a manner of speaking, encompasses *all* of the above capital sins as does pride. What makes it such a common sin is that it is an out-in-the-open desire, far more than being a duplicitous act. In this age of meism, easy connect, and hookups, where shame has been removed from our vocabulary and where sex in many of its deviant forms is practiced from junior high on, our national and our faith's ability to be embarrassed by anything dealing with sex rests in bygone days. Our national moral conscience and moral compass are way off-kilter.

The seven virtues to be eagerly sought to offset our want of the seven capital sins

Once again, we see a twofold classification of the virtues holding out the possibility of offsetting the seven capital sins. The first three are termed "theological virtues," as they are common to Christians and uncommon to non-Christians. The last four are virtues possible to all mankind. They are termed the "cardinal virtues."

The Seven Holy Virtues

The three theological (or spiritual) virtues are faith, hope, and charity. "They inform all the moral virtues and give life to them" (CCC 1841). The "moral virtues" are prudence, justice, temperance, and fortitude.

The spiritual virtues work as follows:

- *Faith* offsets *pride.*
- *Hope* offsets *envy.*
- *Charity* offsets *wrath.*

"Four virtues play a pivotal role and accordingly are called 'cardinal'; all the others are grouped around them. They are: prudence, justice, fortitude, and temperance. 'If anyone loves righteousness, [Wisdom's] labors are virtues; for she teaches temperance and prudence, justice, and courage.' These virtues are praised under other names in many passages id Scripture" (CCC 1805).

The corporal (or cardinal) virtues work as follows:

- *Fortitude* offsets *gluttony.*
- *Temperance* offsets *greed.*
- *Prudence* offsets *sloth.*
- *Justice* offsets *lust.*

In AD 410, Prudentius wrote the following very apt and descriptive list:

Humility cures *pride.*
Kindness cures *envy.*
Abstinence cures *gluttony.*
Chastity cures *lust.*
Patience cures *wrath.*
Liberality cures *greed.*
And *diligence* cures *sloth.*

What we see here is that Christ never (figuratively) builds for us a cross that does not, in a sense, have "wheels." What I'm teaching here is that God is always on our side and always available to us in times of need and temptation.

Isaiah 55:6–10 is a profound teaching to be memorized: "Seek the Lord while he may be found, call upon him while he is near; let the wicked forsake his way, and the unrighteous man his thoughts; let him return to the Lord, that he may have mercy on him, and to our God, for he will abundantly pardon. For my thoughts are not your thoughts, neither are your ways my ways, says the Lord. For as the heavens are higher than the earth, so are my ways higher than your ways and my thoughts than your thoughts. For as the rain and the snow come down from heaven, and return not thither but water the earth, making it bring forth and sprout, giving seed to the sower and bread to the eater."

God will never tempt us beyond our ability to resist sin, *if* we permit God to assist us in our times of need and call, "Jesus, help me!"

CHAPTER NINE

Unlocking Salvation's Door

The Lord is my strength and my praise, and he is become salvation to me: he is my God and I will glorify him: the God of my father, and I will exalt him.

—Exodus 15:2

Enter by the narrow gate; for the gate is wide and the way is easy, that leads to destruction, and those who enter by it are many. For the gate is narrow and the way is hard, that leads to life, and those who find it are few.

—Matthew 7:13–14

But Peter and the apostles answering, said: We ought to obey God, rather than men.

—Acts 5:29

The Ten Commandments

This lesson is included because of the wide range of beliefs in our day regarding sin. Some say sin simply does not exist, and others say mortal sin is impossible for mankind to commit, so what is sin? And what is "a sin"? Of course, the "I am a god" and "there is no god" philosophy adds to this gravely errant understanding. Untold numbers of souls are at risk of eternal hell.

"The Council of Trent teaches that he Ten Commandments are obligatory for [all] Christians and that the justified man is still bound to keep them; the Second Vatican Council confirms: 'The bishops, successors of the apostles, receive from the Lord . . . the mission of teaching all peoples [Mark 16:14–15, Matthew 28:16–20], and of preaching the Gospel to every creature, so that all men may attain salvation through faith, Baptism [John 3:5, Matthew 28:19] and the [full] observance of the Commandments'" (CCC 2068). "What God commands he makes possible by his grace" (CCC 2082)."

To begin, I must share that the Ten Commandments presented to Moses on our behalf are ten categories of possible sins, not the list of the "ten possible sins." Long before Jesus was conceived in the virgin womb of his blessed mother, Mary, by the power of God and the direct intervention of the Holy Spirit (Luke 1:26–36), the great "I AM" presented his chosen people, our Jewish ancestors, ten rules for a spiritual and immortal life. "Moses said to God, 'If I come to the people of Israel and say to them, "The God of your fathers has sent me to you," and they ask me, "What is his name?" what shall I say to them?' God said to Moses, 'I AM WHO AM'" (Exodus 3:13–14). Known originally as the Decalogue (which means "ten words") and presented to Moses in stone, the original Ten Commandments were expanded by men to over six hundred rules by the time of the birth of Jesus. Jesus clarified their intent and explained their current application to our life in his sermon on the mount (Matthew chapter five). We know them today as the Ten Commandments.

"The Ten Commandments state what is required in the love of God and love of neighbor. The first three concern the love of God, and the other seven love of neighbor" (CCC 2067).

The first commandment: "I am the Lord thy God, you shall have no strange gods before me." ""Teacher, which is the great commandment in the law?' And he said to him, 'You shall love the Lord your God with all your heart, and with all your soul, and with all your mind. This is the great and first commandment'" (Matthew 22:37–38). "And the Lord said to Moses, 'Say to all the congregation of the people of Israel, You shall be holy; for I the Lord your God am holy. I am the Lord your God. Do not turn to idols or make for yourselves molten gods: I am the Lord your God" (Leviticus 19:1–4).

A basic understanding of this first rule for a happy eternal life includes knowing that our God is a jealous God. "The Lord is a jealous God and avenging, the Lord is avenging and wrathful; the Lord takes vengeance on his adversaries and keeps wrath for his enemies" (Nahum 1:1–2).

"Other gods" mean more than the molten images of Aaron and are to include anyone and anything that we place above God or permit to hinder our adoration or love of God. Family members, work, lust, greed, envy, jealously, and hatred are some of today's custom-made idols that interfere with our always placing God first.

The first commandment embraces the theological virtues of faith, hope, and charity. "The first commandment [and the virtue of faith] requires us to nourish our faith with prudence and vigilance, and to reject everything that is opposed to it" (CCC 2088). We are directed by Christ himself to "render therefore to Caesar the things that are Caesar's, and to God the things that are God's" (Matthew 22:21). This obligates us to prayer, sacrifice, learning the religious truths and accepting them, avoiding all superstitious practices, and avoiding divination (the art of knowing and declaring future events) and magic. It obligates us to be aware of and obey the church's law.

In faith, this commandment demands that we recognize God as our supreme creator. We cannot explicitly deny his reality and presence (atheism), *including his sacred presence in the Holy Eucharist.* It obligates us to praise, honor, worship, and glorify him in all that we do.

The first commandment and the virtue of hope are concerned with sins of despair and presumption. "By despair, man ceases to hope for his personal salvation from God" (CCC 2091). Presumption takes two forms. Either man presumes upon his own capabilities, without assistance from God, or man presumes upon God's mercy, hoping to gain forgiveness without conversion, repentance, or merit.

The first commandment, as well as the virtue of charity, "enjoins us to love God above everything" (CCC 2093). Not only are we to love God (always the first and primary love of our hearts) but we also are to love our neighbor (everyone, without regard to race, creed, or color) as ourselves. (Cf. Matthew 6:44.) The virtuous practice of charity also prohibits sins of indifference, ingratitude, negligence, acedia (spiritual sloth), and sins of pride.

The second commandment: "You shall not take the name of the Lord your God in vain." Say what you mean, and mean what you say. (Cf. Matthew 5:33–34).

The second commandment prescribes respect for the name of our Lord and forbids all abuse of God's name. Promises and oaths must be kept. We are not to blaspheme God, his saints, or his holy things. The second commandment prohibits perjury and all lying. "Blasphemy is contrary to the respect due God and His holy name. It is [usually] in itself a grave [mortal] sin" (CCC 2148).

In the sermon on the mount, Jesus explains, "Again you have heard that it was said to the men of old, 'You shall not swear falsely, but shall perform to the Lord what you have sworn.' But I say to you, Do not swear at all, either by heaven, for it is the throne of God, or by the earth, for it is his footstool, or by Jerusalem, for it is the city of the great King. And do not swear by your head, for you cannot make one hair white or black. Let what you say be simply 'Yes' or 'No'; anything more than this comes from evil." (Matthew 5:33–37).

The third commandment: "Remember to keep holy the Lord's Day."

In Old Testament times, "the Sabbath day" was Saturday, the seventh day of the week. It was always a day of rest. Today's Jews continue the Old Testament tradition of Saturday as a holy day of praise and rest. Today's Christians use Sunday as our Sabbath day because it was on Easter Sunday that Christ rose from the dead. It was on a Sunday that our life under grace began. "For sin will have no dominion over you, since you are not under law but [now] under grace" (Romans 6:14–15).

"You shall keep my Sabbaths, for this is a sign between me and you throughout your generations, that you may know that I, the Lord, sanctify you. You shall keep the Sabbath, because it is holy for you. Everyone who profanes it shall be put to death. Six days shall work be done, but the seventh day is a Sabbath of solemn rest, holy to the Lord" (Exodus 31:14–17).

"The sabbath was made for man, not man for the sabbath; so the Son of man is lord even of the sabbath" (Mark 2:27–28).

The concise message and directive of the commandments is for love to be obediently applied through an obligatory informed Catholic conscience.

"The Sunday celebration of the Lord's Day and His Eucharist is at the heart of the Church's life" (CCC 2177). Participation in this most holy and awesome gift from God is the single most important and significant source of grace available to us. It is grace from God in a most direct, unique, and special manner, as it is Jesus himself we receive in Holy Communion. We invite Jesus himself into our souls and our bodies—the real Jesus, not simply a symbol. Therefore, this privilege of Sunday and holy day mass imposes on all Catholics a solemn, grave obligation for weekly attendance and full, active participation as minimal worship, praise, and thanksgiving to our triune Godhead. Only serious matter like illness, child care, or dispensation from one's pastor can excuse our not fulfilling this obligation without committing mortal sin.

"You, therefore, must be perfect, as you're heavenly Father is perfect" (Matthew 5:48).

In accord with CIC 1246, the United States Conference of Catholic Bishops decrees that the holy days of obligation to be observed in the United States are as follows (can be changed as these are "church practices," which are changeable).

- The solemnity of Mary, the Mother of God
- The solemnity of the Ascension
- The solemnity of the Assumption
- The solemnity of All Saints
- The solemnity of the Immaculate Conception
- The solemnity of Christmas
- The solemnity of the Epiphany, transferred to the first Sunday following January 1
- The solemnity of Corpus Christi, observed on the second Sunday following Pentecost

When the solemnities of Mary, Mother of God; the Assumption; and All Saints fall on a Saturday or a Monday, they will not be observed as holy days of obligation. Note: The Feast of the Ascension, in many areas, has been moved to the following Sunday.

The Fourth Commandment: "Honor your father and your mother." Children, obey your parents in the Lord, for this is right. This is the first commandment with a promise. "Honor your father and mother as the Lord your God commanded you; that your days may be prolonged, and that it may be well with you" (Deuteronomy 5:16). "Pay all of them their dues, taxes to whom taxes are due, revenue to whom revenue is due, respect to whom respect is due, honor to whom honor is due" (Romans 13:7). This commandment not only enjoins children but also binds parents with specific responsibilities toward their offspring and each other.

Christ never failed to demonstrate, in his own life on earth, all that he commanded us. "All who heard him were amazed at his understanding and his answers. And when they saw him they were astonished; and his mother said to him, 'Son, why have you treated us so? Behold, your father and I have been looking for you anxiously.' And he said to them, 'How is it that you sought me? Did you not know that I must be in my Father's house?' And they did not understand the saying which he spoke to them. And he went down with them and came to Nazareth, and was obedient to them; and his mother kept all these things in her heart" (Luke 2:47–51).

The fourth commandment introduces the all-encompassing, binding law of love. "You have heard it said, 'You shall love your neighbor and hate your enemy.' But I say to you, Love your enemies and pray for those who persecute you, so that you may be sons of your Father who is in heaven; for he makes his sun rise on the evil and on the good, and sends rain on the just and on the unjust. For if you love those who love you, what reward have you?" (Matthew 5:43–46). Love begins at home with patience, forgiveness, and charity. Then like the sun, it is to shine forth for all to see, feel, share, and experience. The Catholic family is the very foundation on which the church exists and grows. It is from the family that the children of God are formed in his likeness. The family is the fountain of vocations so necessary for the growth of the church and our salvation. "Marriage and the family are ordered to the good of the spouses [the unitive purpose] and to the procreation [that is, creation with divine intent and intervention] and education of children. The love of the spouses and the begetting of children create among members of the same family personal relationships and primordial responsibilities" (CCC 2201).

Children are to always show respect for their parents. This is especially true while they remain at home, regardless of age. If a child resides under the roof of his parents, he is to be obedient unto them. "But if a child is convinced in conscience that it would be morally wrong to obey a particular order, he must not do so. As they grow up, children should continue to respect their parents. They should anticipate their wishes, willingly seek their advice, and accept their just admonitions. Obedience toward parents ceases with the emancipation of the children; not so respect, which is always owed to them. This respect has its roots in the fear of God, one of the gifts of the Holy Spirit" (CCC 2217).

"The fourth commandment reminds grown children of their responsibilities toward their parents. As much as they can, they must give them material and moral support in old age and in times of illness, loneliness, or distress. Jesus recalls this duty of gratitude" (CCC 2218).

"Submission to authority and co-responsibility for the common good make it morally obligatory to pay taxes, to exercise the right to vote, and to defend one's country" (CCC 2240). "The citizen is obliged in conscience not to follow the directives of civil authorities when they are contrary to the demands of the moral order, to the fundamental rights of persons or the teachings of the Gospel. Refusing obedience to civil authorities, when their demands are contrary to those of an upright conscience, finds its justification in the distinction between serving God and serving the political community. 'Render therefore to Caesar the things that are Caesar's, and to God the things that are God's.' 'We must obey God rather than men'" (CCC 2242).

"It is a part of the Church's mission 'to pass moral judgments even in matters related to politics, whenever the fundamental rights of man or the salvation of souls requires it'" (CCC 2246).

The fifth commandment: "You shall not kill." "You have heard that it was said to the men of old, 'You shall not kill; and whoever kills shall be liable to judgment.' But I say to you that every one who is angry with his brother shall be liable to judgment; whoever insults his brother shall be liable to the council, and whoever says, 'You fool!' shall be liable to the hell of fire" (Matthew 5:21–22).

Human life is a sacred gift from God. It is to be respected, protected, cherished, and nourished from inception to death. Both inception and death are reserved to a time and place of God's choosing. This commandment prohibits much beyond the recognized murder of the innocent. It clearly includes the protection of all unborn babies. Do not doubt that abortion, avocation of abortion, "blind" support of abortion, or any known association with abortion is likely a grievous sin. (Cf. CCC 2270–2274.)

We are permitted to defend ourselves, our families, and our country with reasonable means that could include lethal force. (Cf. CCC 2264.) The state too, in order to protect its citizens, can use reasonable, even lethal, force. The state does have recourse to the "death penalty," if nonlethal means are insufficient to protect the people safely from the aggressor. All life is sacred, and death is to be an exceptional, rarely applied remedy and never used as a deterrent but only to preserve other lives. (Cf. CCC 2267.)

Life is a gift without a return policy. Illness, old age, and dissatisfaction with life's crosses come from God with a purpose that often only he understands at the time. Our lack of understanding does not give cause or justification for murder, euthanasia, or suicide. Only God can determine the intent of the actions and justly judge the consequences. All forms of murder are intrinsically ordered and carry the high risk of grievous sin. We should not despair if a loved one takes their life, as our God is a merciful judge, and extenuating circumstances are always factored in. "We are stewards, not owners, of life" (CCC 2280).

"Discontinuing medical procedures that are burdensome, dangerous, extraordinary, or disproportionate to the expected outcome can be legitimate; it is the refusal of 'over-zealous' treatment. Here one does not will to cause death; one's inability to impede it is merely accepted. The decisions should be made by the patient if he is competent and able or, if not, by those legally entitled to act for the patient, whose reasonable will and legitimate interests must always be respected" (CCC 2278).

Less obvious is our obligation to take reasonable measures to protect our health by eating correctly, exercising, getting the necessary rest and relaxation, and avoiding nonmedical drugs and excessive alcohol. We need be mindful that our bodies are (and should always be) temples of the Holy Spirit and, at the time of Holy Communion, the abode of Jesus Christ himself.

This commandment also binds us not to gossip, slander, or endanger another's good name. "'You shall love your neighbor as yourself.' Love does no wrong to a neighbor; therefore love is the fulfilling of the law" (Romans 13:9–10). We must also work and strive for peace in our hearts, families, local community, church, and world.

The sixth commandment: "You shall not commit adultery." "You have heard that it was said, 'You shall not commit adultery.' But I say to you that every one who looks at a woman lustfully has already committed adultery with her in his heart" (Matthew 5:27–28).

"Sexuality affects all aspects of the human person in the unity of his body and soul. It especially concerns affectivity, the capacity to love and to procreate, and in a more general way the aptitude for forming bonds of communion with others" (CCC 2332).

While sex within marriage is a very good thing, it is a gift from God to be used only as he as our creator intended. Because most of the folks who will read this book will likely be married or considering marriage, I shall cover this topic in a bit more depth. There exists today a prevailing mind-set that we can decide for ourselves what is right for us. Our bodies "are our own," and as long as we don't hurt anyone, we are "free" to do with them, pretty much as we see fit. That certainly is the message broadcast media flaunts daily, and its acceptance and application is a sure path to hell. Sex outside of marriage is more than simply OK; it's almost the expected behavior in today's new age, "anything goes," "don't judge me, and I won't judge you" society, which is gravely moral wrong.

God creates everything. To create means to make out of nothing. *Our bodies, minds, and souls are created by God and belong to God.* They are simply on loan to us for the express purpose of giving him greater honor and glory and working out his plan for our salvation (Isaiah 43:7, 21). Unlike grace, which is a gift, the basic elements of our existence are ours to use, not to keep. We therefore have only limited rights as designed by God. All use of our minds, bodies, and souls that do not give glory and honor to God are, to some degree, disordered and, to varying degrees, sinful.

"Everyone, man and woman, should acknowledge and accept his sexual identity. Physical, moral, and spiritual difference and complementarity are oriented toward the goods of marriage and the flourishing of family life. The harmony of the couple and of society depends in part on the way in which the complementarity, needs, and mutual support between the sexes are lived out" (CCC 2333). "In creating men 'male and female,' God gives man and woman an equal personal dignity" (CCC 2334). "Sexuality is a source of joy and pleasure" (CCC 2362). Married women have the same right to sexual satisfaction as do their husbands.

Every human person is to practice chastity to the degree and in the manner required by his station in life. (Cf. CCC 2348.) All forms of premarital sex are forbidden, as the express purpose of conjugal love is the unimpeded possibility of procreation. (Cf. CCC 2360–2361.) This includes those who are engaged but not yet married. Masturbation, which is the deliberate stimulation of the genital organs in order to derive sexual pleasure outside of conjugal lovemaking (usually but not always by oneself), has no possibility of procreation, is ordered only for personal gratification, and therefore is gravely disordered.

"Homosexual persons are called to chastity. By the virtues of self-mastery that teach them inner freedom, at times by the support of disinterested friendship, by prayer and sacramental grace, they can and should gradually and resolutely approach Christian perfection" (CCC 2359).

Pornography is dangerous, habit-forming, and disordered as it debases the sacred and beautiful act of love, wrongly stresses personal satisfaction, introduces in some manner a third "person" into the relationship, and profits those who sell their souls for illicit and immoral gain. It is especially dangerous to our youth, who learn to see their opposite gender as mere "sex objects," as acquisitions, and in a sad, unrealistic, morally distorted sense as sex toys.

Married couples may not employ any unnatural means (contraception) to limit the possibility of a pregnancy. To do so is gravely disordered, as it seeks to usurp from God, our creator, his option and control of birth issues. "Fecundity is a gift, an end of marriage, for conjugal love naturally tends to be fruitful. A child does not come from outside as something added on to the mutual love of the spouses, but springs from the very heart of that mutual giving, as its fruit and fulfillment" (CCC 2366).

"Periodic continence, that is, the methods of birth regulation based on self-observation and the use of infertile periods, is in conformity with the objective criteria of morality. These methods respect the bodies of the spouses, encourage tenderness between them, and favor the education of an authentic freedom. In contrast, 'every action which, whether in anticipation of the conjugal act, or in its accomplishment, or in the development of its natural consequences, proposes, whether as an end or as a means, to render procreation impossible' is intrinsically evil" (CCC 2370).

A proper sacramental, consummated marriage cannot and may not be dissolved or terminated. Every station in life brings with it joys, sufferings, sacrifices, and crosses. Each has its own path to heaven and to personal happiness; marriage is but one way to eternal salvation. The noble and natural purpose of marriage is procreation and the growth of God's church. However, not every married union is blessed with children. This too is God's plan, and charitable, self-giving sex is both permitted and encouraged, as chaste conjugal love is the cement of a happy marriage. God insists on being the "author of life." "For you were called to freedom, brethren; only do not use your freedom as an opportunity for the flesh, but through love be servants of one another" (Galatians 5:13).

The seventh commandment: "You shall not steal." "A false balance is an abomination to the Lord, but a just weight is his delight. To do righteousness and justice is more acceptable to the Lord than sacrifice" (Proverbs 11:1, 21:3). "Do not lay up for yourselves treasures on earth, where moth and rust consume and where thieves break in and steal, but lay up for yourselves treasures in heaven, where neither moth nor rust consumes and where thieves do not break in and steal. For where your treasure is, there will your heart be also" (Matthew 6:19–21).

I forget at times to give thanks for being born in America. No other country offers its citizens and its guests so much freedom and opportunity for wealth. Yet we have proven time and again that these two privileges can be a source of sin. Materialism is an invented religion as it is commonly practiced, and we are told continuously that it is all right to do whatever we desire. Is it inconceivable that Jesus, who for a time became a mere man and then gave up his heavenly throne and suffered the most humiliating and excruciating death known to mankind, would not expect that we too endure the crosses he sends us? Each tailored specifically to lead us to heaven? No. Luke 9:23 says, "And he said to all: If any man will come after me, let him deny himself, take up his cross daily, and follow me."

God's rules for obedience of the seventh commandment are common sense, practiced with charity, and applied with love.

"The seventh commandment forbids theft, that is, usurping another's property against the reasonable will of the owner. There is no theft if consent can be presumed or if refusal is contrary to reason and the universal destination of goods. This is the case in obvious and urgent necessity when the only way to provide for immediate, essential needs (food, shelter, clothing . . .) is to put at one's disposal and use the property of others" (CCC 2408).

"Promises must be kept and contracts strictly observed to the extent that the commitments made in them are morally just. A significant part of economic and social life depends on the honoring of contracts between physical or moral persons - commercial contracts of purchase or sale, rental or labor contracts. All contracts must be agreed to and executed in good faith" (CCC 2410).

"The seventh commandment demands respect for the integrity of creation. Animals, like plants and inanimate beings, which are by nature destined for the common good of past, present, and future humanity" (CCC 2415).

The golden rule is this: "So whatever you wish that men would do to you, do so to them; for this is the law and the prophets" (Matthew 7:12). "You shall love your neighbor as yourself" (Matthew 19:19).

The eighth commandment: "You shall not bear false witness against your neighbor." "Do not devise a lie against your brother, nor do the like to a friend. Refuse to utter any lie, for the habit of lying serves no good" (Sirach 7:12–13).

The source of all truth is God himself, and we are to live this truth as taught by the life example of his Son, Jesus. "Men could not live with one another if there were not mutual confidence that they were being truthful to one another" (CCC 2469). "Man tends by nature toward the truth. He is obliged to honor and bear witness to it: 'It is in accordance with their dignity that all men, because they are persons . . . are both impelled by their nature and bound by a moral obligation to seek the truth, especially religious truth. They are also bound to adhere to the truth once they come to know it and direct their whole lives in accordance with the demands of truth" (CCC 2467).

What does the eighth commandment compel? It prohibits giving false witness and perjury. We are obligated to go out of our way to protect another's reputation. We must avoid making rash, unsubstantiated judgments; we are to avoid detraction, which without valid reason discloses another's faults or failings; and we must avoid the sin of calumny by not making remarks contrary to the truth and giving the occasion for making false judgments against them. (Cf. CCC 2477.)

We are to avoid bragging. "Clothe yourselves, all of you, with humility toward one another, for 'God opposes the proud, but gives grace to the humble'" (1 Peter 5:5).

A lie is a direct offense against truth. "A lie consists in speaking a falsehood with the intention of deceiving" (CCC 2482). The sinful seriousness of a lie depends of the intention to do harm and on the amount of harm done. All lies are sinful; some lies can be grievous. All lies should be confessed in the sacrament of penance.

"Every offense committed against justice and truth entails the duty of reparation, even if its author has been forgiven. When it is impossible publicly to make reparation for a wrong, it must be made secretly. If someone who has suffered harm cannot be directly compensated, he must be given moral satisfaction in the name of charity. This duty of reparation also concerns offenses against another's reputation. This reparation, moral and sometimes material, must be evaluated in terms of the extent of the damage inflicted. It obliges in conscience" (CCC 2487; italics mine).

The ninth commandment: "You shall not covet your neighbor's wife/ husband." A thief of hearts you cannot be. "Do not love the world or the things in the world. If any one loves the world, love for the Father is not in him. For all that is in the world, the lust of the flesh and the lust of the eyes and the pride of life, is not of the Father but is of the world" (1 John 2:15–16).

The ninth commandment is an extension and further expression of the sixth commandment, which prohibits all sinful sexual acts, but you have heard Jesus tell us, "'You shall not commit adultery.' But I say to you that every one who looks at a woman lustfully has already committed adultery with her in his heart. If your right eye causes you to sin, pluck it out and throw it away; it is better that you lose one of your members than that your whole body be thrown into hell" (Matthew 5:27–29). Jesus is not telling us to maim ourselves; he is telling us that this is a serious, potentially grievous matter, so listen up.

Both men and women possessing certitude of understanding are bound by this commandment that specifically prohibits sexual covetousness. "To covet" means to desire something or, in this case, someone whom we are not morally entitled to have sexual union with.

Intent and desire can, and often are, equal to actually committing this always mortal sin. It applies equally to the single and married state of life, and to both males and females. It prohibits all intentional, uncontrolled sexual desire for anyone except our spouse, and even then our desires are to be controlled and chastely directed. (We have already explained that sex in marriage can and should be a mutually enjoyable and satisfying experience.) We are not to dream, fantasize, or even willingly think impure thoughts about having sex outside of marriage or with anyone except our spouse. Is this possible? Yes, but only with divine intervention. It cannot be accomplished by our own volition and will.

"If, because of one man's trespass, death reigned through that one man, much more will those who receive the abundance of grace and the free gift of righteousness reign in life through the one man Jesus Christ. For as by one man's disobedience many were made sinners, so by one man's obedience many will be made righteous. Law came in, to increase the trespass; *but where sin increased, grace abounded all the more,* so that, as sin reigned in death, grace also might reign through righteousness to eternal life through Jesus Christ our Lord" (Romans 5:17, 19–21; italics added).

God, by virtue of his perfect justice and mercy, is obligated to offer sufficient grace to permit our salvation. In the same way, we are similarly obligated to cooperate, accept, apply, and use the grace that God intends for each of us.

"The disciples said to him, 'If such is the case of a man with his wife, it is not expedient to marry.' But he [Jesus] said to them, 'Not all men can receive this saying, but only those to whom it [sufficient grace] is [will be] given'" (Matthew 19:10–11). When chastity is committed to by a priest or religious, it is a gift from God, and he extends to them sufficient grace to enable them to live their live chastely, fully, and even joyfully. While God will test each of us, he will not test us beyond our ability to choose "good over evil," grace over sin.

Directed by God, we choose our vocation. If we have chosen wisely, God provides all the necessary grace and help we need to fulfill his call. Virginity is but one way to serve our Lord. It is, as Saint Paul tells us, a more difficult but a more perfect way (1 Corinthians 7:37). All priests in the order of Melchizedek (Hebrews 5:6), those men called by God to holy orders, serve a special need and purpose and are supposed to be willing and knowledgeable about their commitment to celibacy. This is both a chosen sacrifice and a most worthy gift.

More recent times have seen the exception of married priests permitted; when they are already married and coming from another faith, where the practice of married priests existed, they are permitted to remain married and serve as a Catholic priest. This, however, is an exception, not the universal norm.

John 15:16 says, "You did not choose me, but I chose you and appointed you that you should go and bear fruit and that your fruit should abide; so that whatever you ask the Father in my name, he may give it to you."

The tenth commandment: "You shall not covet your neighbor's goods." "Nor thieves, nor the greedy, nor drunkards, nor revilers, nor robbers will inherit the kingdom of God" (1 Corinthians 6:10).

"Do not lay up for yourselves treasures on earth, where moth and rust consume and where thieves break in and steal, but lay up for yourselves treasures in heaven, where neither moth nor rust consumes and where thieves do not break in and steal. For where your treasure is there will your heart be also. No one can serve two masters; for either he will hate the one and love the other, or he will be devoted to the one and despise the other. You cannot serve God and mammon" (Matthew 6:19–21, 24).

This is an easy commandment to understand but difficult to live. If it isn't yours, don't be consumed with desire for it. If God wishes you to acquire more, he shall guide you to it. We can serve only one master, and it had better be God. This is less a prohibition on improving one's state in life than a serious warning from God, and therefore, our priorities must be God, family, and then, and only then, career. A desire to gain more simply to "keep up with or surpass the Jones" is an excuse, not a valid reason. If you adhere to these rules and still acquire wealth, count it as a blessing from God, and give him thanks.

"Envy is a capital sin. It refers to sadness at the sight of another's goods and the immoderate desire to acquire them for oneself, even unjustly. When it wishes grave harm to a neighbor, it is a mortal sin" (CCC 2539). "Vices can be classified according to the virtues they oppose, or also be linked to the capital sins which Christian experience has distinguished, following St. John Cassian and St. Gregory the Great. They are called 'capital' because they engender other sins, other vices. They are pride, avarice, envy, wrath, lust, gluttony, and sloth or acedia" (CCC 1866).

One of the great risks of wealth is endangering one's humility. Humility, coupled with an active prayer life, and charity are keys to holiness and piety. Jesus asks, "For what does it profit a man, to gain the whole world and forfeit his life?" (Mark 8:36)

Know, dear friends, that even this deeper reflection into the commandments neither is intended to nor does it cover the entire scope of possible sins under that "commandment" heading. If and when in doubt, discuss it with your confessor priest (John 20:19–23).

Lesson No. 2

A Brief History of Salvation

Matthew 7:21 says, "Not every one who says to me, 'Lord, Lord,' shall enter the kingdom of heaven, but he who does the will of my Father who is in heaven." This, dear friends, may have been made evident by the sixteenth-century Protestant Revolution, led very successfully by Martin Luther, an apostate Catholic priest who was greatly influenced by an earlier apostate Catholic priest John Wycliffe of the thirteenth century, who too was a heretic; both of them were followed by John Calvin, a nominal Catholic apostate, and they have collectively quite possibly contributed mightily in fulfilling this shocking biblical prophecy for untold numbers of souls of the past, present, and future.

It is necessary to point out, however, that the culpability of their followers diminishes somewhat through time and distance from the original faith founders because now it is what is taught to them, whereas the founders themselves were innovators and inventors who knowingly designed their personal beliefs to compete with Christ's Catholic Church. One can neither run nor hide from the fact that today's Catholic Church, for one thousand years, was the only "Christian true-faith church" up to the time of the great eastern schism in AD 1054.

So as to be both faithful and objective here, I will first share what our Catholic Church teaches on the possibility of salvation.

"'Since Christ died for all, and since all men are in fact called to one and the same destiny, which is divine, we must hold that the Holy Spirit offers to all the possibility of being made partakers, in a way known to God, of the Pascal mystery.' Every man who is ignorant of the Gospel of Christ and of his Church, but seeks the truth and does the will of God in accordance with his understanding of it, can be saved. It may be supposed that such persons would have desired Baptism explicitly if they had known of its necessity" (CCC 1260).

"How are we to understand this affirmation, often repeated by the Church Fathers? Re-formulated positively, it means that all salvation comes from Christ the Head through the Church which is his Body:

Basing itself on Scripture and Tradition, the Council teaches that the Church, a pilgrim now on earth, is necessary for salvation: the one Christ is the mediator and the way to salvation; he is present to us in his body which is the Church. He himself explicitly asserted the necessity of faith and Baptism, and thereby affirmed at the same time the necessity of the Church which men enter through Baptism as through a door. Hence they could not be saved who, knowing that the Catholic Church was founded as necessary by God through Christ, would refuse to enter it or remain in it" (CCC 846).

"This affirmation is not aimed at those who, through no fault of their own, do not know Christ and his Church:

Those who, through no fault of their own, do not know the Gospel of Christ or his Church, but who nevertheless seek God with a sincere heart, and, moved by grace, try in their actions to do his will as they know it through dictates of their conscience – those too may achieve eternal salvation" (CCC 847).

"Humanity alone, of all of God's created creatures was willed for God's own sake" (Fr. Wade Mendez of the Fathers of Mercy on EWTN; see Isaiah 43:7, 21).

Clarifying these three catechism passages, the catechism is not teaching that everyone, in an absolute sense, "must be a Catholic" in order to attain heaven. Being a Catholic, though, can greatly enhance one's chances of attaining heaven because it is God's one true and complete faith, because it is the church he personally founded, and because of the seven sacraments instituted by Jesus precisely to enhance the possibility of one's meriting salvation, his way.

It is saying that literally all salvation does, as it must, flow through the Catholic Church. The reason for this is historically and biblically provable. Jesus established (Matthew 16:18–19), guides (Matthew 28:20), guards, and protects (John 17:18–19) to a much higher degree the only church founded on "the rock" (Matthew 16:15–19). Catholics and other Christians alike express their belief that all salvation is through Jesus Christ (Acts 4:12). What others fail to recognize is that, in order to actually accomplish that reality, their own and everyone else's salvation must then absolutely flow through the "narrow gate," the Catholic Church (singular; Matthew 7:13–15), because she alone has been entrusted with all the keys. Heaven has just one gate, while the other place has lots of gates (Matthew 16:18–19).

So what does the Catholic Church has to do, knowing full well that God desires that all men might be saved? First Timothy 2:3–4 says, "For this is good and an acceptable in the sight of God our Saviour, Who will have all men to be saved, and to come to the knowledge of the truth [singular]." And John 3:17 states, "For God sent the Son into the world, not to condemn the world, but that the world might be saved through him."

With the recent addition of a multitude of differing and competing Christian faiths and knowing of God's desire that all men be saved, which was also an unchangeable, defined doctrine, the church still had to include these newly formed competing faiths in the definition of who conditionally might and could possibly also merit salvation. She had to expand the definition and doctrine of who might be saved, adding on to but not changing the original teaching, to accommodate these new demographics.

This was accomplished, guided by the Holy Spirit, by teaching that those who did not know Christ and/or Christ's one true church and faith through no fault of their own might possibly merit salvation based on their charity. However, this is to be understood with the following caveat: God, who alone can and does make this judgment call, will do so based on what he has made possible for every soul to know, not on what one has chosen as a personal "faith church" preference. Man's excuses are not going to matter to God, who must be good and fair and offers sufficient grace for everyone to know of him.

John 10:9 says, "I am the door; if any one enters *by me*, he will be saved, and will go in and out and find pasture." But "by me" is *literal*. It means doing things God's way, knowing and then doing all that God has put into place, and with humility obeying those God has chosen to teach us for the fullness of his truths.

To claim to "know Christ" means to also know the church he founded and the faith he taught long before it was customized by mortal men to be easier and to grant salvation faster and often with assurance that their salvation cannot be lost. Truth is singular per defined issue. It is God himself who withholds right understanding, until someone is seeking him his way.

My friends, I hadn't expected to begin this lesson in this particular manner, but it is where the Holy Spirit led me. So let's now back up before we again go forward.

Salvation history begins with the nomadic Abram, whom God chose, challenged, and tested. Genesis 12:1 says, "And the Lord said to Abram: Go forth out of thy country, and from thy kindred, and out of thy father's house, and come into the land which I shall shew thee." This then is the beginning of Christianity's salvation history, and it teaches several critical lessons that must be grasped and accepted.

1. God chooses us long before we choose to follow him (if "we" ever do).
2. Complete obedience is expected.
3. Humility is a primary requirement of salvation.
4. There is a corollary between what God expected from Abram and what he expected of Peter and the apostles: "Come! Follow me." And it is the same today for those called by Christ to minister in his name and for his name.
5. God "appeared" to Abram; exactly what form God took in doing this is not known. Genesis 18:1–3 and Genesis 32:24–25, 28–30 hold out the possibility that it may have been in human form, which is certainly not beyond God's capabilities. Haydock's Catholic Commentary suggests it was "angels in human form," termed "God" and meaning "of God" but not actually "God himself." This dates to about four thousand years ago. Personally, I find either possibility to be acceptable. And truth of exactly what form, whether it was actually Yahweh or one of his angels, is not essential to the history we are sharing.
6. Genesis 12:2–5 says, "And I [God] will make of thee a great nation, and I will bless thee, and magnify thy name, and thou shalt be blessed. I will bless those that bless thee, and curse those that curse thee, and IN THEE shall all the kindred of the earth be blessed: So Abram went out as the Lord had commanded him, and Lot went with him: Abram was seventy-five years old when he went forth from Haran. And he took Sarai his wife, Lot his brother's son, and all of his substance [possessions]." There seems to be at least a hint here in God's blessings for the possibility of an eternal reward.

We see here also the beginning of what will become an evident tradition, God choosing just one man to lead and to be "God's voice" and the intercessor between God and man. This is a point of critical understanding when we later see Jesus choosing Peter for this very role but then in a fuller and more perfected manner. We note also that God already had selected his chosen people, demanded full obedience from them, rewarded good action, and, as history tells, punished actions not corresponding to God's divine will.

The next highly significant event is God insisting on a sign of their faithfulness and loyalty to him. And we move forward to Genesis 17:8–11: "And I will give to thee, and to thy seed, the land of thy sojournment, all the land of Chanaan for a perpetual possession, and *I will be their God*. Again God said to [the now-renamed] *Abraham*: And thou shalt therefore shalt keep my covenant, and thy seed after thee in their generations. This is my covenant which you shall observe, between me and you, and thy seed after thee: All the male kind of you shall be circumcised: And you shall circumcise the flesh of your foreskin, that it may be a sign of the covenant between me and you" (italics added).

We see now that God changed Abram's name to Abraham and then demanded evidence of this new covenant relationship (circumcision in Genesis 17:11). It was a test that was to last until the new covenant of baptism of Jesus himself, which overrides but does not negate the original covenant (John 3:5, Matthew 28:18–19).

Jumping ahead, we find God choosing Moses to lead his often headstrong, disobedient chosen people out of the captivity of Egypt.

Exodus 3:2–4, 6–8, 10, 13–15 says, "And the Lord appeared to him [Moses] in a flame of fire out of the midst of a bush: and he saw that the bush was on fire and was not burnt. And Moses said: I will go see this great sight, why the bush is not burnt. And when the Lord saw that he went forward to see, he called him out of the midst of the bush, and said: Moses, Moses. And he answered: Here I am [as should we all when called]. And he said: I am the God of thy father, the God of Abraham, the God of Isaac, and the God of Jacob. I have seen the affliction of *my people* in Egypt, and I have heard their cry [prayers]. I am come down to deliver them. I will send thee to Pharao, that thou mayst bring forth my people. Moses [after protesting that he was not articulate enough and after God empowering Aaron to be the spokesperson for him] said to God: Lo, I shall go to the children of Israel, and say to them: The God of your fathers hath sent me to you. If they should say to me: What is his name? what shall I say to them? God said to Moses: I AM WHO AM. This is my name for ever."

Then we encounter the plagues inflicted unto the pharaoh, and God "hardened" pharaoh's heart, which meant that pharaoh himself, being obstinate and prideful, would not relent, would not obey, and in his self-inflicted hardness of his heart would not believe that it was God punishing him.

There is a corollary here between the pharaoh and today's Protestants: the evidence of one God, one true faith, and one church is right in front of them; but they are often unable to see it, to understand it, to accept it because of the same kind of self-inflicted obstinacy. They too, in varying degrees (it's different with each individual), have chosen to harden their hearts.

Evidence of this is the logic that even God can only have one set of faith beliefs on defined issues because truth is, as it must be, is singular per defined issue. It is also impossible that God could, should, or would have waited some 1,500 *years* after the establishment of Christianity and his church to introduce his "true" faith beliefs. Such is utterly impossible, yet both of these very logical points are missed by very sincere and possibly (spiritually) deadly wrong people.

Simply studying their faith seems to be insufficient. It is necessary that they turn to God in humility and actually begin to seek the truth, which only God can open up to them. God seems to be inclined to grant them his truthful understanding until they "seek the Lord while he *may* be found" (Isaiah 55:6; italics mine).

Following this were the trials and test of a forty-year trek in the desert, a test required by God because of their infidelities, which prompted God to allow them to become a "captive people" in the first place. God still provided for their essential needs, yet their collective pride led to more grumbling. Exodus 16:31 says, "And the house of Israel called the name thereof Manna: and it was like coriander seed white, and the taste thereof like to flour with honey." But they soon grew tired of this and complained to Moses. Numbers 21:5 is where God empowered Aaron to bring forth water from the rock (a prelude to salvation through Peter, "the Rock" (Matthew 19:18–19). And they complained of having only "bread" (manna) and water, so God then gave them "flesh to eat" (Numbers 11:18) daily. Quail descended upon the camp every evening. This event leads to the most Holy Eucharist, the pinnacle of grace, as it really is Jesus himself. And nothing is more efficacious or binding to God, nor is anything more of an aid to one's effort to merit salvation.

Then we have God commanding Moses to build for him a house of divine worship to contain the ark of the covenant, the forerunner to present-day Catholic churches, which all have a tabernacle to hold our "manna," the transubstantiated divine presence of Jesus himself. The opulence that used to be common to Catholic churches (dependent on a capacity to give the best) followed the design commands given by God to Moses in constructing the ark of the covenant; using much gold and the finest fabrics and materials was mandated by God in Exodus chapters 25–28.

So as not to veer too far from our topic of salvation history, we now look at the Old Testament priesthood, from the time of the exodus and forward.

In Exodus 28:1, Aaron and his sons are separated to be priest for God, and they are told to make for them elaborate and distinctive clothing. And in verse 41, Moses is instructed to consecrate the hands of all the priests as a sign of their being chosen by God to serve him and his people.

Subsequently, we find Yahweh using his priest in the act of forgiving his chosen people of their sins. Leviticus 5:13 states, "Thus the *priest* shall make atonement for him for the sin which he has committed in any one of these things, and he shall be forgiven. And the remainder shall be for the *priest*, as in the cereal offering" (italics added). Leviticus 6:7 says, "And the *priest* [italics mine] shall make atonement for him before the Lord, and he shall be forgiven for any of the things which one may do and thereby become guilty." So we see here the desire of God to use his chosen priest to lead not only worship services but other salvation-related tasks as well. Obviously, Jesus chooses to use the priesthood that he establishes through Peter and the apostles for this very same task, but now his priesthood is granted powers and authority never even imagined by Aaron and his sons.

Induced by space limits, we now jump all the way forward to the New Testament. John 15:16 says, "You did not choose me, but I chose you and appointed you that you should go and bear fruit and that your fruit should abide; so that whatever you ask the Father in my name, he may give it to you."

Here's what we learned so far:
*   Beginning with Abram, God decides to select just one tribe, one nation as his "chosen people" from the midst of his humanity (Exodus 6:7).
*   God begins the long process of conversion, education, trials, and tests, some of which are met successfully, others not so.

* As a corrective behavior of judgment, Yahweh permits the chosen people to be enslaved.
* God continues and affirms the tradition he selected of always having one man leading his chosen people. Now it's Moses's turn.
* God provides for all of their necessities, first creating manna, second providing water from "the rock," and third, when they still complained, providing them "flesh to eat." All three of these gifts point and predate Christ's gift of himself, his Catholic Church, and the Catholic Holy Communion. *Manna* points to the bread that is transfigured into his body; *water*, needed for physical salvation, points to the blood of Christ; the *rock* points to Peter, "the Rock" (Matthew 16:18), representing the church, which is critical to our soul's salvation; and of course, the *flesh* of the provided quails reminds us of the very body of Jesus himself. John 6:35, 47–49, 54–56 states, "Jesus said to them, 'I am the bread of life; he who comes to me shall not hunger, and he who believes in me shall never thirst. Truly, truly, I say to you, he who believes has eternal life. *I am the bread of life.* Your fathers ate the manna in the wilderness, and they died. He who eats my flesh and drinks my blood has eternal life, and I will raise him up at the last day. *For my flesh is food indeed, and my blood is drink indeed.* He who eats my flesh and drinks my blood abides in me, and I in him.'"

Next is evidence that God, even in the Old Testament, nearly four thousand years ago, chose to use the priest he had chosen for sin's forgiveness. In these snippets of our Old Testament salvation history, we are given sight of the fact that God does not change. Malachi 3:6 says, "For I am the Lord, and I change not." In brief summary, we see the origins of Christ's plan for humanity's salvation under the new covenant in his blood. One God remains just one true God with just one possible set of "true" faith beliefs (one set of beliefs is all that is logically possible, even for God), and one "chosen people" becomes one chosen church (Matthew 16:18).

Then we have the introduction of sacraments, each instituted by Jesus. All seven are represented in and through these manifestations: manna is to introduce sacramentally the most Holy Eucharist; water is sacramental baptism; flesh, of course, is Jesus himself; and the rock introduces the new church, which holds all the keys to heaven's gate (singular; Matthew 16:18).

Later, in the book of Exodus, we discover that God chose to ordain a new priesthood from Aaron and his sons. And this priesthood is "to God" (Exodus 28:1) and for God's people. They will handle the worship task assigned, the sacraments like circumcision and purification, and even sin forgiveness, found in the books of Numbers and Leviticus, both of which are included in the Jewish Torah.

I'm always amazed at Protestant Bible commentaries when they try to explain away things like one God, faith, and church (Ephesians 4:1–7), replacing just one chosen people or the most Holy Eucharist actually being what it claims (five different authors all testify to it); the body, blood, soul, and divinity of Jesus Christ; or sin forgiveness God's way as taught in both the Old and the New Testaments, which is our next and final segment of this lesson.

Again, we are reminded that God "does not change." Leviticus 5:13 says, "Thus the priest shall make atonement for him for the sin which he has committed in any one of these things, and he shall be forgiven. And the remainder shall be for the priest, as in the cereal offering." Leviticus 6:7 states, "And the priest shall make atonement for him before the Lord, and he shall be forgiven for any of the things which one may do and thereby become guilty."

This then is the foundation for Christ's choosing to follow his own sacred Old Testament tradition of using his chosen priest in the New Testament, who is now empowered with some of God's own authority and powers (similar but not to the same degree as Christ) to actually be able to forgive sins in Christ's name (John 20:21–23).

Matthew **10**:1–4 says, "And he called to him his twelve disciples and gave them authority over unclean spirits, to cast them out, and to heal every disease and every infirmity. The names of the twelve apostles are these: *first, Simon, who is called Peter*, and Andrew his brother; James the son of Zeb'edee, and John his brother; Philip and Bartholomew; Thomas and Matthew the tax collector; James the son of Alphaeus, and Thaddaeus; Simon the Cananaean, and Judas Iscariot, who betrayed him" (italics added).

Matthew 16:18–19 states, "And I tell you, *you are Peter, and on this rock* I will build my church [singular], and the powers of death shall not prevail against it. *I will give you the keys of the kingdom of heaven, and whatever you bind on earth shall be bound in heaven, and whatever you loose on earth shall be loosed in heaven*" (italics added).

John 17:17–19 declares, "Sanctify them in the truth; thy word is truth. *As thou didst send me into the world, so I have sent them into the world.* And for their sake I consecrate myself, that they also may be consecrated in truth."

This then sets up what Jesus himself ordains, commands, and makes possible as his way, the precise manner Christ chooses to have man's sins forgiven: John 20:20–23 says, "When he had said this, he showed them his hands and his side. Then the disciples were glad when they saw the Lord. Jesus said to them again, 'Peace be with you. *As the Father has sent me, even so I send you.*' And when he had said this, he breathed on them, and said to them, '*Receive the Holy Spirit. If you forgive the sins of any, they are forgiven; if you retain the sins of any, they are retained.*'"

These teachings lead to two additional questions: How and why did Jesus do this?

Jesus, being God, can do any good thing. A brief but telling definition of God is this: "God is every good thing perfected." Matthew 10:1–2 says, "And he called to him his twelve disciples and gave them authority over unclean spirits, to cast them out, and to heal every disease and every infirmity. *The names of the twelve apostles are these*: first, Simon, who is called Peter" (italics added). So we see from the above that Jesus had already demonstrated that that he could and then did share his godly powers and authority with his apostles. So what he chose to do in regard to empowering them and, of course, their successors is just another manifestation of Jesus fulfilling his ministry: Matthew 9:13 says, "Go and learn what this means, 'I desire mercy, and not sacrifice.' For *I* came not to call the righteous, but sinners" (italics added).

And here is the exact time, place, and manner that Jesus chose to continue to use his chosen priests, now Catholic priests, to actually forgive or not to forgive man's sins in the name of Christ. John 20:19–23 says, "On the evening of that day, the first day of the week, the doors being shut where the disciples were, for fear of the Jews, Jesus came and stood among them and said to them, '*Peace be with you.*' When he had said this, he showed them his hands and his side. Then the disciples were glad when they saw the Lord. Jesus said to them again, '*Peace be with you. As the Father has sent me, even so I send you.*' And when he had said this, he breathed on them, and said to them, 'Receive the Holy Spirit. *If you forgive the sins of any, they are forgiven; if you retain the sins of any, they are retained*" (italics added).

Having now answered the "how" question, we proceed to the "why" question. Notice please in the above teaching that Jesus said, "Peace be with you," not once but twice in this very brief passage. This was not simply a greeting, like we'd say "hello." No, this was a demonstration of God's will being unified with God's desire for humanity, to actually find and have a peaceful, peace-filled spirit as a reality: John 14:27 says, "Peace I leave with you; *my peace* I give to you; not as the world gives do I give to you. Let not your hearts be troubled, neither let them be afraid" (italics added).

First John 1:8–10 states, "If we say we have no sin, we deceive ourselves, and the truth is not in us. If we confess our sins, he is faithful and just, and will forgive our sins and cleanse us from all unrighteousness. If we say we have not sinned, we make him a liar, and his word is not in us."

First John 5:16–17 says, "If any one sees his brother committing what is not a mortal sin, he will ask, and God will give him life for those whose sin is not mortal. *There is sin which is mortal*; I do not say that one is to pray for that. All wrongdoing is sin, but there is sin which is not mortal" (italics added).

Because God has to be "good" and "just," he cannot judge all sins to be equal in seriousness or to judge them to have the same consequences. Murder and stealing a candy bar cannot merit the same punishment. There is under each of the ten sin category headings, which we know (or ought to) as God's commandments, the possibility of committing mortal sins.

"Mortal sins "are those infractions so grievous as to actually sever our bond with Christ, until such are confessed and forgiven God's way. They are literally a "spiritual death," a way to "kill," which is to say "to condemn," our immortal spiritual souls to hell for eternity.

Mortal sins require the following:
1. The sinner has to know that the act that they are about to do is serious enough to be considered by God as a "mortal sin."
2. Knowing this, the sinner has to freely consent to do it anyway.
3. Then the sinner has to either actually do it or at least desire to "do it" if they could.

While this may give a "pass" to some for lack of foreknowledge, there are mortal sins that are so grievous that everyone ought to know that they are quite possibly mortal sins. They are called "intrinsic evils." Aborting or supporting in any way this activity, adultery, slander, all sexual activity outside of marriage, knowingly and willingly not giving God weekly worship, which he demands in the first and third commandments, are but a few examples of this. This category of sins is nearly always mortal sins.

Among the saddest and more frightening aspects of Protestant theology on sin forgiveness is that their human-engineered methods, methods specifically designed to be far easier and more appealing than Catholic sacramental confession, are neither biblical nor the manner Jesus himself chose to accomplish this critical salvation task. It is quite possible that as the norm for Christ not to accept these man-made innovations as being sufficient to actually do what others promise they will do. "Altar calls," the Sinner's Prayer, the belief that God has already done all the hard work by dying for our sins so all that we have to do is "profess that we believe that Jesus is God" and keep sinning as if it doesn't really matter because "we are saved" and can't lose our salvation are at best speculative and imprudently optimistic.

Folks, here's a news flash: Jesus did not empower Protestant ministers to be able to forgive man's sins. What he did do is, through the Catholic sacrament of "known forgiveness of our sins," he made it possible for restless hearts to be comforted and assured (guaranteed) that their sins have truly and actually been forgiven and forgotten by God, which is why one really ought to be an informed and fully practicing Catholic. Protestants, through an act of "perfect contrition," combined with a firm sense of amendment (a commitment to change your life and really attempt to avoid these sins in the future), can be effective, but only God knows if you have met his criteria sufficiently. That, dear friends, is hardly a recipe for a truly "peaceful mind and heart." God's mercy might cover some degree of ignorance so long as it is not an intentional affront to what he, Jesus, taught.

Our perfect God chose only one God, one set of faith beliefs, and one church so that man could easily discern what it is that he desires. Ephesians 4:1–7 says, "I therefore, a prisoner for the Lord, beg you to lead a life worthy of the calling to which you have been called, with all lowliness and meekness, with patience, forbearing one another in love, eager to maintain the unity of the Spirit in the bond of peace. There is *one body* [meaning one church] and one Spirit, just as you were called to the one hope that belongs to your call, one Lord, *one faith* [meaning only one set of acceptable faith beliefs], one baptism, one God and Father of us all, who is above all and through all and in all. *But grace was given to each of us according to the measure of Christ's gift*" (italics added). And this, my dear friends, explains why so many can't comprehend these realities. God's grace is being withheld until such time as one actually begins to seek God's truths. Amen!

CHAPTER TEN

Godly Gifts: From Profound to Sublime

Go therefore and make disciples of all nations, baptizing them in the name of the Father and of the Son and of the Holy Spirit.

—Matthew 28:19

*Jesus said to them, "I am the **bread of life**; he who comes to me shall not hunger, and he who believes in me shall never thirst.*

—John 6:35

*And when he saw their faith he said, "Man, your **sins are forgiven** you." Which is easier, to say, 'Your **sins are forgiven** you,' or to say, 'Rise and walk'?*

—Luke 5:20, 23

Lesson No. 1

The Seven Sacraments of the Catholic Church

Where the immortal meets mortal; where man meets his God.
"All saints have a past, all sinners a future."

A "sacrament," as defined by the Catholic Church, is an outward sign, instituted by Christ, to give the grace that it signifies. There are seven sacraments: baptism, confirmation, Holy Eucharist, penance, anointing of the sick (extreme unction), holy orders, and matrimony.

"Each Sacrament is the personal saving act of the risen Christ Himself, but realized in the visible form of the Church. [p 54] Should we not be able to conceive how a smile of the man-Jesus, God's Smile, how the God-man's glance at us, can change our whole life?" (E. Schillebeeckx, OP, *Christ, the Sacrament of the Encounter with God*, p. 79)

Why is there a need for sacraments?

Souls and bodies have similar needs. When a body is born, it requires nourishment, guidance, and love. When we become ill, we require medical attention. Our souls have similar needs. They are brought into spiritual life by baptism, made strong by confirmation, nourished by Christ himself in Holy Eucharist, healed by penance, loved in death by extreme unction, and guided in life by our holy priests in holy orders. (Cf. *Catholic Encyclopedia*.)

Why seven sacraments?

The number of sacraments was determined as necessary and instituted by Christ himself. This is a dogma of our faith and was defined at the church's Council of Trent. The Bible is replete with numbers, and they are of specific significance and understanding to the Jewish community, God's chosen people. The number "seven" connotes "complete," even "perfect." That is why so many today, when asked what their lucky number is, reply seven. Christ selected seven as to include the special spiritual needs all of his children by offering extra opportunities for the grace necessary to reach our final goal, which is heaven. Strictly speaking, all the sacraments are not absolutely necessary for our salvation, as "God, grace and the soul are all spiritual beings" (*Catholic Encyclopedia*). Two sacraments, however, are absolutely necessary for adult salvation: baptism and the Holy Eucharist, and baptism is necessary even for infants. (Cf. John 3:5, 6:47–53.) The Eucharist exists for this very reason.

If all the sacraments are not, strictly speaking, necessary, why did Christ institute them?

Grace itself is a free gift from God, who himself is the very origin of all grace. Life is more a spiritual than a physical battle, and grace is an essential weapon of this war for our souls. Christ desires us to win (1 Timothy 2:4) and gives us sufficient assistance to respond to his call.

Free gifts are usually a sign of affection, even of love. Such is the case in the institution of the seven sacraments. Christ loves us so that he wished to offer and make available to us signs of his love and his hope for us. The sacraments require a desire to be loved and a willingness to participate in them in order for them to have their designed effects.

Just what is a sacrament?

The word *sacrament* in Greek means "mystery." In its broadest sense, a sacrament is something hidden and sacred. Sacraments are God's response to man's desire to be led by things corporeal and perceptible, spiritual and intelligible (St. Thomas Aquinas). Sacraments are an outward sign of God's love and desire to save us, by offering special additional graces through their proper administration and acceptance.

There are three essential signs of a sacrament:
1. A sensible sign (able to be perceived by and through the senses)
2. Instituted by Christ as the origin and source of all grace
3. Have the power to produce grace, which is to say that the form and ceremony of each sacrament properly administered and received has the God-given power itself to produce and give the grace that it signifies. "The sacraments act ex opere operato (literally: 'by the fact of the actions being performed)" (CCC 1128) and "confer the grace that they signify" (CCC 1127).

Baptism, the sacrament of entry into unity with God and the sacrament of initiation

"There is one body and one Spirit, just as you were called to the one hope that belongs to your call, one Lord, one faith, one baptism, one God and Father of us all, who is above all and through all and in all" (Ephesians 4:4–6). "Baptism is true entry into the holiness of God through incorporation into Christ and the indwelling of His Spirit" (Pope John Paul II, *Novo Millennio Ineunte*, January 2001).

Some general facts

Christian baptism may only be validly administered and received one time, as this sacrament leaves an indelible mark on the soul. We are permanently sealed and identified as chosen heirs of the kingdom and have been called by name. Faith is a gift from God that can be accepted or rejected by our free will. Baptism is essential for salvation, at least by intent (CCC 1129).

Like a newborn babe, we come into Christ's church spotless and free of the stain of all sin. Even the stain of "original" sin is removed. Baptism should be received as soon after birth as convenient, certainly within one month. The normal form for this sacrament is "holy (blessed) water," and the usual words by the delegated minister (usually an ordained priest or pastor, bishop, or deacon but could even be a Protestant minister) are "I baptize you in the name of the Father, and the Son, and the Holy Spirit" while pouring the water over the head of the person being baptized three times. "He who believes and is baptized will be saved; but he who does not believe will be condemned" (Mark 16:16).

The symbolism

In the liturgy of the Easter Vigil, during the blessing of the baptismal water, the Church solemnly commemorates the great events in salvation history that already prefigured the mystery of Baptism:
Father, you give us grace through sacramental signs,
which tell us of the wonders of your unseen power.
In Baptism we use your gift of water,
which you have made a rich symbol
of the grace you give us in this sacrament. (CCC 1217)

"Jesus answered, 'Truly, truly, I say to you, unless one is born of water and the Spirit, he cannot enter the kingdom of God'" (John 3:5).

The three forms of (one) baptism

1. *Baptism with holy water.* It's the normal, most common, and required form of baptism. It is a grave obligation for each of us to, in charity, baptize an adult that is in danger of death if we are not sure that they have been baptized. This presumes their desire to be baptized. In danger of death, we may also baptize an infant that normally, but not necessarily, presumes that this would be the desire of their parents. Water, even if not blessed, is to be used, saying the words, "I baptize you in the name of the Father and the Son and the Holy Spirit," pouring a small amount of water on the head with each pronouncement.

2. *Baptism of desire.* This is valid if a soul desires to come to the Lord but has no opportunity to be formally baptized. Such might be the case in countries where Christ's faithful are persecuted or if one should die while receiving instruction before coming into the church.

3. *Baptism of blood.* When a child of the Christ sheds their blood in defense of the church and faith that Christ founded, they are baptized in their own blood. Similar to the blood Christ shed on the cross, their blood becomes the blood of salvation (CCC 1258).

Confirmation, the sacrament of anointing

Jesus returned to the synagogues of his home territory in Galilee "in the power of the Holy Spirit," and he read to them from the sacred scrolls where it is written, "The Spirit of the Lord is upon me, because he has anointed me to preach good news to the poor. He has sent me to proclaim release to the captives and recovering of sight to the blind, to set at liberty those who are oppressed." Jesus went on to inform them, "Today this scripture has been fulfilled in your hearing." (Cf. Luke 4:14–21.)

The anointing

The symbolism of anointing with chrism, the same pure oil of olives mixed with balsam and specially blessed by the bishop used in baptism, signifies the Holy Spirit to the point of becoming a synonym for the Holy Spirit. In Christian initiation, anointing is the sacramental sign of confirmation, called "chrismation" in the churches of the East (CCC 695).

We are created to know, love, and serve God in this world in order to be happy with him in the next (Isaiah 43:7, 21). In the service of the Lord, we are termed "the church militant" for good cause. We are soldiers for Christ in the very real and ongoing battle for souls, ours and those of all who are placed in our life path; it is certain that no one is placed in our path without cause. They are there to assist us, to divert us to hell, or to be influenced by us to also join the cause of Christ and his church, the way to salvation. Like baptism, confirmation is a sacrament of initiation into the Catholic Church, and it too leaves an indelible mark on the soul and may only be received once in a lifetime.

Because confirmation, as the indwelling of the Holy Spirit, is a duplication of the gift of himself to the apostles, our first bishops at the first Pentecost, and its purpose is to strengthen and enlighten, this sacrament is commonly bestowed by the local bishop with a special holy oil (pure oil of olives), called chrism or *myron*, which is specially formulated, blessed by the bishop in a dedicated ceremony, and set apart for "the sanctification of men (all in Christian initiation)." *All baptized Christians need to be confirmed, as this sacrament of anointing completes the graces offered at baptism.*

Since Vatican II, there have been three changes in the ceremony for confirmation. The sacrament is preceded by the formal renewal of baptismal promises; during baptism, these promises are often spoken for the candidate by the sponsor because of the age of the baptized. Confirmation is now conferred during the sacrifice of Holy Mass, and Holy Communion is received. This requires that the candidate for confirmation be in the state of grace. The sacrament is still validly received in mortal sin, and the sacramental character is imprinted on the soul if properly motivated by desire and with valid form and matter and purpose, but the grace conferred by the sacrament is not received until that person is again in the state of grace. (Cf. "Basic Catholic Catechism," CCC 1351.)

The effects of confirmation

Confirmation brings an increase and deepening of baptismal grace:
* It roots us more deeply in the divine filiation, which makes us cry, "Abba! Father!"
* It unites us more firmly with Christ.
* It increases the gifts of the Holy Spirit in us.
* It renders our bond with the church more perfect. It gives us a special strength of the Holy Spirit.

Holy Eucharist, the sacrament of Christ himself

"God is the only source of happiness; happiness is in Him alone, and He has reserved the right to bestow it through Himself. And well it is that we have to go to God Himself to find happiness" (Saint Peter Julian Eymard, *Holy Communion*, p. 80). The Eucharist is the sacrament of love par excellence. Certainly, the other sacraments are proofs of God's love for us; they are gifts of God. But in the Eucharist, we receive the author of every gift, God himself (p. 81).

All sacraments and all Catholic doctrine and dogma both lead to and emanate from the blessed sacrament, which is Christ himself.

Complete perfection and perfect love are embodied in this, which is the goal of all sacraments, as well as the most perfect gift of God of himself to us for our nourishment, enlightenment, happiness, and our peace. Nothing—absolutely nothing—can replace the splendor, the majesty, and the power to heal and to save as Jesus himself can in the blessed sacrament of Holy Communion. Therefore, we must, imperatively speaking, unite ourselves with Jesus in the Eucharist as often as we are able, even at great sacrifice, daily if possible, if we are to grow spiritually and know, live, and share our faith. There is no greater source of the supernatural grace we need to get to heaven.

Jesus—in his glorified body and blood, total humanity, and total divinity in the gift of himself—can only be had in the only church that Jesus himself founded, the Catholic Church. Other Christian denominations celebrate only a remembrance of Christ, while we actually share in the real Christ. There exists no better reason to be an informed, practicing Roman Catholic. Nowhere else can one find the real presence of Jesus here on earth.

The fourteenth-century author of *The Imitation of Christ*, Thomas *à* Kempis, reminds us of the great honor that Christ bestows on his holy (Catholic) priests, an honor bestowed the very same evening that he created the perpetual gift of himself, the gift of perpetual earthly residence, the Holy Eucharist, which is brought to earth countless times each day by their hands and their prayers.

"For I received from the Lord what I also delivered to you, that the Lord Jesus on the night when he was betrayed took bread, and when he had given thanks, he broke it, and said, 'This is my body which is for you. Do this in remembrance of me.' In the same way also he took the cup, after supper, saying, 'This cup is the new covenant in my blood. Do this, as often as you drink it, in remembrance of me'" (1 Corinthians 11:23–25).

"The priesthood is a great mystery; how great a dignity is that of a priest! He has been given powers not granted to the Angels: for no one but a priest duly ordained in [the Catholic or Orthodox] church has the power to celebrate the Divine Liturgy, to consecrate the Body of Christ" (Thomas à Kempis). Only a man, properly ordained, has this powerful privilege. As Christ himself ordained the form and format of this most blessed sacrament, its structure cannot be changed by anyone other than the supreme pontiff. The elements of unleavened bread and real wine may not be either altered or substituted. The words of consecration not only may not but also absolutely cannot be changed.

So not to embarrass us or frighten us by his glory and splendor, Jesus Christ chose to become the bread of Life, our most basic of food, for he desires to nourish both our bodies and our souls. In fact, he desires it so very much that he chooses himself to be that very nourishment, in the appearance (form) of bread and wine, which becomes his body and blood in the sacrament of Holy Communion. The same Jesus who died for us would abase himself even more than he did in his holy passion and death in order to remain with us and available to us. Jesus loves us so much that he desires to remain in our midst, visible to all, and available to all in the holy tabernacles of his bride, his church.

Recent changes allow for, even strongly recommend, the daily, if possible, reception of Jesus in Holy Communion. This has become necessary because of the grip and influence Satan has on so many souls today. Conquered by pride, greed, and lust, only the redeemer, Jesus himself, can save us. In our working toward sainthood, the Eucharist, which is Christ himself, must be our closest friend and is certainly our strongest allay. The graces offered and received through proper reception of Christ in the Holy Eucharist are quite special. They can enlighten the mind to God's plans and will for us today, this hour, and even this minute. Our will is strengthened to fight off temptations, discouragement, even depression. Frequent Holy Communion places the soul in total abandonment to God's will, which allows him to use us as he desires and when and how he desires. Through Holy Communion, Christ is directly and personally invited to work miracles in our lives. "Taste and see the goodness of the Lord."

The sacrament of penance, reconciliation, or confession

This is the sacrament of reconciliation with your God, your church, and yourself; the above terms references the same sacrament but with separate definitions. This sacrament alone offers God's guarantee for the known forgiveness of our sins (John 17:18–19, John 20:23).

"'As the Father has sent me, even so I send you.' And when he had said this, he breathed on them, and said to them, 'Receive the Holy Spirit. If you forgive the sins of any, they are forgiven; if you retain the sins of any, they are retained" (John 20:21–23).

With privilege and honor come responsibility and duty. This sacrament attacks our pride by not only asking but also demanding that we both seek forgiveness and in turn forgive others. Asking for forgiveness and forgiving are as closely joined as newlyweds are on their honeymoon. And similarly, there is a certain trepidation, release, and joy in the process. Both require love. "The sacrament of Penance restores the life of grace in us, heals us. But is a violent remedy, a victory dearly bought, which leaves us weary with battle" (Saint Peter Julian Eymard, *Holy Communion*, p. 91).

At the root of fear and refusal to go to confession to a priest is the prideful thought that either we are not sinners—which is, of course, absurd—or this sacrament of penance is simply for those wannabe-pious-type Catholics. The simple truth is that it is not God who benefits from the sacrament of penance; it is us who gain the benefit. God gains nothing but performance of his holy will, while we stand to gain grace, even entrance unto salvation, and to find the inner peace that God intends for us all to possess: "Peace I leave with you; *my peace* I give to you; not as the world gives do I give to you. Let not your hearts be troubled, neither let them be afraid" (John 14:27; italics added).

There are elements of logic and even genius in the form and format of the sacrament of penance. Pride is the inhibiting instigator of refusal, and humility is the balm of relief. Satan tells you "No, you don't need it." Jesus, who is love, says, "Yes, you do." Who do you listen to? Who should you listen to?

This sacrament is absolutely required when we are not in the state of grace because of mortal sin and an obligation for what is termed a Catholic's "Easter duty."

This is a sign of unity with Christ's church, receiving Holy Communion worthily at least once each year. Though not strictly required for those in the state of grace, a minimal annual utilization of the sacrament of penance is strongly recommended. This is normally completed between Ash Wednesday and Trinity Sunday.

Three elements are required on the part of the penitent: contrition, confession, and satisfaction. Confession is only valid when these three elements are present, and confession is made to a duly ordained and authorized priest, who is granted the faculty to hear confessions. In danger of death, any priests may validly hear one's confession. Do not be afraid to ask a priest for a special time or to make an appointment for confession. It is, after all, his job and your salvation. Don't be thwarted by posted confession times. Don't abuse the good service of your priest, but do get to confession regularly.

Contrition: It is true and sincere sorrow for having sinned. Sinning is a desire, at least implicitly, to be separated from the grace of God. All mortal sins must be confessed, and all or at least some venial sins should be confessed. Confessing one's sins to a priest is a needed manifestation of this contrition. It is not sufficient to simply tell God that you are sorry, even if you are sincere. Yet true sorrow is a necessary element of a personal confession. God has determined and designed his forgiveness to come through him by your actions and the actions of the priest in and through the sacrament of penance. You must be sufficiently sorry, willing to accuse yourself, and willing to properly confess at least all of your mortal sins.

Confession: The forms authorized by the church include person-to-person (called auricular confession) or penitent-to-confessor recitation of all serious mortal sins and most, if not all, lesser venial sins. Confession can be "face to face, or in the more traditional veiled format. The priest must say, "I absolve you from your sins," and you then must make "satisfaction" (do the penance assigned).

General absolutions are for emergency situations only, such as war or natural disasters. Even then, they are valid only on the condition that you will make a personal confession as soon as practical reality permits. Some errant clerics, including a few bishops, abuse the privilege of general absolution. These confessions are neither valid nor licit. All serious sins must be, need to be, and should be confessed in a personal confession to have the desired effect of forgiveness by Almighty God.

Satisfaction: It is a "cause and effect" situation. When I was teaching religious education to junior high and high school students, I would bring in sections of 2" x 6" lumber on which I had written, "Your soul." I would then, without discussion, pass out hammers and nails and allow them to hammer as many nails into the boards as they desired, with a caution to be careful and a reminder that we would have to pull out all the nails. Once the nails were removed, we would begin our discussion of the need for the sacrament of confession by explaining what sin is, the two categories of sin, and their effects on the soul and end by explaining that confession removes both sin and the guilt of sin. The "soul boards" before sin were without blemish; the nails (sins) changed that, and confession removed the sins (nails). Looking at the boards, they would see the difference. Nail holes, the effect of sin, remained.

Retribution must be made for damaging our soul, not for the benefit of God but for the benefit of our salvation. Mortal sin kills the soul. It is completely shut off from God, and if a soul dies in this state, it will be damned to hell for all eternity. One might think of the soul as an electric master switch that is very badly corroded. The electricity can't get through. Similarly, a soul in mortal sin prohibits grace from getting through.

The normal form of confession

* The priest greets the penitent, who responds by making the sign of the cross and proclaiming, "Bless me, Father, for I have sinned." He then tells the priest how long it has been since the last confession.
* A scriptural passage is read (often, not always).
* The penitent confesses all mortal sins and most, if not all, venial sins. If only venial sins are present and confessed, true sorrow must be present for at least one of them in order for the

sacrament to be received validly. (In absence of mortal sin(s), one can also confess a prior serious sin.)

* The priest offers encouragement and advice and imposes a penance. The penitent will be welcomed back, like in the story of the son who squandered away his inheritance but was welcomed back with a joyful celebration by his father (Luke 15:11–32). (Jesus himself told us there is more joy in heaven over one repentant sinner than a hundred with no need of repentance. [Cf. Luke 11:7.] Satan imposes a fear not born in either charity or fact. "Be not afraid.")

* The penitent expresses sorrow by making an act of contrition.

* Absolution is given. This is the key. The priest, acting on behalf of Christ, must pronounce the words of absolution: "I absolve you in the name of the Father, the Son, and the Holy Spirit." The confessor will prescribe certain prayers or pious acts for penance. These prescribed acts must be fulfilled.

Like all sacraments, reconciliation requires sacrifice, but the rewards far exceed them. "Go in peace." What an incredible message, and what complete joy!

Anointing of the sick, the sacrament of special graces for the needy

"Is any among you sick? Let him call for the elders of the church, and let them pray over him, anointing him with oil in the name of the Lord; and the prayer of faith will save the sick man, and the Lord will raise him up; and if he has committed sins, he will be forgiven" (James 5:14–15).

"The sacrament of Anointing is a sacrament of the New Law instituted by Christ to give the sick spiritual assistance, strengthen their supernatural life and, if need be forgive their sins. Moreover, if God wills it, anointing restores physical health to the body of the Christian who is seriously ill" (*Basic Catholic Catechism*, p. 123).

Who may receive the sacrament of anointing of the sick?

The sacrament of anointing is available to all baptized people who have reached the age of reason (CIC 891) (usually around the age of seven), are seriously ill, or are of advanced age. It may also be received before surgery, if a dangerous illness is the cause of the surgery. This special gift from God may be received as often as warranted. It may be applied even if the sick person has lost their senses or even if they are unconscious. The sacrament may be applied conditionally, if the priest has a reasonable doubt about the death of the victim.

The form for the sacrament of anointing

The priest uses special olive oil that has been previously blessed by the bishop or an authorized priest. The priest begins by stating, "Through this holy anointing, may the Lord in his love and mercy help you with the grace of the Holy Spirit." The sick person responds, "Amen." The priest continues, "May the Lord who frees you from your sins save you and raise you up." The sick person again responds, "Amen." The forehead and hands are anointed. In case of necessity, one anointing is sufficient, and it may be a different part of the body. However, the entire formula is to be recited each time.

The spiritual effects of the anointing (a "happy death")

"For persons who are unable to confess their sins or even give some sign of sorrow, anointing may be the only way that they can be saved. This assumes that they have unconfessed grave sins on their souls which the sacrament of Anointing certainly removes that the person has at some time been sorry for their sins, at least out of fear of God's punishment" (*Basic Catholic Catechism*, p. 125).

* Forgiveness of the guilt of unremitted sin, even grave sin for which the person has at least imperfect sorrow
* Remission of the temporal punishment still due for remitted sin to such a degree that the expiation can be complete if judged by God
* Supernatural patience to bear with one's suffering
* Extraordinary confidence in God's mercy
* A special infusion of moral courage to resist temptation of the devil (who *never* gives up)

The bodily effects can be restoration of health, if God sees it will be for his greater good, and the salvation of the sick person.

Holy orders, the power of Christ perpetuated

"Do this in memory of me" (Luke 22:19).

It is through holy orders, instituted by Christ on Holy Thursday at the Last Supper when he said and "ordered" his apostles to "do this in memory of me," that the hierarchal priesthood was instituted.

We are reminded by Thomas *à* Kempis, "The priesthood is a great mystery; how great a dignity is that of a priest! He has been given powers not even granted to the Angels: for no one but a priest duly ordained in church [the Catholic Church] has the power to celebrate the Divine Liturgy [to say the Holy Mass], to consecrate the Body of Christ [to transform what was merely unleavened bread and ordinary wine into the real body, blood, soul, and divinity of our Savior, Jesus Christ]."

Christ instituted only one church and one hierarchical priesthood. The sacrament of holy orders was so immense that it was actually instituted by three separate actions, at three separate times, by our Lord. This is especially significant as it demonstrates in the clearest possible manner the intention of our blessed Lord.

Holy Thursday, the Last Supper: "And he took bread, and when he had given thanks he broke it and gave it to them, saying, 'This is my body which is given for you. Do this in remembrance of me.' *And likewise the cup after supper, saying, 'This cup which is poured out for you is the new covenant in my blood'*" (Luke 22:19–20; italics added).

Easter Sunday night: "And when he had said this, he breathed on them, and said to them, 'Receive the Holy Spirit. If you forgive the sins of any, they are forgiven; if you retain the sins of any, they are retained'" (John 20:22–23).

Before Christ's ascension back to the Father: "Go therefore and make disciples of all nations, baptizing them in the name of the Father and of the Son and of the Holy Spirit, teaching them to observe all that I have commanded you; and lo, I am with you always, to the close of the age" (Matthew 28:19–20).

Only men, always a priest

By God's personal choice and unchangeable design, the hierarchical priesthood has always been and must always remain of the male gender only. God could have chosen differently but did not. Holy order is a sacrament whose form was selected by Christ and cannot be changed.

Indisputably, male gender and female gender physiology differs and is yet another valid reason why the Catholic priest is male, who is commanded to "do this in remembrance of *me* [literally, Jesus]," and therefore *must be* male in order to act "persona Christi" (CCC 1548).

There exists no greater truth, no greater blessing in the theology of our beliefs than the doctrine of Christ's real presence—body, blood, soul, and complete divinity—in our midst and only available to us through the mystery and power of God's love and providence, through the hands of his validly ordained Catholic priest.

There exist no reason of greater value or importance for being an informed, practicing Catholic than to be able to really receive worthily the sacred body and blood of our Lord and Savior, the son of Mary, and the crucified Son of God into our bodies in an intercourse more intimate, more noble, more complete than any other. Our Lord and our God, our King and our Savior loves us this much, desires to be with and in us this much, abases himself this much in the manifestation of perfect love. It is Catholic priests who make Jesus available to us in the sacrament of the Holy Communion. There is no greater privilege and no greater honor among men than this.

Always a priest

Because of the indelible mark of ordination on the priesthood, a priest always remains a priest and can never become a layman in the identical sense that we are. There is a formal release process for priests entitled laicization, which if granted allows for cessation of formal duties and may permit marriage. This has been granted to a very large number of priests in the post–Vatican II era because many men who took vows really did not accept the church's teachings on priestly celibacy and chastity, which has long and prudent roots in tradition.

Priestly duties

The main duty of a priest is to live a life of holiness. Example is always the best teacher. Priests receive special graces in order to lead others to Christ. The ordained ministerial priesthood differs in essence from the common priesthood of the faithful because it confers a sacred power for the service of the faithful. The ordained ministers exercise their service for the people of God by teaching divine worship and pastoral governance (CCC 1592).

Marriage, the sacrament of a lifelong commitment and procreation

"And God blessed them, and God said to them, 'Be fruitful and multiply, and fill the earth and subdue it;' To the woman he said, 'I will greatly multiply your pain in childbearing; in pain you shall bring forth children, yet your desire shall be for your husband, and he shall rule over you'" (Genesis 1:28, 3:16).

In this chapter, we will deal primarily with marriage as a sacrament instituted and raised to a level of a lifelong supernatural covenant contract by Jesus himself. "He said to them, 'For your hardness of heart Moses allowed you to divorce your wives, but from the beginning it was not so. And I say to you: whoever divorces his wife, except for unchastity, and marries another, commits adultery" (Matthew 19:8–9). "And he who marries a woman divorced from her husband commits adultery" (Luke 16:18).

Catholic sacramental marriages between two baptized people (one male and one female) are, in a very real sense, brought to fruition by the bride and groom, whom by their choice, under the guidance of the Holy Spirit, commit to the married life. They really "marry" each other by the exchange of their vows of commitment. That is to say that their will and desire to marry, so long as it is unimpeded, is that act which brings the sacrament of marriage into being. "According to Latin tradition, the spouses as ministers of Christ's grace mutually confer upon each other the sacrament of Matrimony by expressing their consent before the Church" (CCC 1623).

Matrimonial

* The parties to a marriage covenant are a baptized man and woman (nothing less, nothing more) free to contract marriage.
* Mutual consent is essential to the marriage. Without free consent, a valid marriage does not exist. Free will of both spouses is absolutely necessary for a valid marriage to take place.
* The words "I take you as my husband/wife" is consent that binds for life. No authority on earth, not even the Catholic Church,

has the power or right to set aside a valid, licit, consummated marriage.

* A sacramental marriage is a liturgical act and therefore is appropriately celebrated in the public liturgy of the Holy Mass, where the body and blood of Christ are made present and received. Therefore, the sacrament of penance is foundational to the sacrament of matrimony.

* The priest (or assisting deacon) receives the consent of the spouses in the name of the church and with the blessings of the church. (In special, limited, and authorized cases, it may even be a layperson.)

Mixed marriage

"As you saw the iron mixed with miry clay, so they will mix with one another in marriage, but they will not hold together, just as iron does not mix with clay" (Daniel 2:43).

Mixed marriages, that of a Catholic and non-Catholic, requires a dispensation from the local bishop, which is most often granted. Our Catholic Church prudently recommends marriage between practicing Catholics because experience and tradition show and prove this to be the best possible union. Mixed marriages may "work," but the union is unnecessarily made difficult because of the inherent differences, priorities, and often different values. Try to have your children associated with other Catholic youth. You and they will likely be happier in unions of both spirit and heart.

There is evidence that by the third generation of a mixed marriage, most offspring of those marriages will not be practicing Catholics. Why? Being an informed, practicing Roman Catholic is difficult and requires commitment, sacrifice, and obedience to the church and God's laws and rules. If one parent didn't have to do it, why should they?

The purpose of marriage is procreation, not only recreation. "The ordering to the natural ends of marriage—the good of the spouses and the procreation and education of offspring—is intrinsically present in masculinity and femininity. This theological characteristic is crucial for understanding the natural dimension of the union. In this sense, the natural character of marriage is better understood when it is not separated from the family. Marriage and the family are inseparable, because the masculinity and femininity of the married couple are constitutively open to the gift of children. Without this openness there could not even be a good of the spouses worthy of the name." (Saint Pope John Paul II, *God Himself Is the Author of Marriage*).

Saint Pope John Paul II repeats what Pope Paul VI, in his encyclical letter *Humanae Vitae*, is telling us in truth and tradition that no married Catholics, for that matter, are to use unnatural methods of birth control. Similarly, masturbation is prohibited, and both are grievously sinful. You might ask why. Because the gift of procreation is divinely created by Almighty God for his good, the creation of his children. *Neither man nor woman has the right to impede God's design and will. God's divine will must always supersede our own often selfish will.*

I struggled with this issue for a long time. In my own Pre-Cana marriage instruction, in the late 1960s (Detroit), we were advised that the use of artificial birth control was a matter of "personal choice," which we exercised until many years later when I read *Humanae Vitae* and discovered that this was a lie. God, as the creator of all life, justly demands the right to decide who will be born and when. Sex is to be mutually enjoyable and is a reward for the pains and difficulties of married and family life. When we impose physical constraints on the will of God, we do so selfishly and become, without due regard to the needs (physical, emotional, and spiritual) of our marriage partners, focused primarily on our own physical "needs." We are really operating at a base nature, unfitting for those created in the image and likeness of God. This is and is intended to be a sacrifice, a sign of our love for each other and for God, our creator. We are to give ourselves to our mates as often as requested willingly, joyfully, and completely unless there is illness or a physical reason not to. Otherwise, we might contribute to our partner seeking to fulfill his or her sexual desires in a sinful manner. Sex should never be a tool of argument or used to attain one's way in marriage. Marriage is for lovers.

"Let marriage be held in honor among all, and let the marriage bed be undefiled; for God will judge the immoral and adulterous" (Hebrews 13:4).

A good marriage is a full partnership, *but* in every organization, in every business, in every society, in most relationships, someone is in charge. Marriage is a partnership, with the man always as the head partner. First Corinthians 11:3 says, "But I want you to understand that the head of every man is Christ, the head of a woman is her husband, and the head of Christ is God" Ephesians 5:22–25, 28, 33 states, "Wives, be subject to your husbands, as to the Lord. For the **husband** is the head of the wife as Christ is the head of the church, his body, and is himself its Savior. As the church is subject to Christ, so let wives also be subject in everything to their **husband**s. Husbands, love your wives, as Christ loved the church and gave himself up for her. Even so **husband**s should love their wives as their own bodies. He who loves his wife loves himself. However, let each one of you love his wife as himself, and let the wife see that she respects her **husband**."

That is the way God intends it to be; and that is why we have complementary but importantly different physical, emotional, and intuitive attributes. The planned feminization of man has had a disastrous effect on marriages, on society, and on the Catholic Church. God made us different for his purposes, and a man leading the family is paramount among them. Still, marriage is not a dictatorship; it is a partnership, with as many as possible joint decisions and shared responsibilities. But the man is to take—absolutely must take (and be permitted, even encouraged to take)—the leadership position.

I will end this discourse with a few more quotes from Father E. Schillebeeckx, OP, in his book *Christ, the Sacrament of the Encounter with God*. "The true riches of a life lived for God, finds its inward meaning in the sacraments. For here we really experience Christ, as our encounter with God, because this theological activity is our only immediate connection with God Himself" (p. 182). "The fruitfulness of a sacrament in grace, then includes all the richness of a Christian life in communion with the Church, the visible sign of grace in which the fullness of Christ is present" (p 183).

"The family that prays together stays together" is far more than an advertising slogan; it reflects God's truth. Amen!

Catholics, Priests, Confession, and Sin

Exodus 28:1–3 states, "*Then bring near to you Aaron your brother, and his sons with him, from among the people of Israel, to serve me as priests* (italics added)—Aaron and Aaron's sons, Nadab and Abi'hu, Elea'zar and Ith'amar. And you shall make holy garments for Aaron your brother, for glory and for beauty. And you shall speak to all who have ability, whom I have endowed with an able mind, that they make Aaron's garments to consecrate him for my priesthood."

Leviticus 5:13 says, "Thus the **priest** shall make atonement for him for the sin which he has committed in any one of these things, and he shall be forgiven. And the remainder shall be for the **priest**, as in the cereal offering." Leviticus 6:7 states, "And the **priest** shall make atonement for him before the Lord, and he shall be forgiven for any of the things which one may do and thereby become guilty."

Hebrews 5:1–6 proclaims, "For every high priest chosen from among men is appointed to act on behalf of men in relation to God, to offer gifts and sacrifices for sins. He can deal gently with the ignorant and wayward, since he himself is beset with weakness. Because of this he is bound to offer sacrifice for his own sins as well as for those of the people. And one does not take the honor upon himself, but he is called by God, just as Aaron was. So also Christ did not exalt himself to be made a high priest, but was appointed by him who said to him, 'Thou art my Son, today I have begotten thee'; as he says also in another place, 'Thou art a priest for ever, after the order of Melchiz'edek.'"

"The Lord, having loved those who were his own, loved them to the end. Knowing that the hour had come to leave the world and return to the Father, in the course of a meal he washed their feet and gave them the commandment of love. In order to leave them a pledge of this love, in order never to depart from his own and to make them sharers in his Passover, he instituted the Eucharist as the memorial of this death and Resurrection, and commanded his apostles to celebrate it until his return; 'thereby he constituted them priests of the New Testament'" (CCC 1337).

But there is a more subtle reality in this necessary link of these two sacraments instituted by Christ. In order to make the Eucharist present to us and available to us, the priest actually becomes, for the instant of the transubstantiation, alter Christus, which is literally "another Christ." This is a miracle within the miracle of the Eucharist. And it is this reality that unbelievers simply do not comprehend. That we do is a great grace from God. Amen! Both the sacrament of ordination and the sacrament of the most Holy Eucharist were instituted at the same time, at the same place, and for the very same reasons—to make Christ's divine presence available to us, to lead us to him today and forever.

John 15:16 says, "You did not choose me, but I *chose you* [italics added] and appointed you that you should go and bear fruit and that your fruit should abide; so that whatever you ask the Father in my name, he may give it to you."

Here's what we learn from the above teachings:

1. It is God who chooses his priests, not, at first, the other way around.
2. The God who "cannot change" (Malachi 3:6), both Yahweh and then Jesus, chose to have priests take a role in the forgiveness of man's sins. This role, however, is dramatically different from the "sons of Aaron" and the priests of the new covenant, Catholic priests, who are now under grace (Romans 6:4), not only the law.

Before we enter into a discussion of these different yet same roles for God's priests, I'll take a detour and discuss the nature of sin itself. This seems to me necessary because sin is largely unrecognized, not understood, and even denied as a reality.

Heaven, hell, and purgatory all exist because of two factors: God's necessary justice and man's freedom to choose good or evil, spiritual life or death (Ecclesiastes 15:18). It is we who decide where we will spend eternity; God only affirms our personal life choices.

First John 1:8–10 states, "If we say we have no sin, we deceive ourselves, and the truth is not in us. If we confess our sins, he is faithful and just, and will forgive our sins and cleanse us from all unrighteousness. If we say we have not sinned, we make him a liar, and his word is not in us." First John 5:16–17 says, "If any one sees his brother committing what is not a mortal sin, he will ask, and God will give him life for those whose sin is not mortal. There is sin which is mortal; I do not say that one is to pray for that. All wrongdoing is sin, but there is sin which is not mortal."

To join the throngs of those claiming that sin simply does not exist is not only foolish; it's also illogical. Why do I say this? Jeremiah 31:33

states, "But this is the covenant which I will make with the house of Israel after those days, says the Lord: I will put my law within them, and I will write it upon their hearts; and I will be their God, and they shall be my people." Hebrews 10:16 declares, "This is the covenant that I will make with them after those days, says the Lord: I will put my laws on their hearts, and write them on their minds."

Whether we recognize God or not, the fact remains that he is the creator of the universe and all of those who inhabit the planet Earth. Truth can be denied, but that does not change its nature. I love what Pope Benedict XVI had to say about "truth": "There cannot be your truth and my truth, or there would be no truth." Certain truths are intrinsic to our very nature as human beings. There are things that everyone can and ought to know as both "good" and "bad." They may not clearly understand the nature of sin, but they just know within themselves that certain choices are better than others. For example, murder is an intrinsic evil, while love is an intrinsic good. And this need not be taught; its reality is simply known by all.

Sin necessarily falls into less and more serious and very broad categories or what we term "venial sins" and "mortal sins." Both are numerous and specifically uncountable. Venial sins will not directly send us to hell, while mortal sins, unconfessed and unforgiven through sacramental confession, will. Venial sins very often—whose actions and bad habits, if not corrected, can lead us and encourage us to sin mortally—ought not to be taken lightly.

Isaiah 43:7, 21 says, "Every one who is called by my name, whom I created for my glory, whom I formed and made. The people whom I formed for myself that they might declare my praise."

In the entire universe, only man has been gifted with these attributes: an intellect, a mind, and a free will, all of which are permanently attached to our souls. This, by the way, is how man emulates our God, which fulfills God's promise to make man "in his own image," which is found in Genesis 1:26–27.

Like God, this "spiritual other self" is immortal or cannot be killed, nor does it ever "die." And it is this "other self" that either suffers the pains of hell or enjoys the wonders of heaven in the presence of our God. Because man alone is enabled to know, love, and serve God, that then becomes the very reason for man's existence. And it becomes man's task to recognize sin, its effects, and its consequences, which only man can do.

Venial sins are often habitual, lessening their degree of culpability, but can weaken our will and lead us to mortal sin if left uncorrected. Please take them seriously; God does. Mortal sins or what the Bible refers to as "sin unto [spiritual] death" are so egregious as to actually sever our personal relationship bonds with Christ, until such time as they are sacramentally confessed and forgiven. I'm speaking here only of the norms of our Catholic faith.

Romans 6:16 states, "Know you not, that to whom you yield yourselves servants to obey, his servants you are whom you obey, whether it be of sin into death, or of obedience unto justice [salvation]."

Because of the high risk of hell capability of mortal sins, they are more difficult to commit. While venial sins can happen accidently, mortal sins have to, in a sense, be premeditated.

Three conditions must exist as the norm for an act to be a mortal sin:

1. It must be a serious matter.
2. One must know before choosing to commit the sin that what they are contemplating is a serious matter and going through with it will be a mortal sin.
3. One then desires to do it anyway. The act need not actually be committed; a sincere desire to commit it is sufficient grounds for it to be grievously or mortally sinful.

Just a bit ago, we addressed "intrinsic" good and "intrinsic" evils and gave the examples of murder and love. Flowing from this innate ability within every human being is the possibility for a mortal sin not meeting the above "normal requirements." Because everyone ought to know, for example, that premeditated murder is always evil, committing such a sin is always a mortal sin, even when one is unaware of the normal conditions for such a sin to exist. This brings up the next salient point: *God will because God must, in fairness and justice, judge each of us not on what we individually choose to believe but on what he has made possible for us to know.*

Sins, in a real sense, have their own "nature." By this, I mean that all sins affect others besides ourselves, creating what we might term a "public nature" for sins. For some sins, this is more evident than for others. Slander, for example, has a very public shadow, while lusting in one's heart for another spouse is less evident in casting a "public shadow." Recognized or not, visible or not, all sin does in some way—whether mysteriously or clearly—affect not only our own soul but also the church, the family of God, and perhaps your own family, neighbors, friends, and associates, by how sin's effects actually affect and change us internally. One might say that "there is no solely private sin."

I mention this as an introduction to a future lesson on purgatory, another subject seldom understood and one denied by Protestantism, whose man-invented ways to attain salvation are far more hopeful wishing than they are realities.

Let us now return to the difference in the Old and the New Testament priesthood, both chosen by God to have an active role in the forgiveness of man's many sins. This difference perhaps is best demonstrated by the Old Testament's consideration for equality being literally "an eye for an eye" mentality. Inflict nothing more, and accept nothing less. When "justice" is explained by Jesus, even the apostles are shocked.

Matthew 18:21–22 says, "Then Peter came up and said to him, 'Lord, how often shall my brother sin against me, and I forgive him? As many as seven times?' Jesus said to him, 'I do not say to you seven times, but seventy times seven.'" To add some perspective to this, numbers in the Bible, especially but not exclusively in the Old Testament, had their own meanings beyond that which is evident to us today. The number "seven," for example, meant full, complete, and perfected; so Peter thought that saying "seven times" would certainly be sufficient when compared to literally "getting even." But Jesus *shocks* them by saying, "Not seven but seventy times seven," meaning indefinitely or always.

That example does not relate directly to today's topic but does demonstrate the dramatic differences in God's expectations while his chosen people were under "the law" and the demonstrably different expectations that same God establishes now that we, the new "chosen people," are under his flow of grace (Romans 6:14–15).

In the Old Testament, God's priests essentially covered over their sins. It was God who directly forgave them. And his expectations were much lower than under the new covenant under grace. The Jewish nation had an annual day of atonement, where they went to the "wailing wall," confessed verbally their sins, repented, and sought God's mercy. Yom Kippur is still practiced today.

In the times that the Jewish nation was captive and outside of Jerusalem, there was a different procedure and different method that God found acceptable: Leviticus 16:20–24 says, "And when he has made an end of atoning for the holy place and the tent of meeting and the altar, he shall present the live goat; and Aaron shall lay both his hands upon the head of the live goat, and confess over him all the iniquities of the people of Israel, and all their transgressions, all their sins; and he shall put them upon the head of the goat, and send him away into the wilderness by the hand of a man who is in readiness. The goat shall bear all their iniquities upon him to a solitary land; and he shall let the goat go in the wilderness. Then Aaron shall come into the tent of meeting, and shall put off the linen garments which he put on when he went into the holy place, and shall leave them there; and he shall bathe his body in water in a holy place, and put on his garments, and come forth, and offer his burnt offering and the burnt offering of the people, and make atonement for himself and for the people."

This practice, I believe, led to the common expression "scapegoat." And because his people were under the law bereft of grace, God chose to accept this as sufficient for his forgiveness of their sins.

Now that we are under grace (Romans 6:14–15), God's expectations are much greater for each and all of us, and the powers entrusted with all the keys to heaven's singular *gate* (Matthew 16:18–19) have more authority and far greater responsibility.

Matthew 13:11–15 states, "And he answered them, 'To you it has been given to know the secrets of the kingdom of heaven, but to them it has not been given. For to him who has will more be given, and he will have abundance; but from him who has not, even what he has will be taken away. This is why I speak to them in parables, because seeing they do not see, and hearing they do not hear, nor do they understand. With them indeed is fulfilled the prophecy of Isaiah which says: "You shall indeed hear but never understand, and you shall indeed see but never perceive. For this people's heart has grown dull, and their ears are heavy of hearing, and their eyes they have closed, lest they should perceive with their eyes, and hear with their ears, and understand with their heart, and turn for me to heal them.""""

These last two verses (14 and 15) apply directly to Protestantism and their "quick fix" means and methods for sin forgiveness, which, while easier, are not biblical and certainly not God's method, which is clearly articulated in the Bible. It seems that they look for the Old Testament's God of mercy but overlook that we are living under a new covenant and under grace, and because God is giving us so much more (the seven sacraments), he must also expect obedience to his desires and his expressed manner to be known, practiced, and taught.

John 20:20–23 states, "When he had said this, he showed them his hands and his side. Then the disciples were glad when they saw the Lord. Jesus said to them again, 'Peace be with you. *As the Father has sent me, even so I send you.*' And when he had said this, he breathed on them, and said to them, '*Receive the Holy Spirit. If you forgive the sins of any, they are forgiven; if you retain the sins of any, they are retained*'" (italics added).

Matthew 10:1-7 says, "*And he called to him his twelve disciples and gave them authority over unclean spirits, to cast them out, and to heal every disease and every infirmity.* The names of the twelve apostles are these: first, Simon, who is called Peter, and Andrew his brother; James the son of Zeb'edee, and John his brother; Philip and Bartholomew; Thomas and Matthew the tax collector; James the son of Alphaeus, and Thaddaeus; Simon the Cananaean, and Judas Iscariot, who betrayed him. *These twelve Jesus sent out*, charging them, 'Go nowhere among the Gentiles, and enter no town of the Samaritans, but go rather to the lost sheep of the house of Israel. And preach as you go, saying, "The kingdom of heaven is at hand"'" (italics added).

John 10:1–8 declares, "'Truly, truly, I say to you, he who does not enter the sheepfold by the door [singular] but climbs in by another way, that man is a thief and a robber; but he who enters by the door is the shepherd of the sheep. To him the gatekeeper opens; the sheep hear his voice, and he calls his own sheep by name and leads them out. When he has brought out all his own, he goes before them, and the sheep follow him, for they know his voice. A stranger they will not follow, but they will flee from him, for they do not know the voice of strangers.' This figure Jesus used with them, but they did not understand what he was saying to them. So Jesus again said to them, 'Truly, truly, I say to you, *I am the door of the sheep* [italics mine]. All who came before me are thieves and robbers; but the sheep did not heed them.'"

This teaching from John chapter 10 above is an affirmation by Jesus that he expects all Christians to actually know and obey his teachings and not usurp his authority or to invent alternate ways to compete with his already chosen and established instructions. This, in turn, requires teachers who are empowered by God to perform this task fully, clearly guided by the Holy Spirit. It is biblical and notable that today's Catholic Church alone has this mandate: Matthew 28:18–20 states, "And Jesus came and said to them, 'All authority in heaven and on earth has been given to me. Go [you] therefore and make disciples of all nations, baptizing them in the name of the Father and of the Son and of the Holy Spirit, teaching them to observe all that I have commanded *you*; and lo, I am with *you* always, to the close of the age'" (italics added).

Now back to today's Catholic priesthood. Today's Catholic priests, in apostolic tradition, are empowered by Christ to actually forgive man's sins and, even more sublime, to also make Jesus actually and really present to us in Catholic Holy Communion. They, in a theological sense, become "alter Christus" (another Christ). And Jesus has committed himself as the personal warranty of this truth: John 17:18–19 says, "As thou didst send me into the world, so I have sent them into the world. And for their sake I consecrate myself, that they also may be consecrated in truth." No other faith or church can make this claim and support it factually. *"And he called to him his twelve disciples and gave them authority over unclean spirits*, to cast them out, and to heal every disease and every infirmity. 'Peace be with you. *As the Father has sent me, even so I send you.'* And when he had said this, he breathed on them, and said to them, *'Receive the Holy Spirit. If you forgive the sins of any, they are forgiven; if you retain the sins of any, they are retained'"* (italics added).

Here is why: Christ knew, before choosing Peter and appointing him as the head of his new faith and church, that he would soon give his life for us (Matthew 17:22–23). Because it is Christ expressly or implicitly who gives us his seven sacraments, which necessitate enormous powers and authority, he literally had to (in divine justice) entrust Peter, the apostles, and through them the absolutely necessary successors (compare Matthew 10:1–8 with Matthew 28:18–20) the sufficient gifts, powers, and authority to fulfill his final command to them to *go* and teach the entire world what he has taught to them (Matthew 28:16–20). Amen!

Catholic sacramental confession is God's chosen method for sin forgiveness and ought to be understood as the "norm" for sin forgiveness. Jesus chose to do this for several critically important reasons:

1. The one professing their sins can know, with absolute certitude, that their sins have been forgiven and can have complete peace of mind. Jesus says, "My peace I give to you. Your sins have been forgiven; go and sin no more."

2. Having to confess one's sins to a priest (either behind a veil or face to face, your choice) is difficult and embarrassing; this very

fact is intended to work as a deterrent and an inhibitor to lessen future sins (John 14:29, John 5:14).

3. Sacramental confession, truly known sin forgiveness, is a gift from God that grants us peace of mind, heart, and soul. Thank you, Jesus!

Catholics and Purgatory: Fact or Fiction?

Let's begin this lesson by asking a question: why purgatory, assuming it even exists? And here is the answer in a single word: "love."

God's love for his "mirror image" humanity (Genesis 1:26–27) exceeds our ability to comprehend it. I mean, can we really understand God in choosing to become a mortal human, being like us in every way but sin (Hebrews 4:15)? To make a comparison, it will be far worse than taking Einstein's mind, intellect, and free will and putting them inside a common earthworm—all that talent and ability and no way to use or express it.

Then even should we be able to comprehend this mystery, the plot thickens. Our God, Jesus, then decided that even the incarnation is not enough (John 19:28), so he willed to suffer his passion and then even gave his mortal life so that we now might be saved and be forgiven (Matthew 20:18–19). The debt of Adam and Eve's "original sin" is paid in full through Christian baptism, although its other imposed penalties will exist until the "End Times," thus permitting humanity to prove and demonstrate their love of God.

Whipped nearly to death, crowned with thorns, and then nailed to a cross all out of love for mankind—this is God whom we're talking about, the very same God who created the entire universe, the very same God who keeps me and you alive. Wow!

In an absolute sense, neither God's divine sense of right and wrong nor his need and want required him to create purgatory. Heaven and hell, yes; purgatory, no. Permit me to explain this further. When God chose to create man, something that he did not absolutely have to do because God is perfect and can neither be more nor less perfected, God desired to be recognized for who he was, for who he is. And man, this "mirror image" of himself, was created to freely choose to fulfill and complete this "want" of God.

Isaiah 43:7, 21 states, "Every one who is called by my name, whom I created for my glory, whom I formed and made. The people whom I formed for myself that they might declare my praise."

Here is a telling but brief description of our God: "God is every good thing perfected." Every word used in this brief but accurate description of our God is a part of the "telling" of who and what God is.

"God." Exodus 3:14 says, "God said to Moses, 'I am who I am.' And he said, 'Say this to the people of Israel, "I am has sent me to you."'" Revelation 1:8 states, "'I am the Alpha and the Omega,' says the Lord God, who is and who was and who is to come, the Almighty." Our God is the first and the last; nothing would or can exist without him, not one thing.

"Is." Everything ties back into God.

"Every." Without God, there would be nothing at all in "existence"—past, present, or future.

"Good thing." Not only is God "good" but good and goodness also exist because of him and to honor him.

"Perfected." This, dear friends, is the critical point of this lesson. Because God gives to us "perfect love," as he can do nothing less, God then desires this same degree of love to be returned to him.

In the entire universe, only one thing, only humanity has the ability to give to God that which God sought: to be known and loved. Only man is gifted with a mind, intellect, and free will. Each of these spiritual realities "mirror" God, our creator, who too is spirit and truth (John 4:23–24). Just as God shared small portions of his power and authority with the apostles (Matthew 10:1–6), God shares these godly attributes with humanity and with an expectation (but not a command) that they be used to love, worship, honor, and glorify him. God insist that these be freely given, not forced.

In order for "love" to "be perfected," it must be freely given. And this reality explains both the creation of humanity and the existence of our "spiritual other self." These attributes of mind, intellect, and free will are a part of and inseparable from our souls and are given to us in the hope that we will use them to love and glorify God.

Man was created out of the dust of the earth and, upon death, returns to dust: Genesis 3:19 says, "In the sweat of your face you shall eat bread till you return to the ground, for out of it you were taken; you are dust, and to dust you shall return." If you have never considered this, it may be a bit of a surprise to discover that when the Bible speaks of meeting Jesus "face to face," it means intuitively, as our bodies are returned to the dust from which we came. I'm speaking here before the promised "End Times of the world." First Corinthians 13:12 states, "For now we see in a mirror dimly, but then face to face. Now I know in part; then I shall understand fully, even as I have been fully understood."

So how does all of this relate to purgatory? That, dear friend, is a great question. God, in fulfilling his need for divine justice and fairness and having given man the necessary attributes to recognize both good and evil to enable them to freely choose whichever had greater appeal to them, had only to create heaven and hell to meet the needs of divine justice. Sirach 15:17 declares, "Before a man are *life and death* [italics mine], and whichever he chooses will be given to him."

So why then did God choose to create purgatory, and why is it not in the Bible? God created purgatory out of his love for man, who alone can love him in return. God's love for humanity includes each and every one of us. First Timothy 2:4 says, "Who desires all men to be saved and to come to the knowledge of the truth [singular per defined issue]."

One of the hidden or seemingly less known teachings of our Catholic faith is the realization that because God is "perfect," so too must the state and the condition of our souls be either perfect or perfected at the time of our death in order for us to access heaven.

Matthew 5:48 says, "You, therefore, must be perfect, as your heavenly Father is perfect." Ephesians 1:4 states, "Even as he chose us in him before the foundation of the world, that we should be holy and blameless before him."

Man dies in one of the following possible conditions:

1. With a perfect soul: this soul proceeds immediately to heaven (the minority).
2. With an imperfect soul (no mortal sins but because of the temporal punishment owing to our sins): this soul, if only heaven and hell existed, couldn't access heaven.
3. With a lost soul (unconfessed and unforgiven sin): it is we who choose our eternity, not God. God only affirms our life choices.

It is category number two that concerns and explains the existence of purgatory. Our God is a god of love and mercy; indeed, these attributes are stronger than his divine justice, stronger but not strong enough to override or replace it. So without purgatory, untold numbers of souls will be unable to attain heaven as they die worthy neither of hell nor of heaven, as heaven only accepts perfected souls because God himself is perfect and can accept nothing less.

Any soul that dies without unconfessed and unforgiven mortal sin is imperfect yet not to a degree worthy of eternal damnation. It is this majority group that Christ chooses most ardently to be included among the saved souls who can attain heaven if and when they become perfected. Purgatory then is, to be graphic, to be seen as a "soul wash," a place and manner to be over time for imperfect souls to be perfected. Souls in purgatory are all heaven bound but only after the detour of purgatory perfecting their souls.

What we have to know about sin

All sins have a hidden "public nature" called the "temporal punishment" because all sins affect others besides the sinner. For some sins such as adultery or abortion, the "others" are evident. For more private sins like jealously or envy, not so much. Yet each and every sin affects God's church, those around us, and our very souls. And every sin, large and small, accrues a debt that must be repaid in order to perfect our souls.

Even when a sin is sacramentally confessed and forgiven, this latent debt or *temporal punishment* for committed sins exists on God's "balance sheet" (the book of life; Revelation 20:15). And God is his own comptroller. Only God knows the extent of our hidden sins' debt, only God knows what and how much payment has been made toward paying off this debt, and only God knows when in divine justice that debt is paid in full.

While we are still on planet Earth, the God-approved church permits us to make partial and even full repayment through prayer, works of charity, and indulgences, which take two forms: partial and full, also called plenary indulgences. Each offered indulgence has its own conditions, which must be fully satisfied to gain their benefit.

More information on this can be found at https://www.ewtn.com/Devotionals/mercy/general_conditions.htm.

The sad reality is that a great many people either are unaware of the "temporal punishment because of all of our sins" or perhaps unaware of how urgent is the need to do what we can while we can. A great many souls of good and faithful servants die with less-than-perfect souls. So purgatory is an unmerited second chance for these souls to still attain heaven after being purged. Souls for the dead can be prayed for by those left on earth, and masses can be offered for their intent.

OK, *but* is it biblical? Have you ever attempted to find the terms mass, confession, Holy Communion, pope, catechism, Catholic or Protestant, or even Bible itself in the Bible? None of them are in there. Yet all of them are realities. John's Gospel ends the final two chapters (20:31–33, 21:24–25) by specifically teaching us that "not everything is in the Bible."

John 20:30–31 says, "Now Jesus did many other signs in the presence of the disciples, which are not written in this book; but these are written that you may believe that Jesus is the Christ, the Son of God, and that believing you may have life in his name." John 21:24–25 declares, "This is the disciple who is bearing witness to these things, and who has written these things; and we know that his testimony is true. But there are also many other things which Jesus did; were every one of them to be written, I suppose that the world itself could not contain the books that would be written."

So we ought not to expect to find every belief and every teaching in the Bible. That said, purgatory is spoken about in the Bible; the term "purgatory" is one of many theological terms. Revelation 21:27 says, "But nothing unclean shall enter it, nor any one who practices abomination or falsehood, but only those who are written in the Lamb's book of life." Matthew 5:26 states, "Truly, I say to you, you will never get out till you have paid the last penny." Matthew 5:48 says, "You, therefore, must be perfect, as your heavenly Father is perfect." Hebrews 2:10 declares, "For it was fitting that he, for whom and by whom all things exist, in bringing many sons to glory, should make the pioneer of their salvation perfect through suffering." First John 3:2–3 proclaims, "Beloved, we are God's children now; it does not yet appear what we shall be, but we know that when he appears we shall be like him, for we shall see him as he is. And every one who thus hopes in him purifies himself as he is pure." And 1 Corinthians 3:13–15 states, "Each man's work will become manifest; for the Day will disclose it, because it will be revealed with fire, and the fire will test what sort of work each one has done. If the work which any man has built on the foundation survives, he will receive a reward. If any man's work is burned up, he will suffer loss [purgatory], though he himself will be saved, but only as through fire."

It is my prayerful hope, dear friends, that this explains sufficiently, for you, this important doctrine of our Catholic Church.

CHAPTER ELEVEN

Holy Mary, Mother of God

Thus hath the Lord dealt with me in the days wherein he hath had regard to take away my reproach among men. And in the sixth month, the angel Gabriel was sent from God into a city of Galilee, called Nazareth, To a virgin espoused to a man whose name was Joseph, of the house of David; and the virgin's name was Mary. And the angel being come in, said unto her: "Hail, full of grace, the Lord is with thee: blessed art thou among women." *Who having heard, was troubled at his saying, and thought with herself what manner of salutation this should be. And the angel said to her: Fear not, Mary, for thou hast found grace with God. Behold thou shalt conceive in thy womb, and shalt bring forth a son; and thou shalt call his name Jesus. He shall be great, and shall be called the Son of the most High; and the Lord God shall give unto him the throne of David his father; and he shall reign in the house of Jacob for ever. And of his kingdom there shall be no end. And Mary said to the angel: How shall this be done, because I know not man? And the angel answering, said to her:* The Holy Ghost shall come upon thee, and the power of the most High shall overshadow thee. And therefore also the Holy **one which shall be born of thee shall be called the Son of God.**

—Luke 1:25–35; emphasis added

Mary and Our Catholic Faith

"Pat, I have enjoyed your e-mails. They are very informative and have been helpful. While I have come to the conclusion that the Catholic Church is indeed the church of Jesus Christ, I feel that there are teachings that just aren't square with sacred scripture, and I can't in good conscience set them aside. [1] Mary. This is one we've talked about, but I can't see her being anything but Jesus' Mom. I don't believe [2] her "immaculate conception" [3] or that she didn't have other children. [4] Is she blessed among women? Yes. [5] Does she deserve glorification or prayers? No."

We'll address the points as I have numbered them.

"I can't see her being anything but Jesus's mom."

Luke 1:26–31, 34–35 says, "In the sixth month the angel Gabriel was sent from God to a city of Galilee named Nazareth, to a virgin betrothed to a man whose name was Joseph, of the house of David; and the virgin's name was Mary. And he came to her and said, *'Hail, full of grace, the Lord is with you!'* But she was greatly troubled at the saying, and considered in her mind what sort of greeting this might be. And the angel said to her, 'Do not be afraid, Mary, *for you have found favor with God.* And behold, you will conceive in your womb and bear a son, and you shall call his name Jesus. And Mary said to the angel, 'How shall this be, since I have no husband' And the angel said to her, 'The Holy Spirit will come upon you, and the power of the Most High will overshadow you; *therefore the child to be born will be called holy, the Son of God'"* (italics added).

God was under no obligation to become "incarnate man." However, once that decision had been reached, God then had to choose just one woman out of literally billions of choices. Never before and never again would one woman be selected to become the literal mother of God.

And Mary was to become not only the "mother of God"; when Christ was crucified, shortly before dying for us, Jesus shouted, "I thirst!" proclaiming his desire to do even more than die for us. This "more" was twofold: his church and all that it encompasses and his mother, whom Jesus chose to share with humanity because no one else could do more on behalf of Jesus than Mary can, directing souls to her son. John 19:25–27 says, "So the soldiers did this. But standing by the cross of Jesus were his mother, and his mother's sister, Mary the wife of Clopas, and Mary Mag'dalene. *When Jesus saw his mother, and the disciple whom he loved standing near, he said to his mother, 'Woman, behold, your son!'* Then he said *to the disciple, 'Behold, your mother!'* And from that hour the disciple took her to his own home."

Careful note is to be taken of the very precise words that Jesus chose while in the shadow of his death. Jesus is addressing his mother, yet Jesus refers to her as "woman," the term for the world's female gender. The apostle John is identified as "the disciple," meaning by gender all of humanity's "men." As if this is not clear enough, it's as if Jesus is saying, "OK, take Mary, your mother, to be the 'mother of humanity.'" And that, dear friend, is wow!

"I don't believe her 'immaculate conception.'"

Why do you suppose that practice of one's religious beliefs is termed "faith"? It is because every "faith" has, to a varying degree, mysteries attached to it. Even the Jehovah's Witnesses, a cult whose beliefs are all logical, at least to them, have the mystery of their founder having godly visions.

We are not meant to comprehend fully all that God allows us to know, for the simple fact that not being able to fully discern this or that builds reliance upon our God. And that, my friend, is as it ought to be.

Unbelieving is a weakness of one's faith. It is telling God, "God, I don't believe that you actually can do that." And God can, as we ought to know, do any "good thing." I wonder perhaps if you might not have an incorrect understanding of what exactly the term "immaculate conception" actually means.

IMMACULATE CONCEPTION. Title of the Blessed Virgin as sinless from her first moment of existence. In the words of Pope Pius IX's solemn definition, made in 1854, "The most holy Virgin Mary was, in the first moment of her conception, *by a unique gift of grace and privilege of almighty God, in view of the merits of Jesus Christ the Redeemer of mankind, preserved free from all stain of original sin* [italics added]." This means that since the first moment of her human existence the mother of Jesus was preserved from the common defect of estrangement from God, which humanity in general inherits through the sin of Adam. Her freedom from sin was an unmerited gift of God or special *grace*, and an exception to the law, or *privilege*, which no other created person has received.

Neither the Greek nor Latin Fathers explicitly taught the Immaculate Conception, but they professed it implicitly in two fundamental ways. Mary, they said, was most perfect in purity of morals and holiness of life. St. Ephrem (c. 306–73) addressed Christ and Mary with the words "You and Your mother are the only ones who are totally beautiful in every way. For in You, O Lord, there is no stain, and in Your mother no stain." Mary was described as the antithesis of Eve. Again in Ephrem, "Mary and Eve [were] two people without guilt. Later one became the cause of our death, the other cause of our life." While implicit in the early writers, the Immaculate Conception had to be clarified before becoming explicit dogma. Main credit for this goes to the Franciscan John Duns Scotus (c. 1264–1308), who introduced the idea of pre-redemption in order to reconcile Mary's freedom from original sin with her conception before the coming of Christ. (*Fr. John A. Hardon's Catholic Dictionary*)

"I don't believe that she didn't have other children."

It is the teaching of the Roman Catholic Church that the term "brothers" refers not in the sense that we today understand and accept it as to only mean "blood brothers or sisters"; rather, it applied to cousins, close friends, and the like.

Luke 8:19–2q says, "Then his mother and his brothers came to him, but they could not reach him for the crowd. And he was told, 'Your mother and your brothers are standing outside, desiring to see you.' But he said to them, 'My mother and my brothers are those who hear the word of God and do it.'" Here, I and Jesus use the term generically, meaning all of humanity.

Acts 1:14 states, "All these with one accord devoted themselves to prayer, together with the women and Mary the mother of Jesus, and with his brothers." Here, the term applies to both the apostles and the disciples of Jesus.

First Corinthians 9:5 says, "Do we not have the right to be accompanied by a wife, as the other apostles and the brothers of the Lord and Cephas?" Here, the term applies to the disciples of Jesus.

First Timothy 5:1 declares, "Do not rebuke an older man but exhort him as you would a father; treat younger men like brothers." Once again, we see the term "brother" applied generically as to mean "all men."

The first recorded argument was between St. Jerome [who gave us the first Bible in the then-common language of Latin] and another fourth-century theologian, Helvidius, who had written that after the virgin birth of Jesus, Mary had other children with her husband, Joseph. St. Jerome disagreed, indicating that by the fourth century at least some of the church community believed that Mary had stayed a virgin for the rest of her life. These children of Mary, Jerome said, were from Mary of Clopas, Jesus' aunt and his mother's sister, making them cousins. He claimed that the Greek word *adelphios* could refer to cousins, not just biological siblings.

Epiphanius, bishop of Salamis and a contemporary of Jerome and Helvidius, threw another possibility into the hat. He argued that the siblings weren't cousins, but Joseph's children from a previous marriage, making them the step-siblings of Jesus. Joseph isn't mentioned outside of the birth of Jesus, causing some to believe that he was much older than Mary and died before Jesus' public ministry. It is conjecture, but some apocryphal works, such as the Protoevangelium of James, the Gospel of Peter, and the Infancy Gospel of Thomas, all seem to indicate a tradition of belief that Jesus' brothers and sisters were the children of Joseph. (U.S. Catholic)

"Is she blessed among women? Yes."

On this point, we agree.

"Does she deserve glorification or prayers? No."

Mary, the mother of God, is truly "the great intercessor." Evidence of this abounds in the miracles surrounding Mary's apparitions. Lourdes and Fatima come to mind. Multiple miraculous healings are recorded at both locations. In Fatima, see http://www.marypages.com/fatimaEng1. htm. In Lourdes, see http://www.catholicpilgrims.com/lourdes/ bd_lourdes_apparitions.htm.

Once again quoting *Father Hardon's Catholic Dictionary,*

APPARITION. Supernatural vision. It is a psychical experience in which a person or object not accessible to normal human powers is seen and ordinarily also heard. When apparitions are claimed, the Church's policy is to require proof of the fact, since illusions and hallucinations are so common, and the influence of the evil spirit is also to be taken into account. Yet from the Scriptures on there have been numerous, well-attested apparitions that were certainly of divine origin.

A common but understandable, perhaps, misconception of Mary and Catholics' relationship to her is that we Catholics "worship Mary," which, were it true, would constitute a form of idolatry. But that, dear friend, is not what we Catholics do. The term "worship" in the practice of the Catholic faith is reserved to and for God alone.

"You shall worship the Lord your God" (CCC 2135). Words like "honor," "venerate," "reverence," "respect," even "love" can apply to Mary; but the term "worship" is for God alone.

Evidence of this Catholic practice is biblically supported in two distinct ways. The charge that Catholics are "idolaters" is explained away in the following manner: God himself, on two separate occasions, "commanded" Moses to build for him, that is, for God, idols.

Exodus 25:18, 20 says, "And you shall make two cherubim [angels] of gold; of hammered work shall you make them, on the two ends of the mercy seat. The cherubim shall spread out their wings above, overshadowing the mercy seat with their wings, their faces one to another; toward the mercy seat shall the faces of the cherubim be." Numbers 21:8–9 states, "And the Lord said to Moses, 'Make a fiery serpent, and set it on a pole; and every one who is bitten, when he sees it, shall live.' So Moses made a bronze serpent, and set it on a pole; and if a serpent bit any man, he would look at the bronze serpent and live."

So obviously, if God commands Moses to build for him idols, there must be another discerning factor. That factor is the end use of the "idol." As shown above, the idols built by God were directly and indirectly to give recognition and honor to God, respectively. That is exactly what Mary does.

By a wide margin, the most common "Mary prayer" is the Hail Mary, which is solidly biblical:

Hail Mary [Luke 1:28], full of grace [Luke 1:28], the Lord is with you [Luke 1:27]. Blessed are you among all women [Luke 1:42], and blessed is the fruit of your womb, Jesus [Luke 1:42]. Holy Mary [Luke 1:28], mother of God [Luke 1:35], pray for us sinners [our Catholic petition], now and at the hour of our death. Amen [I believe].

Catholic beliefs concerning Mary would be better served if, instead of proclaiming praying "to" Mary (which is a fact), we were to proclaim that Catholics pray "through" Mary to God (which is a far clearer fact of the same truth). All prayers have God as their end.

Why do Catholics even bother to pray through Mary or the saints?

We do this because it benefits us. Mary and the declared saints are in the very spot we endeavor to be: in the divine presence. The "communion of saints"—which is made up of the saints in heaven, the souls in purgatory, and the pilgrim souls on earth—makes up a sort of "family." And family members help other family members. And that is what Mary and the saints do for us. They take our prayers and petitions, add their own on top of them, and then present them to God on our account. And in doing so, it increases the efficacy of merit of them.

Mary is honored not for who she is but rather for what she is, what she suffered in unity with her son Jesus, and especially what she modeled perfectly for us to emulate. Mary is the most fertile seed in the most fertile ground. Mark 4:3–9 says, "'Listen! A sower went out to sow. And as he sowed, some seed fell along the path, and the birds came and devoured it. Other seed fell on rocky ground, where it had not much soil, and immediately it sprang up, since it had no depth of soil; and when the sun rose it was scorched, and since it had no root it withered away. Other seed fell among thorns and the thorns grew up and choked it, and it yielded no grain. And other seeds [like Mary] fell into good soil and brought forth grain, growing up and increasing and yielding thirtyfold and sixtyfold and a hundredfold.' ***And he said,*** 'He who has ears to hear, let him hear.'"

Mary is the "mediatrix of all graces" and "the dispenser of grace," not the creator of grace, not even the one who determines who is to be offered grace, who aids, directs, and assists us in doing God's will. Matthew 5:48 says, "You, therefore, must be perfect, as your heavenly Father is perfect."

Mary, better and more effectively than any other saint, is located closer to the throne of her son, Jesus, and has better access to him than anyone else. We simply undervalue the bond that unites this mother and Jesus, her son.

What we Catholics hold as truth about Mary is that (1) she is "ever virgin" and that (2) she was assumed, body and soul, into heaven. The key word here is "assumed," which is God's doing, not Mary's. These are graces and gifts from a loving son. Further, we believe that God chose to permit Mary to cooperate continually in humanity's salvation by being *his* dispenser of *all* graces and the example for us par excellence. For the benefit of those who might wish to see what we actually teach, here are some selected teachings of the *CCC* (*Catechism of the Catholic Church*) on Mary.

148 The Virgin Mary most perfectly embodies the obedience of faith. By faith Mary welcomes the tidings and promise brought by the angel Gabriel, believing that "with God nothing will be impossible" and so giving her assent: "Behold I am the handmaid of the Lord; let it be [done] to me according to your word." Elizabeth greeted her: "Blessed is she who believed that there would be a fulfillment of what was spoken to her from the Lord." It is for this faith that all generations have called Mary blessed.

490 To become the mother of the Savior, Mary "was enriched by God with gifts appropriate to such a role." The angel Gabriel at the moment of the annunciation salutes her as "full of grace." In fact, in order for Mary to be able to give the free assent of her faith to the announcement of her vocation, it was necessary that she be wholly borne by God's grace.

506 Mary is a virgin because her virginity is *the sign of her faith* "unadulterated by any doubt," and of her undivided gift of herself to God's will. It is her faith that enables her to become the mother of the Savior: "Mary is more blessed because she embraces faith in Christ than because she conceives the flesh of Christ."

510 Mary "remained a virgin in conceiving her Son, a virgin in giving birth to him, a virgin in carrying him, a virgin in nursing him at her breast, always a virgin."

964 Mary's role in the Church is inseparable from her union with Christ and flows directly from it. "This union of the mother with the Son in the work of salvation is made manifest from the time of Christ's virginal conception up to his death"; it is made manifest above all at the hour of his Passion:

Thus the Blessed Virgin advanced in her pilgrimage of faith, and faithfully persevered in her union with her Son unto the cross. There she stood, in keeping with the divine plan, enduring with her only begotten Son the intensity of his suffering, joining herself with his sacrifice in her mother's heart, and lovingly consenting to the immolation of this victim, born of her: to be given, by the same Christ Jesus dying on the cross, as a mother to his disciple, with these words: "Woman, behold your son."

The book *The Deceiver* by Fr. Livio Fanzaga read as follows:

We should keep very much in mind an essential and irremovable aspect of the work of redemption completed by Christ, that it is realized with the intimate, constant, and fundamental collaboration of the Virgin Mary. Divine Wisdom has decided the woman [Mary], the new Eve, should be placed side by side with the new Adam [Christ] in the struggle against Satan for the liberation of humanity. As Christ is the Redeemer so Mary is the "co-redeemer" [through the merits of Jesus]. From the moment of the Incarnation until Christ's death on the Cross, the Mother is beside the Son and shares each moment of the deadly conflict . . . It is affirmed and it is true: It will not be the woman who crushes the head of the serpent, but Her Seed [Jesus].

Saint Pope John Paul II in *Ecclesia de Eucharistic* (54–55) says the following:

If the Eucharist is the Mystery of [our Catholic] faith which so greatly transcends our understanding as to call for sheer abandonment to the word of God, then there can be no one like Mary to act as our support and guide in acquiring this disposition . . . At the Annunciation Mary conceived the Son of God in the physical reality of His Body and Blood, thus anticipating within herself what to some degree happens sacramentally in every believer who receives, under the signs of bread and wine, the Lord's body and blood. As a result, there is a profound analogy between the fiat, which Mary said in reply to the angel, and the amen which every believer says when receiving the body of our Lord . . . In continuity with the Virgin's faith, in the Eucharistic mystery we are asked to believe that the same

Jesus Christ, Son of God and Son of Mary, becomes present in his full humanity and divinity under the signs of bread and wine.

"May the name of Mary be ever on our lips; remembrance of her ever in our hearts" (Fr. John A. Hardon, *Catholic Prayer Book*, "The Fourth Station").

CHAPTER TWELVE

The Four Last Things

Watch ye therefore, because you know not the day nor the hour.
— Matthew 25:13

I call heaven and earth to witness against you this day, that I have set before you is life *and* death, *a blessing and curse; therefore choose life, that you and your descendants may live.*
— Deuteronomy 30:19; emphasis added

The Four Last Things: Death, Judgment, Heaven, and Hell

And I will strike her children dead. And all the churches shall know that I am he who searches mind and heart, and I will give to each of you as your works deserve.

—Revelation 2:23

We are formed in the image of our God. Genesis 1:26–27 says, "Then God said, 'Let us make man in our image, after our likeness; and let them have dominion over the fish of the sea, and over the birds of the air, and over the cattle, and over all the earth, and over every creeping thing that creeps upon the earth.' So God created man in his own image, in the image of God he created him; male and female he created them." Have you ever pondered just how this might be possible? After all, man being "like God" is quite a stretch. Or is it?

John 4:23–24 tells us the secret. "But the hour is coming, and now is, when the true worshipers will worship the Father in spirit and truth, for such the Father seeks to worship him. *God is spirit* [italics added], and those who worship him must worship in spirit and truth."

If, as the Bible says, "man is made of dust, and to dust he shall return," what's left of us for either eternal heaven or eternal hell? In order for man to know God and to choose for ourselves either heaven or hell, certain attributes are necessary, godlike attributes. And rest assured, this is our choice, not God's, who would have everyone saved (1 Timothy 2:4).

In the entire universe, God chose only one thing that could and therefore would incur the moral obligation to love or hate him. That one thing is humanity, created in the very image of our God. God blesses every human soul with a mind (not speaking here of our brain), an intellect (not meaning one's IQ), and a free will, all of which are attachments to our immortal souls. Each of these attributes, like God himself, is spirit (John 4:23–24) and eternal. And like our God, they cannot be killed and do not die. I call this our "other self," and it is this "other self" that faces eternal heaven or eternal hell and that emulates our God, until the final judgment, when our then glorified and perfected bodies will be reunited with our immortal souls.

Death

Genesis 2:7 says, "Then the Lord God formed man of dust from the ground, and breathed into his nostrils the breath of life; and man became a living being." Genesis 3:19 states, "In the sweat of your face you shall eat bread till you return to the ground, for out of it you were taken; you are dust, and to dust you shall return."

Death can be defined as "the absence of life." However, such a definition falls short of the magnificent glory of humanity. It defines correctly man's brief stay on earth but misses man's purpose to exist, which is "to take the God test." We exist with the ability to know God, if no other way than through the majestic and enormous universe that God has placed us in, which exists for the possibility of anyone paying attention to make the evidence of God obvious.

Once having identified a source, a power so far surpassing our own limitations and understanding, we are then obligated to seek that source, that power, and identify it. Because God has written many of his laws on our minds and hearts, man is able, if he chooses and cooperates, to discover God. Jeremiah 31:33 says, "This is the covenant which I will make with the house of Israel after those days, says the Lord: I will put my law within them, and I will write it upon their hearts; and I will be their God, and they shall be my people." Hebrews 10:16 states, "This is the covenant that I will make with them after those days, says the Lord: I will put my laws on their hearts, and write them on their minds."

This discovery of God's truths, always singular per defined issue, must be enlightened by God's "free gift" of grace, which alone can led one to his true faith. Ephesians 2:8 says, "For by grace you have been saved through faith; and this is not your own doing, it is the gift of God." Grace depends on the divine will. Matthew 7:7 states, "Ask, and it will be given you; seek, and you will find; knock, and it will be opened to you." We can be assured that they who seek and those who knock will be heard.

Our God is a god of intentionally simplistic choices. In the Old Testament, he allowed only one chosen people, one set of faith beliefs, and one God. In the New Testament, the only change he made is to terminology; "chosen people" became "my church" (singular). Matthew 16:18 declares, "And I tell you, you are Peter, and on this rock I will build my church, and the powers of death shall not prevail against it."

Our God, who can be briefly described as "all good things perfected," obligates himself to "offer" every soul sufficient grace so that they might know him. But this is just an offer, not a command. God does not force anyone to love him. Such would violate the very gifts or the "spiritual attributes" God grants every soul, specifically that man might find and love him. And, dear friends, it is on the basis of grace offered and received or rejected that the eternity of our souls rest. We, not God, choose for ourselves heaven or hell, and God only affirms our life choices:

Judgment

Revelation 2:23 states, "And I will strike her children dead. And all the churches shall know that I am he who searches mind and heart, and I will give to each of you as your works deserve."

Hebrews 6:10 says, "For God is not so unjust as to overlook your work and the love which you showed for his sake in serving the saints, as you still do."

First Peter 1:17 declares, "And if you invoke as Father him who judges each one impartially according to his deeds, conduct yourselves with fear throughout the time of your exile."

Matthew 19:17 states, "And he said to him, 'Why do you ask me about what is good? One there is who is good. If you would enter life, keep the commandments.'"

Man's eternal destination is not a predestination that God makes for us; no, this we decide for ourselves.

What, I believe, is largely beyond our ability to fully comprehend is the fact that God in passing judgment considers every act, every thought, every sin—both of commission and omission—every good work, and even our good and evil intentions. He also factors in grace offered and accepted and grace offered and rejected in arriving at an objectively fair disposition of our eternal souls from the time of our "age of reason" (estimated to be around seven years of age) until the moment of our death.

James 2:15–17 says, "If a brother or sister is ill-clad and in lack of daily food, and one of you says to them, 'Go in peace, be warmed and filled,' without giving them the things needed for the body, what does it profit? So faith by itself, if it has no works, is dead." ***Acts of charity will cover many sins.***

Isaiah 55:6–10 states, "Seek the Lord while he may be found, call upon him while he is near; let the wicked forsake his way, and the unrighteous man his thoughts; let him return to the Lord, that he may have mercy on him, and to our God, for he will abundantly pardon. For my thoughts are not your thoughts, neither are your ways my ways, says the Lord. For as the heavens are higher than the earth, so are my ways higher than your ways and my thoughts than your thoughts. For as the rain and the snow come down from heaven, and return not thither but water the earth, making it bring forth and sprout, giving seed to the sower and bread to the eater."

So long as we have breath in our bodies and control of our minds, there is time to save our souls from hell. No sin is unforgiveable except for intentional denial of God himself. *Repent and convert; today is the day.*

Heaven

The place and condition of perfect supernatural happiness. This happiness consists essentially in the immediate vision and love of God, and secondarily in the knowledge, love, and enjoyment of creatures. Until the final resurrection, except for Christ and his Mother, only the souls of the just are in heaven. After the last day, the just will be in heaven in body and soul. Although the same God will be seen by all and enjoyed by all, not everyone will have the same degree of happiness. The depth of beatitude will depend on the measure of God's grace with which a person dies, and this in turn will be greatly conditioned by the merits that one earns during life on earth. Heaven is eternal because it will never cease. It is continuous because its joys never stop. It is communal because the happiness is shared with the angels and saints and the company of those who were known and loved on earth. (*Father Hardon's Catholic Dictionary*)

Hell

The place and state of eternal punishment for the fallen angels and human beings who die deliberately estranged from the love of God. There is a twofold punishment in hell: the pain of loss, which consists in the deprivation of the vision of God, and the pain of sense, which consists in the suffering caused by outside material things. The punishment of hell is eternal, as declared by Christ in his prediction of the last day (Matthew

25:46), and as defined by the Fourth Lateran Council, stating that the wicked will "receive a perpetual punishment with the devil" (Denzinger 801). The existence of hell is consistent with divine justice, since God respects human freedom and those who are lost actually condemn themselves by their resistance to the grace of God. (*Father Hardon's Catholic Dictionary*)

Choose well my friends.

Seeking Truth

For the law was given through Moses; grace and truth came through Jesus Christ.

—John 1:17

This book's final lesson aims to alert us Catholics to the lies that surround us. I wish to make us aware of the challenges that face us, which will require supernatural and sacramental graces to overcome. Each of us, in the manner called by our God, is commanded and, in some fashion determined by the Holy Spirit (1 Corinthians 12), is equipped to have a role in the "new evangelization." Each of us is called to come to the aid of the, at present, sickly body of Christ. Our gifts and our talents are from God on loan and not our very own possessions, which must be used to build up and to restore Christ's church to its potential glory and prominence.

What I share below is a candid overview of the crisis that we are in the midst of. Prayer, sacrifices, and being actively involved in the core of the today's amoral society are Christ's expectations for each and every one of us. Let us not, dear friends, sin by omission. The body of Christ needs us now, right now.

Matthew 28:16–20 says, "Now the eleven disciples [remaining apostles after Judas hanged himself] went to Galilee, to the mountain to which Jesus had directed them. And when they saw him they worshiped him; but some doubted. [This was before Pentecost.] And Jesus came and said to them, 'All authority in heaven and on earth has been given to me. ["And I now pass it on to you"; see also John 17:18, 20:21.] Go therefore and make disciples of all nations, baptizing them in the name of the Father and of the Son and of the Holy Spirit, teaching them to observe all that I have commanded you [meaning both taught and commanded]; and lo, I am with you always, to the close of the age."

There was a time when logic ruled or was at least considered more relevant, when common sense regularly made sense, when right *was* right, and when wrong *was* wrong. Those times, dear friends, were "the good old days." The title I choose for this lesson sadly reflects today's "new reality."

Pope Francis said, "[There can be] no peace without truth."

Upon being elected as our pontiff, Pope Benedict XVI shared this thought in his first public address: "There cannot be your truth and my truth, or there would be no truth." He also said, "Truth is not determined by a majority vote." "In this way it became clear to me how important it is that we don't lose the concept of truth, in spite of the menaces and perils that it doubtless carries with it. It has to remain as a central category. As a demand on us that doesn't give us rights but requires, on the contrary, our humility and our obedience and can lead us to the common path," declared Pope Benedict XVI. Another time, he said, "The human person finds his perfection "in seeking and loving what is true and good."

So what's happened to change the once-bright light of truth? Today's benchmark for "truth," much like the setting sun at day's end, just keeps getting lower and lower. Why and how this happened is an important heads-up to those of us, now in the minority, who remain concerned about the fate of truth and its consequences upon humanity and who understand that salvation cannot rest on the foundation of man-made, human-engineered (which is a precise term) faith beliefs, which are accepted because they call for a more simple, a less taxing, a far easier, "make me feel good" path to salvation based on half truths, lies, and misunderstandings. Salvation's "narrow gate" (Matthew 7:12–15) seems hidden, bypassed, overlooked, unsought, and even at times nonexistent.

What some might find surprising are the large numbers of who "buy into" false philosophies and religious teachings, on which rest the outcome of their eternal soul. God is one, so how can one God hold more than just one set of faith beliefs on the same long-defined issues? And could our perfect God actually have waited for King Henry VIII; Wycliffe, Luther, Calvin, or Smith; and a time lapse of more than a thousand years after Christ's earthly visitation to introduce his truth? How absurd, illogical presumptions these human-engineered upstart faiths are. Partial truths cannot substitute for the entire truth on any issue. Yet a great many unsuspecting, uniformed souls buy into these faiths, believing and making them "their truth."

There exist a myriad of differing sets of faith beliefs that compete, contradict, and redefine God's necessarily and completely logical singular truths found in its fullness only in our Catholic faith (Ephesians 4:5).

Jesus gave an unchangeable, exclusive command to the apostles in Matthew 28:18–19 to go and teach the world all that he personally taught them. The apostles and their successors alone are fully guided and guarded by both Jesus (Matthew 28:20) and the Holy Spirit (John 14:26); in doing so, Christ used clear and precisely chosen words so as not to be easily misunderstood, yet many obviously are unaware of the existence of Satan's mighty influence on their chosen beliefs. This handiwork of Satan used prideful, pride-filled men to attempt to destroy that which is indestructible, and the gates (plural) of hell shall not prevail against "it" (singular).

The further one gets from their "founding fathers," the less culpable they are. In our time, they are "only" being taught errors, while their founders were inventing lies and falsehoods. It is God who permits their hardened hearts and minds. Until one makes an attempt to seek God and his truths, God seems reluctant to grant them the necessary and essential graces to break the bond of ignorance that is holding them back.

Saint John Paul II and Pope Benedict XVI spoke of the critical importance of "truth" if society is to exist as a free and healthy society. Saint John Paul II said the following:

"Truth must be the foundation stone, the cement to solidify the entire social edifice.

"Truth cannot contradict truth."

"The truth is not always the same as the majority decision."

"Life is entrusted to man as a treasure which must not be squandered, as a talent which must be used well."

"Faith and reason are like two wings of the human spirit by which is soars to the truth."

"True freedom is not advanced in the permissive society, which confuses freedom with license to do anything whatever and which in the name of freedom proclaims a kind of general amorality. It is a caricature of freedom to claim that people are free to organize their lives with no reference to moral values, and to say that society does not have to ensure the protection and advancement of ethical values. Such an attitude is destructive of freedom and peace."

"Stupidity is also a gift of God, but one mustn't misuse it"

A while back, my lifelong mentor and friend Al purchased for me a subscription to the *Wanderer*, a weekly "very traditional" Catholic newspaper. In volume 146 no. 18 of May 2, 2013, there is an article by Donald De Marco entitled "The Holy Spirit, Interpreter of Scripture." The title really got my attention because, while it's true, its reality seems to me to be largely unrecognized by a large segment of the "Christian" population worldwide.

Here are some of what he wrote.

Saint Augustine observed that although he has met people who have been deceived, he never met anyone who wanted to be deceived. [This explains, in part, why there are so many non-Catholic Christians.]

The natural inclination toward truth [and away from deception] is fundamental. In fact, one can say that the human being is the one who seeks the truth. Why then is deception so widespread and such a common occurrence? We may begin to understand this curious phenomenon from the standpoint of human weakness and the immensity of truth.

Human Weakness: Although man is naturally inclined to seek the truth, his search will be in vain if he is not equipped with a number of virtues. The first and most important of these is humility. The humble person recognizes that truth is not of his own making, but something that exist prior to and apart from him. God's created order stands against man's subjective preferences. "The Fall" was preceded by deception. Our primal parents' original sin was the pride that obscured the fact that the serpent had deceived them. Humility then is needed to avoid the blindness of pride.

[The second needed virtue is] Docility: It is the virtue that allows us to be teachable . . . .

The Immensity of truth: According to Socrates, the Father of Moral Philosophy, and a person of firm integrity, "when people are deceived and form opinions wide of the truth, it is clear that error has slid into their minds through the medium of certain resemblances to that truth." It is easy consequently, for human beings not to distinguish between a whole truth and a partial truth that resembles truth but does not fully coincide with it.

When the great Russian novelist, Fyodor Dostoyevsky, submitted his manual script, "Crime and Punishment," to the publisher, he appended a succinct and accurate description of his masterpiece. It was according to the author, a story of a university student whose mind is infected with incomplete ideas that float on the wind. Ideas may seem true because they partake of a wider truth, though they do not represent it fully.

I will add faith and reason. In his encyclical letter "Fides et Ratio" (Faith and Reason), Saint John Paul II states that it is becoming increasingly commonplace in today's world for people to "rest content with partial and provisional truths, no longer seeking to ask radical questions about the meaning and ultimate foundation of human personal and social existence."

Scripture provides a reliable test where by the truth of Christ can be distinguished from the deceptions of false messiahs. This involves recognizing the different effects of fruits that proceed from the people of God and those who have been deceived. In Galatians 6:7–8, we read, "Be not deceived, God is not mocked. For what things a man shall sow, those also shall he reap. For he that soweth in his flesh, of the flesh also shall reap corruption. But he that soweth in the spirit, of the spirit shall reap life everlasting." And in Matthew 7:15–20, we find, "Beware of false prophets, who come to you in the clothing of sheep, but inwardly they are ravening wolves. By their fruits you shall know them. Do men gather grapes of thorns, or figs of thistles? Even so every good tree bringeth forth good fruit, and the evil tree bringeth forth evil fruit. A good tree cannot bring forth evil fruit, neither can an evil tree bring forth good fruit. Every tree that bringeth not forth good fruit, shall be cut down, and shall be cast into the fire. Wherefore by their fruits you shall know them."

There is also the need for the Holy Spirit. Saint Thomas Aquinas in his *Summa Theologica* wrote on the necessity for grace. "Every truth by whomever spoken is from the Holy Ghost as bestowing the natural light, and moving us to understand and speak the truth."

The Holy Spirit safeguards the coherence of faith and reason, knowledge in this world and the entire plan of revelation. By their faults, the action of the Holy Spirit and the operation of the Catholic Church offer invaluable aids in protecting man from deceptions. It is because truth is, must be, and shall always be "singular" per defined issues, so we informed and fully practicing Catholics need to recognize the exalted gift of God's mercy in our lives, as we alone have God's chosen leader and the holder of the very keys to heaven's gate (Matthew 16:15–19), we alone have the fullness of God's truth (Matthew 28:16–20), and we are exceedingly blessed with the seven sacraments instituted by our God to aid and direct our path to salvation.

Searching for "the truth" can be challenging, even a daunting task. It remains a massive effort to find "suitable passages" than can be skewed to prove that we Catholics are wrong and they are right. Protestant founders, theologians, and pastors have already decided that they do know more and that they do know better than God, his Bible, and, of course, the Catholic Church; and they seem unaware that what they hold is "their" but not "the" truth," which requires ignoring what else the Bible has to say on this or that particular teaching. Second Timothy 3:16–17 and Matthew 4:4 teach that the entire Bible is to be utilized.

The second aspect revolves around "one-upmanship"—the constant struggle to be different, to be "better than," to be more appealing, to be easier than that other church, the other faith, or the other flock. It's a constant fight for bodies and souls. What began as a fight with those "damned Catholics" has evolved to a fight with every "Christian" who is teaching anything they don't agree with. It's all about what "they believe." *And* it doesn't often leave room for "truth." Like Pilate exclaimed, "What is truth?" (John 18:38)

Plenty of clear, concise warnings are regularly bypassed, ignored, and presumed not to be applicable to themselves and their flocks:

"You will do well to pay attention to this as to a lamp shining in a dark place, until the day dawns and the morning star rises in your hearts. First of all you must understand this, that no prophecy of scripture is a matter of one's own interpretation, because no prophecy ever came by the impulse of man, but men moved by the Holy Spirit spoke from God." (2 Peter 1:19–21)

"Who answered and said: It is written, Not in bread alone doth man live, but in every word that proceedeth from the mouth of God." (Matthew 4:4)

"All scripture, inspired of God, is profitable to teach, to reprove, to correct, to instruct in justice, That the man of God may be perfect, furnished to every good work." (2 Timothy 3:16–17)

In closing this lesson, I will quote Archbishop Fulton Sheen, whom I greatly admire: "Truth remains 'the truth' even if no one believes it; while 'a lie' remains a lie even if everyone beliefs it."

The lesson for us is to not become discouraged. Truth is singular, and we Catholics have it in its fullness on *all* matters of faith beliefs and/or moral teachings. When God grants the opportunity, share it clearly, factually, and always with charity. Look for God's truth where it can be found—in his Catholic Church. Know, my friends, that a "partial truth" is much closer to being "a lie" than it is to being "the truth."

While some of my comments may seem uncharitable, that is not my intent. I feel it is essential to the lesson to point out with clarity the quicksand foundation many choose to build upon and what we are up against in sharing God's truths with them. Keep in mind that only God can cause a conversion, and while he permits us to assist him, he is to get the gratitude and glory, never us. Much of these lessons apply also to lapsed and apostate Catholics, as well as our non-Catholic Christian friends.

God will, because God must, make judgment based not on our personal beliefs but on what he makes possible for us to know and believe. We must pray for the mercy of God for all of these endangered souls. May God grant his wisdom and understanding to both them and us. Amen!